THE
BOND
BOOK

EVERYTHING YOU NEED TO KNOW ABOUT
TREASURIES
MUNICIPALS
GNMAs
CORPORATES
ZEROS
FUNDS
& MORE

ANNETTE THAU

IRWIN
Professional Publishing®
Chicago • London • Singapore

ISBN 1-55738-809-1

Printed in the United States of America

BB

3 4 5 6 7 8 9 0

TAQ

**To
Fred**

Contents

Preface

While working as a bond analyst, I started exploring the literature on investing in bonds. I found two types of books. The first, meant for institutional investors, consisted primarily of highly sophisticated mathematical tools. The second, meant for individual investors explained in detail how to evaluate credit risk, that is, the likelihood that when you buy a bond, you will get your money back.

As I started studying the bond market, it became clear to me that interest rate risk (that is, rates going up and down), and not credit risk, has become the major risk to any bondbuyer. In addition, so many new instruments have come on the market (for example, junk bonds, GNMAs, and zero coupon bonds) within the last decade that any book written earlier is obsolete.

I looked in vain for a book that would explain in clear English some of the basic concepts used by professionals in managing bond portfolios; and that would contain information on the major types of securities available to any individual investor, so that the merits and disadvantages of each could be compared. Because I was unable to find such a book, after working for several years as a bond analyst, I decided to write the book that I would have liked to read.

This book is meant to be practical. It assumes little or no knowledge of any bond investment, but it explains all of the critical information required to buy any security, be it a Treasury bond, a municipal bond, or a bond fund.

Several basic themes run through the book. First, I explain in detail the risks that underlie the purchase of any security. The main reason for this is that it is patently silly to lose money because you are buying a security thought to be riskless only because the risk factors are unknown. After you read this book, this will no longer happen.

Second, this book will define areas of opportunity. Just as you can lose money because you don't realize that an investment is risky, you can also earn less because you are restricting yourself unnecessarily. There may be areas of opportunity that you just don't know are out there.

Third, at minimum, any investor needs to understand enough technical information to be able to discriminate between sound analysis and hot air. You will learn a lot of technical terms and concepts so that, in the future, no one can intimidate you. If you sound like an informed investor, the next time you talk to a bond salesman, he will be much more likely to be honest with you and less likely to try to sell you a bill of goods.

This will, in turn, enable you to locate knowledgeable salespeople. You will learn to find such salespeople by asking questions. This book will suggest many. Their answers will tell you whether they have the technical expertise that you are looking for.

Fourth, another theme is how to obtain information. Many chapters contain sample tables and graphs along with explanations on how to interpret them. Similar tables appear in the three bibles of the financial press, that is, the *Wall Street Journal*, the *New York Times*, and *Barron's*; and also in the financial pages of many major daily newspapers. Also, references for additional research (books and newsletters) are listed at the end of many chapters so that if you wish to pursue any topic in greater depth, it will be easy for you to do so.

I kept in mind that investors differ both in the amount of time they have to devote to investing and the amount of personal interest. I have pointed out throughout those techniques that minimize risk for safety-minded investors who have limited time to devote to investing.

Ultimately, this book should enable you to select the instruments that match your tolerance for risk and your overall investment goals and strategies. If you wish to purchase only the safest securities, you will learn what those are. If you love risk, well then, you will learn what instruments in the bond market will provide the highest amount of leverage.

A word about the organization of the book. It is divided into four parts. The first, consisting of five chapters, is introductory, and it is basic to understanding everything that follows. It explains the fundamentals of bond investing, namely, what a bond is and how it originates; how the bond market works; what you must know before buying or selling bonds; the specifics of interest rate risk and credit risk; key concepts used to measure bond returns; and the key data you will want to consult in the financial pages of your newspaper. That part of the book should be read first, in entirety.

The second part of the book discusses the major individual securities purchased by individual investors, in order of appeal: Treasuries, municipals, GNMAs, and corporate bonds. One chapter is devoted to each security. The third part of the book analyzes the major types of bond funds. Most of that is devoted to mutual funds, but closed-end bond funds and unit investment trusts are discussed as well. The fourth part of the book, portfolio management, deals in a more general way with management of bond investments and illustrates how the information contained in various sections of this book may be put together and used. Parts 2, 3, and 4 may be read in any order desired.

Some vocabulary notes are in order. First, a word about the term "bond": the term designates any debt instrument or fixed-income security available on the market. Unfortunately, no nifty term exists to cover this type of instrument. For the sake of variety, the terms bond, fixed-income security, or debt instrument are used interchangeably throughout the book.

Second, it was necessary to decide how to deal with gender to refer to men and women as investors, or as salespeople. I considered using "he/she" but rejected it as too clumsy. Instead, I decided to use either "he" or "she" in random fashion. This should introduce some variety in the text. It is not meant to offend anyone.

Finally, I have no axe to grind. This is not a book for bonds or against bonds. Bond investments are more complex and less predictable than is generally realized. This book will explain how and why. You may, after reading it, decide to allocate more of your portfolio, or less, to bonds, or to change the mix. What I hope is that whatever you decide, the information contained in this book will enable you to invest in a more informed manner and in turn, increase your returns.

So, many happy returns!

Annette Thau
Teaneck, N.J.
October, 1991

Acknowledgments

I would like thank the many individuals whose help was invaluable while I was writing this book.

First of all, I would like to thank those persons who not only spent hours answering questions; but who also subsequently read portions of the manuscript. This book benefited enormously from their many insights and suggestions. These individuals include: William T. Reynolds, director of the Municipal Division and managing director of T. Rowe Price Associates; John Charlesworth, chief debt strategist, Merrill Lynch Private Client Group; Richard Wilson, managing director of Research and Private Placements at Fitch Investors Service, Inc.; Thomas Herzfeld, president, Thomas Herzfeld Advisors, Inc.; Gregory Hickok, formerly head of the municipal division of the Chase Manhattan Bank, N.A., and now president of Hydra-Clean; John Campbell and Jim Musson, vice presidents at Dean Witter Reynolds; and Michael Lipper, president, Lipper Analytical Services.

I would also like to thank the many individuals who agreed to be interviewed, some a number of times, while I researched this book. They were incredibly generous with their time. They include Fred Stoever, president, Stoever Glass Securities; the late Steven Hueglin, principal, Gabriele, Hueglin and Cashman; Richard Potter, senior vice president and director of fixed-income portfolios at the Fiduciary Trust International; Theresa Havell, president, Fixed-Income Funds, Neuberger and Berman Management, Inc.; Gary Pollack, vice president, Bankers Trust; and Jeffrey Baker, vice president, the Chase Manhattan Bank, N.A.

For their assistance, I would also like to thank Jeanne Person, Judy Otterman and Y. Y. Ma, vice presidents at Salomon Brothers, Inc.; Susan Scarborough and Jonathan Bitting, vice presidents at Citibank, N.A.; Michele Worthy and Sandy West, of the Investment Company Institute; Natalie R. Cohen, vice president at Enhance Reinsurance Co.; Mark Cohen, vice president at Fitch Investors Service, Inc.; and Gail Hessol, senior vice president, industrial ratings, for Standard and Poor's Corp.

Most special thanks go to Tom Murphy, who not only acted most capably as my literary agent, but who also read several versions of the manuscript; and to my husband, Fred, for cheering me on through all the stages of writing this book.

Any errors are, of course, entirely my own responsibility.

PART I

The Basics

This part of the book is introductory and basic to understanding all that follows. Its purpose is to explain the fundamentals of bond investing. Chapter 1 defines bonds and explains how they are originated and sold. Chapter 2 explains the workings of the bond market and what you must know before buying or selling bonds. Chapter 3 is at the heart of the book: it explains why bond prices go up and down through a detailed discussion of interest rate risk and credit risk. Chapter 4 is an introduction to basic bond mathematics. It defines the key concepts used to measure return from bond investments as well as bond cash flows. Chapter 5 is an introduction to some of the key data you will want to consult when you read the financial pages of your newspaper.

1

The Life of a Bond

This chapter

- *defines a bond*

- *explains how bonds are issued and trade*

- *defines some key terms used in buying and selling bonds: maturity, par, coupon, indenture and prospectus.*

First, what is a bond?

Basically, a bond is a loan or an IOU. When you buy a bond, you lend your money to a large borrower such as a corporation or a governmental body. These borrowers routinely raise needed capital by selling (or using Wall Street vocabulary by "issuing") bonds for periods as brief as a few days to as long as 30 or 40 years. The distinguishing characteristic of a bond is that the borrower (the issuer) enters into a legal agreement to compensate the lender (you, the bondholder) through periodic interest payments in the form of coupons; and to repay the original sum (the principal) in full on a stipulated date, which is known as the bond's maturity date.

The process of issuing bonds is complex. Because the sums involved are so large, issuers do not sell bonds directly to the public. Instead, bonds are brought to market by an investment bank (the underwriter). The investment bank acts as an interme-

3

diary between the issuer and the investing public. Lawyers are hired by both parties (that is, the issuer and the underwriter) to draw up the formal terms of the sale and to see to it that the sale conforms to the regulations of the Securities and Exchange Commission (the SEC).

To illustrate the process, let us say that the State of New Jersey needs to borrow $500 million in order to finance a major project. New Jersey announces its intention through trade journals and asks for bids. Underwriters (major broker-dealer firms such as Merrill Lynch, Goldman Sachs, Morgan Stanley, Shearson Lehman, etc.), or smaller, less well-known firms (there are dozens of them) compete with each other by submitting bids to New Jersey. A firm may bid for the business by itself in its own name. More often, firms form a group called a syndicate, which submits a joint bid. The State awards the sale to the lowest bidder, whether that is a single firm or a syndicate. The underwriters then get busy selling the bonds.

The underwriter (or the syndicate) handles all aspects of the bond sale in effect buying the bonds from the issuer (New Jersey) and selling them to the investing public. The investing public is made up of large institutions (banks, pension funds, insurance companies) as well as individual investors and bond funds. Once the bonds have been sold, however, the underwriter retains no connection to the bonds. Payment of interest and redemption (repayment) of principal are—and will remain—the responsibility of the issuer (New Jersey). After the sale, the actual physical payment of interest, record-keeping chores, and so forth etc. are handled for the issuer by still another party, a fiduciary agent, which is generally a bank that acts as the trustee for the bonds.

The exact terms of the loan agreement between the issuer (the State of N. J.) and anyone who buys the bonds (you or an institution) are described fully in a legal document known as the "indenture," which is legally binding on the issuer for the entire period that the bond remains outstanding.

First, the indenture stipulates the dates when coupons are paid, as well as the date for repayment of the principal in full; that is, the bond's maturity date. The indenture then discusses a great many other matters of importance to the bondholder. It describes how the issuer intends to cover debt payments; that is, where the money will come from. The State of New Jersey, for example, would specify that it intends to raise the monies through taxes and would describe its economy. The indenture also describes a set of conditions that would enable either the issuer or the bondholder to redeem bonds at full value before their stipulated maturity date. These topics are discussed in greater detail in the sections dealing with "call" features and credit quality.

All of the major terms of the indenture, including the payment dates for coupons, the bond's maturity date, call provisions, sources of revenue backing the bonds and so on, are summarized in a document called a "prospectus." It is a good idea to read the prospectus if you can. For bonds bought at issue, a prospectus is easily obtained. But for older issues, the prospectus is usually unavailable. When the prospectus is printed before the sale, it is known as a "preliminary prospectus," or a "red herring" because certain legal terms are printed on the cover of the prospectus in red ink.

The most elementary distinction between bonds is based on what kind of entity issued the bonds. Bonds issued directly by the U. S. government are classified as Treasury bonds; those issued by corporations are known as corporate bonds; and those issued by local and state governmental units, which are generally exempt from federal taxes, are called municipals or munis for short. The actual process of selling the bonds differs somewhat from sale to sale but generally conforms to this process.

Many bonds are issued in very large amounts, typically between $100 million and $500 million for corporates and munis, and billions for Treasuries. To sell the bonds to the public, the investment bank divides them into smaller batches. By custom, the smallest bond unit is one bond, which can be redeemed at maturity for $1,000. The terms "par" and "principal" value both refer to the $1,000 value of the bond at maturity. In practice, however, bonds are traded in larger batches, usually in minimum amounts of $5,000 (par value).

Anyone interested in the New Jersey bonds may buy them when they are first brought to market (at issue), or subsequently, from someone who has decided to sell them. Bonds purchased at the time of issue are said to have been purchased in the "primary market." Bonds may be held to maturity, or resold, anytime between the original issue date and the maturity date. Typically, a bondholder who wishes to sell his bonds will use the services of a broker, who pockets a fee for the service. There is a market in older issues, called the "secondary market." Some bonds (for example, 30-year Treasuries) enjoy a very active market. For most bonds, however, the market becomes moribund and inactive once the bonds have "gone away" (that is an expression used by traders) to investors. It is always possible to sell an older bond; but if the bond is not actively traded, then commission costs for selling are very high. Pricing, buying, and selling bonds, as well as bond returns, are discussed in greater detail in Chapters 3 and 4.

During the time that they trade in the secondary market, bond prices go up and down continually. Bonds seldom, if ever, trade at par. In fact, bonds are likely to be priced at par only twice during their life: first, when they are brought to market (at issue), and second, when they are redeemed. But, and this is an important but, regardless of the purchase price for the bonds, they are always redeemed at par (or at a price close to par stipulated in the indenture).

But, you may well ask, if the issue price of a bond is almost always $1,000, and the maturity value is always $1,000, why and how do bond prices change? That is where the story gets interesting, so read on.

2

Buying and Selling Bonds

This chapter discusses

- *the institutional nature of the bond market*
- *the individual investor and the bond market*
- *bond pricing and commissions*
- *terms used in buying, selling, and discussing bonds.*

THE BOND MARKET: AN OVERVIEW

While people speak of the bond market as if it were one market, in reality, there is not one central place or exchange where bonds are bought and sold. Rather, the bond market is a gigantic over-the-counter market, consisting of networks of independent dealers, organized by type of security, with some overlaps. U. S. Treasury securities, for example, are sold through a network of "primary dealers" who sell directly to large institutions and to large broker-dealer firms. The broker-dealer firms, in turn, resell the bonds to the investing public and to smaller institutional investors. Some corporate bonds are sold on each of the stock exchanges and through bond dealers. Municipals are sold by dealers, by banks and by brokerage firms. Whereas stocks sell ultimately in one of three independent exchanges (the New York Stock Exchange, the American Stock Exchange, or the NASDAQ), bonds are sold primarily dealer to dealer.

This market is so vast that its size is difficult to imagine. Although the financial press reports mainly on the stock market, the bond market is several times larger. Overwhelmingly, this is an institutional market. It raises debt capital for the largest issuers of debt, for example, for the U. S. government, for state and local governments, and also for the largest corporations in the United States. The buyers of that debt are overwhelmingly large institutional investors such as pension funds, insurance companies, banks, corporations and, increasingly, mutual funds. These buyers and sellers routinely trade sums that appear almost unreal to a nonfinance professional. For example, U. S. government bonds trade in blocks of 1 million dollars, and 100 million dollar trades are not unusual. The smallest blocks are traded in the municipal market, where a round lot is $100,000. Another way of characterizing this market is to call it a wholesale market.

Enter the individual investor. In the bond markets, individual investors, even those with considerable wealth, are all little guys, who function in a market designed for far larger traders. Indeed, many of the new fixed-income securities created over the last ten years were specifically tailored to the needs of pension funds or insurance companies, and may not be appropriate for individual investors. The individual investor faces many disadvantages when compared to institutions. For instance, commission costs are much higher. Or, as another example, institutions have developed a vast amount of quantitative data and mathematical models, on which they base buying and selling strategies. Individual investors do not have access to the same kinds of sophisticated tools or information.

Individuals may purchase bonds from a number of sources, such as full-service brokerage firms, banks, or firms that specialize in debt instruments; and discounters. (U. S. Treasuries may also be bought directly from a Federal Reserve Bank.) In this connection, a comparison with stocks may be helpful. If you want to buy a stock listed on the New York Stock Exchange—say International Business Machines (IBM)—any broker can sell you IBM, and any broker knows and can tell you the price of the last transaction. Whether you deal with a large brokerage firm or a small brokerage firm, you can buy IBM at the market price (although commissions may differ). Moreover, you can look up the high, low and closing price of IBM for the previous day in the financial pages of any of the major daily newspapers in the country.

However, the situation is very different for bonds. First, the availability of bonds varies from dealer to dealer. If you want to buy a specific type of bond (say, an intermediate muni with a rating of A or better), you may have to approach several dealers before you find one who has what you want. Discount brokers generally do not maintain inventories. If you want to buy a certain type of bond, their traders have to buy it from another dealer; if you want to sell the bond, their traders ask for bids from other dealers. Large brokerage firms or firms whose main business is selling bonds typically maintain inventories of bonds so that the individual investor is able to select from a wider selection. They may also be able to obtain desirable new issues whereas smaller firms may not.

Pricing also varies from dealer to dealer. Dealers mark up their bonds independently. The markup depends on their own cost, the size of the order, and how much profit they need to earn. Commission costs, moreover, are hidden so that the buyer does not know either the cost to the dealer, or the size of the markup. When you shop for that A-rated intermediate muni, you are likely to be offered a variety of bonds with different yields and prices by different dealers.

Pricing information is extremely difficult to obtain. Bond prices are not as widely reported as stock prices. The tables that appear in the financial newspapers—including most of those listed in this book—list a few representative issues. But the prices apply to institutional size trades of one million dollars or more. Most bonds other than Treasuries trade infrequently; and pricing such issues—either for sale or purchase—can be extremely difficult. There is only one way to protect yourself on price: comparison shop, routinely and extensively.

Finally, many stockbrokers who also sell bonds don't really understand the bond market very well. It may be because many new types of fixed-income instruments have been created within the last ten years. Or it may be because a broker ultimately earns a lot more in commissions from selling stocks than from selling bonds. Whatever the reason, it is important to find salespeople who deal mainly with bonds and who really know the product.

Finding a good source for bonds requires effort. Try to locate either a firm that specializes in bonds, or within a bank or brokerage firm, an individual who specializes in selling bonds to individual investors. Take the trouble to interview brokers and discuss your needs with them. Ask a lot of questions (this book will suggest many). If you are not satisfied with the answers, find a different broker.

Also be aware that there is nothing wrong with bargaining, for example, asking the broker if she can do a little better. To a broker, a smaller commission is better than no sale. Commissions in the bond market are always negotiable. Even if you have always done business with a particular firm (or a particular broker), it pays to shop around and be as well-informed about market conditions as possible. You are more likely to negotiate a better price if your broker realizes that you know where prices should be.

You can judge the quality of a firm partly by what that firm tries to sell you. If you tell a broker that stability of principal is important to you, and you are consistently offered only high yielding—and therefore risky—securities, go elsewhere. Certain firms—referred to unceremoniously as "bucket shops"—are known for their high-pressure tactics. Such firms typically rely on cold-calling, telephoning strangers in order to spot buyers who will buy without investigating carefully. Typically, such a cold caller will tell you that he is offering you a unique opportunity to buy a terrific bond; but that if you do not purchase this bond immediately, the opportunity will disappear. Never buy anything over the phone from a person or a firm that you do not know well or without comparing prices with several dealers.

In summary, to locate a good source for bonds:

- locate a firm that specializes in bonds;

- or locate an individual within a larger firm who specializes in selling fixed-income securities to individual investors;

- interview brokers and discuss your needs; if you are not satisfied, find a different broker;

- comparison shop and be prepared to negotiate a price.

THE VOCABULARY OF BOND TRANSACTIONS

Par, Premium and Discount Bonds

The "par" value of a bond is its value at maturity; that is, $1,000. When a bond begins to trade, it normally ceases to sell at par. If it sells at less than par (less than $1,000), it is said to be selling at a "discount." If it sells at more than par (above $1,000), it is called a "premium" bond.

"Bid," "Ask" and "Spread"

Commission costs for buying or selling bonds are hidden. The price is quoted net. Indeed, if you ask a broker about the commission, you may be told that there is no commission. But that is not the case.

Prices of all fixed-income instruments—including mutual funds—are always quoted in pairs: the "bid" and the "ask" (also called the "offer"). The difference between the bid and the ask is known as the "spread." It represents the commission. Technically, the bid is what you sell for; the ask, the price at which you buy. But it is not difficult to remember which is the bid and which is the ask. Just remember this: if you want to buy, you always pay the *higher* price. If you want to sell, you receive the *lower*.

For example, a bond may be quoted at "98 bid/100 ask." If you are buying the bond, you will pay 100; if you are selling, you will receive 98 (see below for the answer to 98 and 100 what).

Technically, the bid/ask spread is a market spread, which means that it is the cost of buying or selling for the broker. A broker starts with the market spread, and figures out how much additional commission she needs to charge in order to sell a bond to you at a profit. Suppose, for example, that the market spread is "98 bid/100 ask." If you are selling an inactively traded bond (and that description applies to most bonds), then the broker makes sure that she buys it from you cheaply enough so that she will not lose money when she resells. She might then quote a spread to you of "97 bid/101 ask." For that reason, commission costs to an individual investor may often be wider than the market bid/ask spread.

For an individual investor, commission costs range from 1/2 of 1 percent (or even less) for actively traded Treasury issues, to as much as 4 percent on inactively traded long-term bonds. Commissions vary for many reasons:

- The dealer's cost and his markup.

- The type of bond being sold (corporate, Treasury or muni).

- The amount of the bond being traded (that is, the size of the lot).

- The bond's maturity.

- Its credit quality.

- The overall direction of interest rates.

- Demand for a specific bond.

- Demand for a particular bond sector.

As a rule, bonds that have very low risk have narrower (that is, lower) commission (spreads); bonds that are riskier, or less in demand sell at wider (that is, higher) spreads. Any characteristic that makes a bond less desirable makes it more expensive to sell. For example, lower quality bonds are more expensive to resell than bonds with higher credit quality. Bonds with longer maturities have higher markups than short-term bonds. Selling a small number of bonds is more expensive than selling a large quantity (or a round lot). Market conditions are also important. For instance, if interest rates are rising, spreads normally widen; if interest rates are dropping, spreads usually narrow.

Let's illustrate with some concrete examples. Treasury bonds sell at the narrowest spreads (less than 1/2 percent or even less), no matter how many bonds, or the direction of interest rates. High quality intermediate munis (AA or AAA, maturing between three and seven years) sell at commissions of between 3/4 percent to perhaps 2 percent. Thirty-year munis sell at spreads of between 3 percent and 4 percent. The more strikes against a bond, the more difficult it is to sell. Trying to sell a long maturity, low-credit quality bond in a weak market is a worst case scenario because you may have to shop extensively just to get a bid.

The size of the spread (or commission) reflects what is known as a bond's "liquidity"; that is, the ease and cost of trading a particular bond. A narrow spread indicates high demand and low risk; the dealer is sure she can resell quickly. Conversely, a wide spread indicates an unwillingness on the part of the dealer to own a bond without a substantial price cushion. An unusually wide commission (4 percent or more) constitutes a red flag. It warns you that at best, a particular bond may be expensive to resell and, at worst, headed for difficult times. The dealer community that earns its living buying and selling bonds has a very active information and rumor network that is sometimes quicker to spot potential trouble than the credit rating agencies.

Note also that when you buy a bond at issue, even though the commission is built into the deal, commission costs are usually closer to the actual market price for that bond, at that point in time than when bonds trade in the secondary market. Hence, the individual investor may receive a fairer shake by buying at issue than by buying in the secondary market.

It is difficult to obtain information on spreads and pricing. Dealers are understandably reluctant to reveal markups. But pricing is extremely variable. It bears repeating that the only way to protect yourself is to comparison shop and do some arithmetic. A difference of 2 percent in the spread may not seem like a lot; but on a $10,000 investment, that's $200. On a $100,000 investment, it's $2,000. Such differences in markups are common. Moreover, as will be shown in a later section, commission costs are a major factor in determining how much your bond investments actually earn.

Always try to find out the bid/ask spread when you are buying a bond. If the broker does not directly quote the spread, ask what you could resell the bond for if you had to resell it that afternoon (or the next day).

Discussing Bonds

When the broker "shows" you a bond (that is the term generally used), she will say something like: "I want to show you this great bond we just got in. It is the State of Bliss 9 1/4 of 95, and it is priced at 96 bid and 97 ask." Well, what did she say?

Actually, that statement is easily decoded. Bonds are always identified by several pieces of information; namely, the issuer (State of Bliss); the coupon (9 1/4); the maturity date, of "95"; and the price, quoted as 97.

Let us examine each of these details more closely. First, the coupon. Coupons are always quoted in percentages. That percentage is set at issue, and it is therefore a percentage of par. The percentage value, however, is immediately translated into a fixed dollar amount; and that amount remains the same throughout the life of the bond no matter what happens to the price of the bond. In the previous example, the 9 1/4 coupon represents 9 1/4 percent of $1,000, that is, $92.50. Unless stipulated otherwise, coupons are paid semi-annually. You will receive half of that amount, that is $41.25, twice a year, for as long as the bond remains outstanding.

The maturity date is designated by the last two digits. In this instance, it is 95. This has to be 1995, not 2095 since bonds, with few exceptions, are not issued for maturities above 30 years. A maturity date of "00" would indicate the year 2000; "08" would be 2008, and so on.

Finally, the price was quoted as 97. Bond prices are quoted in percentages, and again, percentages of par. So the quote of 97 should be interpreted as 97 percent (or .97) times $1,000, which equals $970. To compute price, add a zero to the percentage quote.

You can now translate what the bond broker is telling you. She would like to sell you a State of Bliss bond, maturing in 1995, with a coupon of $92.50, at a price of $970.

Accrued Interest

Let us suppose you decide to buy the State of Bliss bonds. When you receive your confirmation notice, it is probable that the price will turn out to be somewhat higher than the $970 that you were quoted. No, the broker is not ripping you off. The difference between the price that you pay and the $970 that you were quoted is "accrued interest." Let's explain.

You will remember that coupon payments are usually made twice a year. But actually, bonds earn (the Wall Street word is "accrue") interest every single day. The owner of a bond earns or accrues interest for the exact number of days that he owns the bond.

Now suppose you are buying the State of Bliss bonds three months after the last coupon payment was made (and therefore, three months before the next coupon payment occurs). In three months, you will receive a coupon payment for the past six months; but you will have earned that interest for only three months. The gentlemanly thing to do is to turn over three months worth of interest to the previous owner.

In fact, that is what you do when you buy the bond. Only you do not have any choice in the matter. The three months of interest due to the previous owner are automatically added on to the purchase price. The buyer pays the seller the accrued interest. When you (the buyer) receive the next coupon payment, the interest you receive will cover the three months worth of interest you earned and the three months of interest that you paid the previous owner.

Accrued interest is easily computed. For bond pricing purposes (not for notes), the year has 360 days. To compute accrued interest, divide the annual coupon by 360 days; multiply that by the number of days accrued interest is owed. Add accrued interest to the purchase price.

Accrued interest is paid on par, premium and discount bonds. The amount of accrued interest depends entirely on the coupons, divided by the number of days interest is owed. It has nothing to do with the price.

Call Risk

"Call risk" is the risk that bonds will be redeemed ("called") by the issuer before they mature. Municipal and corporate bonds are subject to call; Treasuries generally are not. Some older 30-year Treasuries may be callable five years before they mature; but the Treasury no longer issues any callable bonds.

The ability to "call" bonds protects issuers by enabling them to retire bonds with high coupons and refinance at lower interest rates. Calls are unwelcome to bondholders. A call normally reduces return because bonds are called when interest rates drop. A high interest rate, thought to be "locked in," disappears, and the bondholder is forced to reinvest at lower rates.

If a bond was purchased at par or at a discount, there is no loss of principal. But if it was purchased at a premium (say for $1200), an unexpected early call can result in a substantial loss of principal, since bonds are redeemed at or close to par. If the $1200 bond is redeemed at par, then that translates into a $200 loss per bond.

The prospectus spells out call provisions by stipulating both specific call dates and call prices, which are typically somewhat above par. But call provisions for certain types of bonds (chiefly corporates) are sometimes obscure. Call features of both municipal and corporate bonds will be discussed in greater detail in the chapters dealing with these securities.

When a bond is offered, the broker should quote not only the yield-to-maturity (see Chapter 4), but also the yield to the earliest call date. In practice, the yield-to-call is normally quoted for munis; but seldom for corporates. If the coupon rate is a lot higher than current interest rate on similar bonds, it is prudent to assume that the bond will be called and to evaluate the bond based on the yield-to-call. If for example, a broker offers you a bond with a 10 percent coupon, maturing in 10 years, callable in one year, and interest rates are now at 8 percent for similar maturities, you should assume the bond will be called.

How can you protect yourself against calls?

- First, check call provisions carefully.

- Be particularly careful in checking call provisions if you are purchasing premium bonds; that is, bonds whose price is well above par.

- Buy deeply discounted bonds; that is, bonds with very low coupons selling well below par. They are much less likely to be called than high coupon bonds. Remember that the coupon represents the cost of money to the issuer. The issuer is therefore most likely to call the bonds with the highest coupons rather than those with lower coupons.

The Form of a Bond: Certificate, Registered and Book-Entry

If you bought a bond before 1980, you received as proof of ownership an ornate document with coupons attached at the side. This document was known as a "certificate." The certificate did not have your name on it. To collect interest, it was necessary to physically clip the coupons and to send them to the trustee who would then mail you the interest payment. (That is the origin of the term "coupon.") The certificate functioned like a dollar bill. It was presumed to be owned by the bearer. Those bonds were also known as "bearer bonds."

In the early 1980s, certificates began to be issued with the name of the owner imprinted on the certificate. Those are called "registered" bonds. Interest payments are sent automatically to the owner of record.

With the spread of computerization, the process has become even more automated. Many bonds are now issued in "book-entry" form. No certificates are issued. Instead, when you buy a bond, you receive a confirmation statement with a number on it. That number is stored in a computer data bank and is the only proof of ownership. Coupon payments are wired automatically to the checking or bank account that the owner designates. Notification of calls is automatic.

The form of a bond varies with the issuer. All Treasuries are now issued in book-entry form whereas approximately 65 percent of municipals are still issued in certificate form. A few older munis are still available in bearer form, but the supply is diminishing as these bonds mature.

You may hold certificates in your own possession or leave them in your account with a broker. Brokers always prefer holding the certificates. There are two good reasons for letting them do so. First, if the firm is covered by the Securities Insurance Protection Corporation (SIPC), and most are, the bond is protected against loss; that is, against physical loss of the certificate—not against a decline in price due to market conditions. Second, the firm is more likely than you to be immediately aware of calls. If a bond is called, the firm should immediately redeem the bonds. That should protect you against loss of interest.

Leaving a bond in a brokerage account does not prevent you from selling the bond through a different broker. To transfer a book-entry bond, you need only to notify your broker to transfer it by wire to any other firm.

If your bond is in certificate form, however, the matter becomes more complicated because you need to deliver the certificate within five days after the sale. And six weeks or more may be needed to obtain the document because it is usually not stored in the branch office. Selling through the firm holding your bond eliminates having to actually get your hands on the document, and it permits you to sell at any time. If you want to sell through a different broker, then you must allow enough time to obtain the certificate.

Basis Points

Interest rates rise from 9 percent to 10 percent. How much have they gone up?

No, they have not gone up 1 percent. On a percentage basis, that increase represents a percentage difference of 11.1 percent.

This may seem like nitpicking. But suppose, for example, that interest rates rise from 9 percent to 9.12 percent? How would you label that increase, using percentages?

The answer to that question would be either imprecise or confusing. Since institutional investors make or lose thousands of dollars on seemingly minute percentage changes, they have divided each percentage point into 100 points, each of which is called a "basis point." The difference between an interest rate of 9 percent and one of 10 percent is 100 basis points; between 5 percent and 6 percent, it is still 100 hundred basis points. An increase in interest rate yield from 9 percent to 9.12 percent represents an increase in yield of 12 basis points.

The term basis point is used to compare both price and yield. If, for example, you are comparing two different bonds, you might note that the three-year bond yields 6.58 percent, whereas the two-year bond yields 6.50 percent. In this instance, the three-year bond yields 8 basis points more than the two-year bond. The yield of the two-year bond might be 7 percent one day and 7.01 percent the next, a difference of one basis point.

Yields of any bond are likely to vary from day to day by no more than one or two basis points. A rise or a decline in yield from one day to the next of more than 10 basis points constitutes a major price move. Remember that changes in yield translate into changes in price and vice-versa.

Experienced investors and salespeople think in basis points. It is far easier and more precise than using percentages. Using the term will immediately mark you as a knowledgeable investor. It will be used through the rest of the book.

3

Volatility: Why Bond Prices Go Up and Down

This chapter discusses

- *interest rate risk*
- *credit ratings and bond returns*
- *a short history of interest rates*

Bond prices fluctuate in response to two factors; namely, changes in interest rates and changes in credit quality. People who purchase bonds tend to worry a lot about the safety of their money. Generally, however, they tie safety to credit considerations. Rarely do investors fully understand how changes in interest rates affect price. Since the late 1970s, changes in the interest rate environment have become the greatest single determinant of bond returns. Managing interest rate risk has become the most critical variable in the management of bond portfolios. In this chapter, we'll see why and how.

INTEREST RATE RISK—OR, A TALE OF PRINCIPAL RISK

"Interest rate risk," also known as "market risk," refers to the propensity bonds have of fluctuating in price as a result of changes in interest rates.

> All bonds are subject to interest rate risk.
> *All bonds are subject to interest rate risk.*
> **All bonds are subject to interest rate risk.**

Why am I repeating this statement so many times?

Because if nothing else makes an impression, but you learn that all bonds are subject to interest rate risk, regardless of the issuer, or the credit rating, or whether the bond is "insured" or "guaranteed," then this book will have served a useful purpose.

The principle behind this fact is easy to explain.

Let us suppose you bought a 30-year bond when 30-year Treasuries were yielding 4 percent. Further suppose that you now wish to sell your bond and that interest rates for the same maturity are currently 10 percent. How can you convince someone to purchase your bond, with a coupon of 4 percent, when he can buy new issues with a 10 percent coupon?

Well, there is only one thing you can do: you mark down your bond. In fact, the price at which a buyer would buy your bond, as readily as a new issue, is that price at which your bond

---

Exhibit 3.1
What Would Happen to the Price of a $1,000 Par Value Bond with a 9 Percent Coupon if Interest Rates Were to Rise to 10 Percent, or to 12 Percent

Maturity	10%	12%
2 years	$983	$949
5 years	962	892
10 years	939	831
15 years	924	796
20 years	915	776
30 years	906	758

would now yield 10 percent. That would be approximately 30 cents on the dollar, or about $300 per bond.

But, you will object, if I sell my $1,000 bond for $300, I have lost $700 per bond! That is precisely the point.

Significant changes in the interest rate environment are not hypothetical. During the past decade, swings of 1 percent (100 basis points) have occurred on several occasions over periods of a few weeks or a few months. During the late 1970s and 1980s, rates moved up and down, in sharp spikes or drops, as much as 5 percent (500 basis points) within a few years.

The following questions and answers discuss management of interest rate risk.

Is there anything you can do to protect your money against interest rate fluctuations?

Yes. You can buy bonds with maturities that are either short (under one year) or short-intermediate (between two and seven years).

Again, the reason for that is easy to explain. While all bonds are subject to interest rate risk, *that risk is directly correlated to maturity length.* As maturity length increases, so do potential price fluctuations. Conversely, the shorter the maturity of the bond you buy, the lower the risk of price fluctuations as a result of changes in interest rate levels.

Exact formulas exist for determining price given coupon and maturity, and price is very easy to calculate with a financial calculator. The formula is of no importance. What is important is that price fluctuations for bonds are correlated directly to maturity length. If interest rates rise, the value of bonds with very short maturities (under a year) changes only a little. That is why such bonds are considered cash equivalents. Each additional year in the maturity of a security increases price fluctuations when interest rates go up or down. A rough rule of thumb is that a 100 basis point rise in yield, (say from 8 percent to 9 percent), will result in a loss of value of 10 percent of principal (a loss of $100 per $1,000 par value bond) for bonds with 30-year maturities. Steeper rises in interest levels devastate the price of long-term bonds.

To illustrate, let's look at Exhibit 3.1. This table shows how changes in interest rate levels would affect the price of a $1,000 (par value) bond with a coupon of 9 percent for different maturities under two different scenarios: first, if interest rates were to rise relatively modestly to 10 percent and second, if interest rates rise more sharply, to 12 percent.

Exhibit 3.1 shows that if interest rates rise from 9 percent to 10 percent, the price decline would be insignificant ($17) for the two-year bond. The ten-year bond, however, would lose $71 (about 6 percent of its principal value); the 15-year bond, about 8 percent; and the 30-year bond, almost 10 percent. If a sharper rise in interest rates were to occur, from 9 percent to 12 percent, the declines would be correspondingly larger: from $51.00 (5 percent) for the two-year bond; through $169 (17 percent) for the 10-year bond; to almost $250 (25 percent) for the 30-year bond.

What happens to bond prices if interest rates decline?

This phenomenon, happily, operates in reverse. As interest rates decline, bond prices rise. This is illustrated in Exhibit 3.2.

Exhibit 3.2 demonstrates changes in price for various maturities under two different scenarios: first, if interest rates decline from 12 percent to 10 percent; and second, if they decline from 12 percent to 8 percent. Again, the price fluctuation is minor for the two-year maturity. But it rises gradually through the maturity

---

Exhibit 3.2
What Would Happen to the Price of a $1,000 Par Value Bond with a 12 Percent Coupon if Interest Rates Were to Decline to 10 Percent, or to 8 Percent

Maturity	10%	8%
2 years	$1035	$1071
5 years	1076	1159
10 years	1123	1268
15 years	1152	1342
20 years	1170	1392
30 years	1189	1450

---

spectrum. If rates were to drop from 12 percent to 10 percent, the value of the two-year bond would increase by $35.00 (3.5 percent). The value of the ten-year bond would rise by $123.00 (12 percent). But the value of the thirty-year bond would rise by $189.00 (19 percent). A decline in interest rates from 12 percent to 8 percent would result in substantial price increases for all maturities, from $71.00 (7 percent) for the two-year bond, to $450.00 (45 percent) for the 30-year bond.

In this instance, the holder of a bond would benefit from holding the longest maturities, because the longer the maturity, the higher the gain. That is the reason that investors anticipating a decline in interest rates position themselves at the long end, in order to realize the largest capital gains.

So now we have the two faces of interest rate fluctuations: risk and opportunity. It may sound paradoxical, but a rising or strong bond market is one in which interest rates are falling because that causes bond prices to rise. You can sell a bond for more than you paid for it and make a profit. A weak bond market is one in which interest rates are rising, and as a result, prices are falling. If you have to sell your bonds, you have to do so at a loss. In either case, the changes in price are directly correlated to maturity length.

If long-term bonds are so risky, why would anyone purchase them?

Mainly because many investors believe that long-term bonds provide the highest yields (or maximum income). That, however, is not necessarily true. If all other factors are equal, long-term bonds have higher coupons than shorter-term bonds of the same credit quality. But, intermediate bonds in the A to AA range often yield as much as AAA bonds with far longer maturities, and they are much less volatile.

You might, of course, want to purchase long-term bonds primarily because of their volatility, if you think interest rates are about to decline. Then, long-term bonds would position you for the largest capital gains. That would imply that you consider potential capital gains as important (or more so) than dividend yield, and in all likelihood, that you intend to resell the bonds before they mature.

How do interest rate fluctuations affect me if I buy and hold a bond until maturity?

If you hold bonds to maturity, you recover your principal in full. No matter what kind of roller coaster ride interest rates take during the life of a bond, its value will always be par when the bond is redeemed. Bonds purchased either above par (premium bonds) or below par (discount bonds) are also redeemed at par. The price of discounts gradually rises to par; the price of premiums falls to par. These changes occur in small annual increments and are reflected in the current price of any bond.

I own bonds issued years ago, when coupon rates were 4 percent. Rates are now much higher. Can't I sell my old bonds and buy new ones with higher coupons in order to earn more income?

The swap by itself will not result in higher yields if you buy a bond that is comparable in maturity length and credit quality; the transaction will be a wash. This is because you would sell at that price at which the buyer of your old bonds would be "indifferent" (using a word from economics) to buying your bond, or one carrying a higher coupon, meaning at the exact price which would result in the prevailing yield. Therefore, your income from the bonds would not change.

For example, let us assume you own bonds with a par value of $10,000 and a coupon rate of 4 percent. That means that annually, you receive interest (coupon) income of $400.00. Assume further that interest rates have risen to 8 percent. You sell your bonds for approximately $500 per bond, for a total of $5,000, which you now reinvest. You now own $5,000 (par value) bonds, and you will now receive annual interest of 8 percent; that is, $400. Therefore, even though you are now earning a coupon rate of 8 percent, you will earn be the same dollar amount as before the swap. Moreover, you would be out the transaction costs (commissions) incurred in selling the old bonds and buying the new bonds.

This does not mean that you should never consider swaps. There are other valid reasons for swapping. For instance, on the preceding transaction, you would realize a capital loss of approximately $5,000 and that might be used for tax purposes to offset capital gains on other transactions. Or, you might swap to upgrade credit quality. You might increase yield by buying lower quality bonds, or by buying different bonds.

Please note two caveats. In the preceding example, you would have taken an enormous hit to principal. Also, costing out a swap accurately is complex. For more on swaps, see Chapter 14.

CREDIT RATINGS: HOW CREDIT QUALITY AFFECTS THE VALUE OF YOUR BONDS

There is widespread misunderstanding about what credit ratings really mean, and how credit ratings affect the returns that you earn and the overall riskiness of your portfolio. This section explains what credit ratings mean. It then discusses two related topics: how credit ratings are assigned; and the relationship between credit ratings, credit risk and overall returns. Finally, this section answers some of the most frequently asked questions concerning credit ratings.

Credit Risk and Credit Ratings: What Ratings Tell You

Investors generally rely on bond ratings to evaluate the credit quality of specific bonds. Credit ratings indicate on a scale of high to low the possibility of default; that is, the possibility that debt will not be repaid on time. Failure to redeem principal at maturity would constitute a default. Failure to make interest payments on time (that is, to pay coupons to bondholders) would also constitute a default. In plain English, ratings answer two questions: how likely am I to get my money back at maturity? how likely am I to get my interest payments on time?

Not all bonds are subject to default risk. Any security issued *directly* by the U. S. government is considered free of default risk. Although these bonds are not rated, they are considered the safest and highest quality securities that you can buy, because a default by the U. S. government is deemed impossible.

Bonds issued by entities other than the U. S. government, for example, corporate bonds and municipal bonds, are rated by several agencies that specialize in evaluating credit quality. The best known rating agencies are Moody's, Standard & Poor's (S & P), and Fitch. Two others, Duff and Phelps and Crisanti and Maffei have more specialized niches; they mainly serve institutional clients. Bonds are rated when issuers initially come to market; and subsequently, as issuers bring additional issues to market. Issuers pay the agencies for the rating.

On a scale going from the best credit quality to the lowest, Exhibit 3.3 lists the symbols used by each of the major credit rating agencies. These symbols are on the left hand side. The right hand side of Exhibit 3.3 is a translation, into plain English, of what the ratings mean.

Standard & Poor's adds plus (+) and minus (-) signs to its ratings. A "+" signifies higher quality; a "-" signifies somewhat lower quality. For instance, a rating of "B+" is slightly higher than a rating of "B." A rating of "B-" is slightly lower than a "B" rating. Moody's adds a "1" to indicate slightly higher credit quality; for instance, a rating of "A1" is a higher quality credit rating than an "A" rating.

Most prudent individual investors limit their purchases to bonds that are at minimum rated "investment grade," which cor-

---

Exhibit 3.3
Credit Quality Ratings and What They Mean

Moody's	Standard & Poor's	Fitch	
Aaa	AAA	AAA	Gilt edged. If everything that can go wrong, goes wrong, they can still service debt.
Aa	AA	AA	Very high quality by all standards.
A	A	A	Investment grade; good quality.
Baa	BBB	BBB	Lowest investment grade rating; satisfactory; but needs to be monitored.
Ba	BB	BB	Somewhat speculative; low grade.
B	B	B	Very speculative.
Caa	CCC	CCC	Even more speculative. Substantial risk.
Ca	CC	CC	Wildly speculative. May be in default.
C	C	C	In default. Junk.

responds to BBB (Standard & Poor's) and Baa (Moody's). The term "investment grade" stems from the fact that fiduciary institutions, such as banks, are permitted by law to invest only in securities rated at the minimum "investment grade." That rating denotes a fair margin of safety. Note that some ads for bond funds use the term "investment grade" to imply extraordinarily high quality, which is misleading.

How Ratings Are Assigned

Ratings are assigned on the basis of extensive economic analysis by the rating agencies. While the general principles are the same, the exact approach differs for munis and for corporates. This section describes how munis are rated.

Ratings are assigned through a three-part process. First, the agencies identify the specific revenues that will be available for payment of debt service: taxes, fees and so on. They then estimate those revenues over the life of the bond. Finally, revenues are compared to costs of debt service. Remember that costs are known. Costs are the interest payments on the bonds and these were fixed when the bonds were issued. Revenues, on the other hand, must be forecast based on models of future economic activity.

The more money that is predicted to be available for debt service, compared to costs of debt service, the higher the rating. An issuer whose revenues are estimated to equal ten times costs of debt service would be assigned a very high rating. But, if revenues are forecast to be less than the costs of debt service, and therefore insufficient to cover debt service, the rating would be somewhere below investment grade.

. . . and Why They Are Subject to Change

When forecasting economic conditions for the next six months or for perhaps one year, experts stand on reasonably secure ground. But the further they predict into the future, the more imprecise and unreliable their forecasts become. Any prediction of economic conditions that goes out more than five years becomes guesswork. Bear in mind, however, that bonds are rated for their entire life, even if that is 30 years.

As a result, some forecasts turn out to be incorrect. When ratings are reviewed, they change. As the economic fortunes of the issuer vary, so will the ratings. Over time, changes in ratings can be major. For example, State of Louisiana bonds were rated AAA in the middle 1980s. In early 1990, they were rated barely investment grade. Occasionally, changes in rating are more sudden. For instance, State of Massachusetts ratings went from AA to barely investment grade within the space of one year. The most dramatic rating changes have occurred recently in the corporate bond sector where bonds of some corporations that were taken over in a leveraged buyout were downgraded very sharply almost overnight.

Credit Ratings and Bond Returns: How Credit Ratings Affect Interest Income

Above all, credit ratings affect the cost of borrowing; that is, the interest rate that will have to be paid by the issuer to attract buyers. The interest cost to the issuer, you will remember, is the coupon you will earn.

The principle for this is easy to explain. Think of a bond as a loan (which you will recall, is what it is), and imagine that you are a bank that is lending to a borrower. You would ask a lot of questions relating to the probability of repayment. To whom would you rather lend money: to a struggling businessman with no collateral who wants to start a business or to IBM? To someone who has one million dollars in the bank and wants to borrow money for a yacht? Or to John Doe, with barely enough earnings to cover his mortgage payments and who wants to borrow money for home improvements? The answer is obvious. Now, suppose you are the struggling businessman or John Doe. Chances are that if your banker turns you down, you will find a different banker, who will charge you higher interest costs. You may even go to your neighborhood loan shark (or equivalent) who will lend you the money, but charge you a much higher interest rate than the bank.

This is also true for bonds. The most creditworthy issuers, say large states with diverse economies, blue chip corporations with very little debt, or the U. S government borrow at a lower cost. Less creditworthy clients have to pay higher interest. Consequently, bonds with the highest quality credit ratings always carry the lowest yields; bonds with lower credit ratings yield more.

How Changes in Ratings Affect the Price of Bonds

If bonds are downgraded, (that is, if the credit rating is lowered) the price declines. If the rating is upgraded, the price goes up. In fact, bond prices sometimes change if there is even a strong possibility of an upgrade or a downgrade. This is is because anxious investors sell bonds whose credit quality is declining, and they buy bonds whose credit quality is rising.

Unless there is a genuine risk of default, however, price changes in response to upgrades or downgrades are far less major than those occurring due to changes in interest rate levels. With rare exceptions, ratings go up one notch or go down one notch in the rating scale, and prices go up or down perhaps 1 percent or 2 percent per bond in response to rating changes. The change in price corresponds to the amount necessary to bring the yield of a bond (and therefore its price) in line with other bonds rated at the same level. For bonds rated AA, for example, a downgrade to A+ may not even drop the price at all.

This point needs to be emphasized because many individual investors are needlessly worried about relatively minor downgrades and this fear is sometimes exacerbated by the financial press. For instance, a recent article in a widely circulated journal stated that the price of certain municipal bonds was likely to decline by as much as 20 percent if their credit quality deteriorated. This statement overstates the danger. While such a decline is possible, it would represent an unusual occurrence. According to dealers, the worst decline to occur in the municipal market over the past few years involved a succession of downgrades that dropped the price of 10-year Philadelphia bonds by about 7 percent over a period of one year.

There is one notable exception to the preceding statements. During the takeover craze of the 1980s, corporate bond prices were exceptionally volatile because of the possibility of downgrades due to takeovers. This unique situation is discussed in detail in the chapter on corporate bonds.

The following questions and answers deal with some common concerns concerning ratings.

Doesn't a downgrade mean my bonds are no longer safe?

That is usually not the case. The rating scales used by the agencies are very conservative. Distinctions between rating levels are often based on nuances. Any bond rated A or higher continues to have good margins of safety, even after a downgrade.

However, certain downgrades are more significant than others, and should be viewed as red flags. Those would include any downgrade that drops a bond rating to below investment grade; a downgrade of more than one notch (say from AA to A-); or a string of downgrades in close succession. If any of these were to occur, you might want to review whether you wish to continue owning that security.

My bonds are insured, or AAA, or government guaranteed. Won't that guarantee that principal remains safe?

No. What is guaranteed is that interest payments will be made on time and that principal will be redeemed in full at the bond's maturity. There is no connection between that guarantee and what happens to the price (or value) of bonds due to fluctuations in interest rates. If interest rates rise, the value of your bonds will decline. If interest rates decline, the value of your bonds will rise. Period. No exceptions.

I am repeating this point because this is one of the most widely misunderstood aspects of investing in bonds. Many investors assume that if bonds are insured, or obligations of the United States government, then, somehow, the bonds are not risky, and will not fluctuate in price. That is a major and costly mistake. Changes in interest rates affect *all* bonds, whether they are those of Fly-by-Night airlines or obligations of the U. S. Government. The major variant in the size of the decline (or appreciation) will be the maturity length of the bonds.

How frequently do defaults occur?

Very few bonds actually default. (I am excluding junk bonds which have been issued in large quantities for a relatively short period of time, but which have experienced significantly higher default rates). Since World War II, and despite a few well-publicized defaults, bond defaults have been relatively rare, particularly for bonds rated at least investment grade. Indeed, according to one study published by Moody's, since 1970, default rates for bonds *currently* rated at least A+ (or higher) have been virtually nonexistent. (While some bonds that were initially highly rated eventually defaulted, these had been downgraded prior to the actual default. Hence, it is prudent to monitor the ratings of bonds in your portfolio).

Moreover, even when defaults occur seldom do bond investors lose 100 percent of their money. Indeed, there is a good deal of speculation in the bonds of defaulted or bankrupt issuers. That is because such bonds may be purchased very cheaply, perhaps as little as 10 to 30 cents on the dollar. Many defaults have taken the form of a suspension of coupon payments. Such bonds are said to be trading flat. If coupon payments are resumed, the price of the bonds can soar. Bondholders may also benefit from the sale of assets of issuers under bankruptcy proceedings. Finally, some bankrupt companies emerge successfully from bankruptcy proceedings, leading to a bonanza for bondholders.

I want maximum income and maximum safety. My broker advises me to buy 30-year bonds with AAA ratings and just hold them to maturity. Isn't that the safest thing to do?

No. That is a costly and high-risk strategy. It is costly because AAA rated bonds yield less than bonds with lower ratings (but with similar maturities). You are therefore sacrificing income. And it is high risk because interest rate risk is a far greater threat to the integrity of principal than default risk. When you buy 30-year bonds, you have no "visibility;" you cannot know what will happen to interest rates over the next 30 years. In addition, you cannot know what rating changes will occur over the next 30 years.

If safety and predictable income are a major concern, it is safer to buy bonds with maturities of five to ten years, rated at least investment grade or somewhat higher, depending on your preferences and tolerance for risk. Interest income from such bonds is likely to be close to (and occasionally higher) than that of AAA rated bonds with long maturities, so you will not be sacrificing income. But risk to principal is dramatically lower.

Does all of this mean that I should ignore credit ratings?

No. But I have tried to put credit ratings in perspective. Remember that ratings are opinions. The rating agencies do not have any connection to actual debt service payments, which are made by the issuer. Nor do the ratings constitute any kind of recommendation to either buy or sell a particular security. A low rating does not mean that default will occur; and a high rating guarantees nothing, not even that a downgrade won't occur.

Here is a summary of what you will want to remember concerning ratings:

- When you purchase bonds, you should check credit ratings by the major agencies. Most of the time, the ratings are close. If they are not, then to be safe, assume the lowest rating is accurate.

- Buy bonds rated investment grade (or higher) depending on your risk tolerance. A rating of A or better represents a sound rating, particularly for bonds with maturities under five years.

- Be sure that you understand the main reasons for the rating. What sources of revenue will pay debt? What is the credit history of the issuer? Has it been upgraded or downgraded? Why?

- When you own a bond, monitor its rating. Ask your broker to let you know if any rating changes occur (and check periodically). If a significant downgrade occurs, such as those previously mentioned, and you feel uncomfortable holding, you may want to considering selling that security.

- Diversify. Don't put all your assets in one bond. If you have a total of $50,000 to invest, it is more prudent to buy five $10,000 lots than one $50,000 lot. Buy bonds of different issuers to diversify credit risk. And buy bonds with different maturities to diversify interest rate risk.

A SHORT HISTORY OF INTEREST RATES

We read all kinds of discussions concerning interest rate levels. Pundits expound on whether they are high or low, and above all, where they are headed. Without some knowledge of historical interest rate levels, discussions concerning interest rate risk appear somewhat unreal. Exhibit 3.4 presents a simplified history of interest rates between 1926 and 1989.

The interest rate shown is for the U. S. government's 30-year bond. That maturity is the longest issued by the U. S. Treasury. It is also the most widely traded bond, not only in the United States but worldwide. (The United States is the only major government which still issues a 30-year bond). Because it is such a key secu-

Exhibit 3.4
A History of Interest Rates between 1926 and 1989

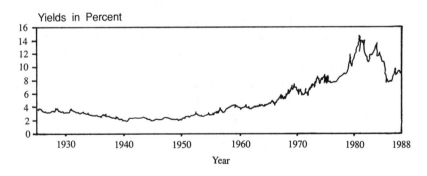

Source: *Stocks, Bonds, Bills & Inflation, 1989 Yearbook™*, *Ibbotson Associates, Chicago (annually updates work by Roger G. Ibbotson and Rex A. Sinquefield). All rights reserved,* p. 41.

rity, the most recently issued 30-year Treasury bond is known as the "bellwether long bond," or the "long bond," for short.

Exhibit 3.4 shows that between 1926 and 1940, during the depression, the yield on the long bond declined gradually from a little under 4 percent to around 2 percent. Between 1940 and 1950, interest rates barely budged. But in 1950, rates began a long and almost uninterrupted rise. They rose first slowly, then more steeply, from 2 percent in 1950, to 4 percent in 1960. (Remember, in those days, bank passbook accounts paid 2 to 2 1/2 percent interest). By the late 1960s, yields began to fluctuate violently, rising to 8 percent in 1970 and then going sharply and steeply upwards. In 1982, the long bond yielded 16 percent! Note that during that period, yields on tax-exempt bonds with 30-year maturities reached 12 to 14 percent.

The period between 1950 and 1982 represents a bear market in bonds that lasted well over 30 years. During many of those years, bonds were said not to "have earned their coupon" meaning that the principal value of bonds declined by more than the interest income received. During the disastrous 1970s, the worst of those three decades, satirists described long-term bonds as "fixed rate instrument(s) designed to fall in price" and "certificates of confiscation." Bondholders suffered staggering losses as bonds purchased in the 1960s and 1970s with coupons of 4 percent to 6 percent declined by 50 percent or more ($500 per $1,000 bond) as interest rates approached 16 percent.

Note further that these bondholders suffered a double whammy. Not only was the value of their bonds sharply down, but to add insult to injury, they were earning meager returns of 4 percent to 6 percent while interest rates went into the double digits even on short-term and on tax-exempt securities. The final blow was that during that period, double digit inflation was eroding the purchasing power of every dollar.

In 1982, however, bond yields began a very sharp decline. Bond prices soared! Since 1986, the yield on the long bond has fluctuated somewhat less violently, confined, with some exceptions, to a trading range between 8 percent and 9 percent although it briefly touched 10 1/2 percent in 1987, just before the 1987 stock crash.

The returns earned on long-term bonds between 1982 and 1990 have no precedent in the history of the United States. First, because yields reached historically high levels. And second, because anyone who purchased bonds during the late 1970s or early 1980s, at coupon rates between 11 percent and 16 percent for Treasuries (and correspondingly high rates in other sectors of the bond market) is either continuing to earn unprecedented rates of interest if those bonds are still in their possession; or, if the bonds were sold, reaped exceptional capital gains. (During the late 1980s, U. S. Treasury bonds with coupons of 15 percent to 16 percent sold for as much as $1700 per bond, for a capital gain of 70 percent).

"Real" and "Nominal" Rates of Return

The terms "real rate" and "nominal rate" are sometimes used to refer to rates of return on bonds. These terms represent a method of adjusting bond yields for the rate of inflation. The nominal rate measures the actual dollars earned, based on interest rate yields. To obtain the real rate, subtract the inflation rate from the nominal rate. For example, the coupon rate on the government 30-year bond is currently close to 8.25 percent. That is the nominal rate. Subtracting the current rate of inflation, which is around 5 percent, results in a real rate of return of about 3.25 percent.

The relationship between the real rate of return and the nominal rate has varied enormously during the century. So has the level of interest rates. Interest rate levels are governed, first of all, by what is happening to prices (that is, inflation or deflation). Second, interest rate levels are governed by expectations of what will happen to prices. Until 1950, even though interest rates were low, bonds earned a real rate of return, because inflation was low. As inflation began to rise, the real rate of return began to decline, despite a rise in nominal rates. The real rate of return throughout the 1960s and 1970s was negative even though rates were high and rising. Moreover, inflation eroded the purchasing power of older issues. That was the main reason interest rates rose so steeply: few investors were willing to purchase long-term bonds because the the nominal rate did not appear high enough to compensate for anticipated increases in yield as a result of continuing high inflation.

In spite of the interest turbulence of the 1960s, 1970s and 1980s, attitudes of many investors concerning bonds continue to be shaped by conditions prevailing more than 30 years ago when interest rates moved less over a period of years than they did during some months of the 1980s. Many investors still don't fully realize how devastating inflation and concomitant increases in interest rates can be to investors who own long-term instruments.

For the decade of the 1980s, the real rate of return on long maturity, fixed-income instruments has been about 3 percent above the rate of inflation. In 1988, with inflation running at about 4 percent, and interest rates on the long bond at around 8 1/2 percent, real rates were about 4 1/2 percent. The comment was sometimes made that real rates of return were unusually generous, compared to historical standards. It is likely, however, that the high real rate of return reflected the belief on the part of professionals that inflation rates would gradually increase.

Indeed, compared to the rates of inflation prevailing in the 1950s, (below 2 percent) the rates of inflation of the 1980s (between 3 percent and 5 percent) are a disaster. In fact, rates of inflation much lower than these were considered a disaster twenty years ago. In contrast, in West Germany and Japan, inflation rates in the 1980s have averaged under 2 percent a year and any rise above that level is viewed with extreme alarm.

Unless there is an extended period of actual deflation, nominal rates will probably continue to remain three or four percentage points above the inflation rate. No one knows whether the next 30 years will see deflation, or go back to double-digit inflation. More importantly, no one has ever consistently predicted interest rates correctly over a period of 30 years; that is, over the life of a long-term bond.

The strategies described in this book are predicated on the assumption that interest rates cannot be predicted, but that you can manage your bond portfolio so that no matter what happens to interest rates, you will not be seriously hurt.

SUMMARY

Individuals who purchase bonds tend to buy and hold and worry mainly about credit quality. Such an attitude made sense at a time when interest rates barely budged. The interest rate volatility that now dominates the credit markets has become the major risk factor that bond investors face. Interest rate changes have wreaked far more devastating losses on bond portfolios, and far more often, than credit risk.

Investors concerned about the safety of their principal should limit their purchases to bonds with maturities of between two and seven years.

4

Many Happy Returns: Fundamentals of Bond Math

This chapter discusses

- *simple and compound interest*

- *yield (current yield and yield-to-maturity)*

- *compounding*

- *total return*

Discussions of bond returns begin and end with numbers. If your eyes glaze over when numbers and formulae appear, you may be tempted to skip this chapter. But that would be a mistake because it is impossible to evaluate bonds without an understanding of bond math. But fear not. I, too, am a charter member of the math anxiety crowd. The mathematics in this section is at the level of arithmetic, or at most, elementary algebra. More importantly, the emphasis is on concepts that help you to evaluate what you will actually earn, not on mathematical formulae.

BOND CASH FLOWS

When you buy a bond, you earn money from three sources. The first source has already been been mentioned. It is the simple interest derived from coupons, usually paid twice a year. The second source arises from the difference between the purchase price of a bond, and its sale or redemption price. This difference may result in capital gains. The third source is earned when coupons are reinvested, thereby creating still another source of revenue known as "interest-on-interest." Let's look at each in turn.

Simple Interest

Let's start with simple interest (that is, the coupon payments).

Let us say you invest $10,000 in a four-year bond, paying 8 percent a year, semi-annually. In return, you will receive two coupons (or interest) payments of $400 each, at six-month intervals every year. If you hold the bond until it matures, you will receive eight coupons that total $3,200. Those eight coupons are the simple interest.

Compound Interest: or the Magic of Compounding

If the coupons are spent, only the simple interest is earned. But if the coupons are reinvested, those produce additional interest; subsequently, if those earnings are reinvested, you earn interest on that interest, and so on. That entire income stream is called, logically enough "interest-on-interest," or "compounded interest."

This illustrates the basic way in which compounding works. But it does not make clear how significantly interest-on-interest increases the total amount of money that is earned on the original investment. The simplest way to explain the process is with some examples.

Let's assume that you are reinvesting each $400 coupon received on your $10,000, 4-year bond, also at 8 percent. Exhibit 4.1 shows how much you earn every six months. At the end of the first year, interest-on-interest totals an unexciting $16.00. By the end of the second year, interest-on-interest amounts to $98. By the end of the third year, it is $253. And by the end of the fourth year,

Exhibit 4.1
**Interest and Interest-on-Interest on a 4-Year, $10,000 Par Value,
8% Bond. Coupons are Reinvested at 8%.**

Period	Time	Coupon (A)	Interest-on-Interest (cumulative) (B)	Total Interest (cumulative) (A + B)
1	6 months	$400	$ 0	$400
2	1 year	400	16	816
3	18 months	400	48	1248
4	2 years	400	98	1698
5	30 months	400	166	2166
6	3 years	400	253	2653
7	42 months	400	359	3159
8	4 years	400	485	3685

it is $485. To place that in perspective, consider the following. By the end of the fourth year, the interest-on-interest of $485 increases the total interest earned by a factor of about 15 percent (compared to simple interest alone). Moreover, whereas at the end of the first year, interest-on-interest represents only 2 percent of the total amount of interest earned, by the end of the fourth year, interest-on-interest of $485 comprises about 13 percent of the total interest.

That, however, is only the beginning. The amount of interest-on-interest earned is directly related to the time allowed for compounding: the longer the time frame, the greater the percentage produced by interest-on-interest. If the 8 percent, $10,000 bond mentioned in the preceding example is allowed to continue to compound (semi-annually) for 10 years at 8 percent, in 10 years, interest-on-interest comprises 33 percent of total interest earned; in 20 years, 58 percent; and in 30 years, it reaches 75 percent.

Increasing the frequency of compounding (compounding four times a year, for example, instead of twice a year; or as some banks do, compounding daily) would translate into higher returns. So would increasing the rate, either of the original coupon or of the interest-on-interest. This would be true both on an absolute basis (more total dollars would be earned) and on a relative basis (the percentage that would consist of interest-on-interest would grow). Even apparently minute percentage differences, compounded over long periods of time, make a significant difference. For example, over a 10-year period, increasing the interest rate from 7 percent to 7.5 percent would increase total interest earned by almost 5 percent; after 20 years, by somewhat over 10 percent; and after 40 years (for the investor with a long-term perspective), by an astonishing 20 percent.

Compounded interest has been called the eighth wonder of the world. And yet, it works for everyone. It requires no special aptitude and it is totally automatic. In fact, only two ingredients are required: reinvesting and time.

The rate at which assets compound is critical to the total actually earned. Money reinvested (tax free) at 4 percent, semi-annually, will double every 17.5 years; at 6 percent, every 11.7 years; at 8 percent, every 8.8 years; and at 10 percent, every 7 years. Over very long periods, as Exhibit 4.2 shows, compounding achieves extraordinary results.

Compounding has been heavily advertised for zero coupon bonds; but it applies equally to all financial investments, whether stocks, bonds, or savings accounts. Whenever you examine information concerning an investment (a mutual fund, stocks, or bonds), the merits of that investment are usually illustrated with tables showing that if you had invested in that particular vehicle,

---

Exhibit 4.2
The Power of Compound Interest

	At 8% Compounded Semiannually:	
$1,000 will grow to	$2,000+	in 9 years
$1,000 will grow to	7,106	in 25 years
$1,000 will grow to	50,504	in 50 years
$1,000 will grow to	2,550,749	in 100 years

Source: Sidney Homer and Martin Leibowitz, *Inside the Yield Book*, Englewood Cliffs: Prentice Hall, 1973, p. 32. Reprinted with permission.

---

you would now be (or you will become) very rich. All those tables basically illustrate the magic of compounding. The differences in the final result are not necessarily due to the particular product that is being advertised. Rather, those differences are the result of two variables; namely, the actual rates at which that instrument compounds (that is, the actual reinvestment rates) and the amount of time.

YIELD

When you buy a bond, you are quoted a "yield." That term appears in a number of phrases: dividend yield, current yield and yield-to-maturity. Each has a very precise meaning. Let's look at each in turn.

Coupon Yield

Coupon yield is set when a bond is issued. It is the interest rate paid by a bond, listed as a percentage (for instance, 8 1/2, 10 3/4). That percentage is a percentage of par, and it designates a fixed-dollar amount which never changes through the life of the bond. A 10 percent coupon will always be $100, (paid out in two $50 increments) for the entire life of the bond, no matter what happens to price.

Current Yield

Almost as soon as a bond starts trading in the secondary market, it ceases to trade at par. Current yield is simply coupon divided by price.

Let us assume you purchase three bonds: the first at par ($1,000); the second at a premium ($1,200); and the third at a discount ($800), each bearing $100 in annual coupons. Dividing the coupon ($100) by the price results in a current yield of 10 percent for the par bond; 8.33 percent for the premium bond; and 12.5 percent for the discount bond. Current yield is equal to coupon yield for the par bond; higher than dividend yield for the premium bond; and lower than dividend yield for the discount.

Current yield is quoted for fixed-income securities of any maturity, whether short or long. In none of the preceding examples was the bond's maturity specified. That is because current yield is based only on coupon and price. Current yield, therefore, fails to measure two important cash flows earned from bonds: interest-on-interest and capital gains or losses.

Yield-to-Maturity

Yield-to-maturity (YTM) is a far more comprehensive measure of return than "current yield." It estimates the total amount that you will earn over the entire life of a bond, from all possible sources of income, namely, coupon income, interest-on-interest, and capital gains or losses due to the difference between the price you pay when you purchase the bond, and par (the redemption price).

Calculating yield-to-maturity (YTM) with paper and pencil involves a tedious trial-and-error algebraic procedure. In practice, no one actually uses the formula. Before the advent of calculators, the investor (or his broker) used bond yield tables to come up with an approximate YTM. Today, the process has been simplified (and made more accurate) through the use of financial calculators.[1] The YTM is the measure of return most widely quoted by brokers although, as will be seen later, it is not usually quoted for corporate bonds or for muni "dollar" bonds.

However, the important point to remember about YTM is the information that yield conveys. Many investors believe that YTM

---

1. A good financial calculator can be purchased for $30.00 to $80.00. Specifically request one that is set up for calculating bond yields. For example, let's use a calculator to compute the yield-to-maturity of a 10-year bond. Let's assume the bond is purchased at the discounted price of $800 and redeemed at maturity at par ($1,000). This bond has one $100 coupon per year. All of those numbers are fed into the calculator as follows:

- Price of $800 is plugged in as PV (present value).
- Par price of $1,000 (the redemption value) is plugged in as future value (FV).
- The dollar amount of the coupon payment is entered as payment (PMT).
- Finally, enter the number of years to maturity (10 years).
- Solve for yield-to-maturity by hitting (i), the interest key.

Result: the yield-to-maturity is 13.8 percent, which is higher than the coupon rate of 10 percent, due to the capital gain of $200.00. The better financial calculators enable you to compute YTM with great precision, by plugging in the specific dates from date of purchase to date of maturity.

is a prediction of what they will actually earn. That is not the case. The actual return is likely to differ from the YTM, perhaps considerably, because the YTM will only be realized under certain conditions. Those conditions are: 1. that you hold the bond to maturity; 2. that the coupons are reinvested (rather than spent); and that 3. coupons are reinvested at the yield-to-maturity rate. Let's briefly look at each assumption.

1. That you hold the bond to maturity.

The YTM quote is based on the redemption price of par. If you sell a bond before it matures at a price other than par, then the capital gain or loss will considerably alter what you actually earn. If, for example, you purchase a bond at par, and sell it at a premium, say $1,200, the $200 difference is a capital gain of approximately 20 percent. That boosts actual return by a very significant amount. But if you buy a bond at par and sell it at a loss, say, for $800, you lose about 20 percent. Clearly, that will mean that you would earn far less than the YTM initially quoted.[2]

2. That you reinvest coupons and

3. That you reinvest them at the YTM rate.

YTM calculations are based on the assumption that coupons are never spent; they are always reinvested.

Clearly, if you spend coupons, then the interest-on-interest goes out the window. You will then earn less than the anticipated YTM. How much less depends both on how many coupons you spend and on the maturity of the bonds.

In addition, the assumption is made that that the coupons are reinvested at the quoted YTM rate. This may sound like double talk. However, what this means is that if a broker quotes a YTM of 7 percent for a bond, then that yield will be earned only if each and every coupon is reinvested at a rate of 7 percent, that is, at the same rate as the quoted YTM. Clearly, that is highly unlikely to happen. Some coupons will be reinvested at more

---

2. For tax purposes, when you sell bonds, capital gains and losses are usually treated as ordinary capital gains and losses. If the sale price is higher than the purchase price, the sale results in a taxable capital gain. Note, however, that if you buy a premium bond, the YTM is quoted net. Even though the redemption price is lower than the purchase price, that difference is not treated as a capital loss for tax purposes.

than 7 percent; others, at less than 7 percent. If you reinvest coupons at a higher rate, you will actually earn more than the bond's stated yield-to-maturity. If you reinvest coupons at lower rates, you will earn less.

Both of these factors alter what you actually earn, compared to the anticipated YTM. Exhibit 4.3 shows what the actual yield would be for a 25-year par bond, with a 7.5 percent coupon, under a variety of reinvestment assumptions. The YTM quoted at the time of purchase is 7.5 percent.

As Exhibit 4.3 shows, the anticipated 7.5 percent YTM is realized only if all coupons are reinvested at 7.5 percent (line 4). If no coupons are reinvested (line 1), the anticipated 7.5 percent YTM is cut to 4.27 percent. On the other hand, if coupons are reinvested at a higher rate than 7.5 percent, the actual yield rises: to 7.77 percent if coupons are reinvested at 8 percent; but more significantly, to 8.91 percent if coupons are reinvested at 10 percent. The higher the reinvestment rate, the higher the actual return.

Exhibit 4.3
How the Reinvestment Rate Affects Actual Yield over the Life of a 25-Year, 7.5 Percent Par Bond

Dollars per $1,000 Bond for the Life of the Bond

Assumed Reinvestment Rate (Semiannual Basis)	Coupon Income (A)	Interest-on-Interest (B)	Total Interest (A + B)	Interest-on-Interest as Percent of Total Interest	Actual Yield
0.0%	$1,875	$ 0	$1,875	0%	4.27%
5.0	1,875	1,781	3,656	49	6.25
6.0	1,875	2,355	4,230	56	6.73
7.5	1,875	3,426	5,301	65	7.50
8.0	1,875	3,850	5,725	67	7.77
10.0	1,875	5,976	7,851	76	8.91

Source: Frank Fabozzi, et al., *The Handbook of Fixed-Income Securities*, 2nd ed., Homewood, IL: Dow Jones Irwin, p. 596. Adapted with permission.

The amount of total earnings due to interest-on-interest varies both with the maturity of a bond and with the reinvestment rate. It is less significant for shorter than for longer bonds. For example, for an 8 percent bond maturing in one year, interest-on-interest represents only 2 percent of total return. For the same bond, with a five-year maturity, interest-on-interest represents 17 percent of total return. When the same bond matures in 20 years, however, interest-on-interest represents 58 percent of total return; and when it matures in 30 years, interest-on-interest represents 75 percent of total return.[3]

Reinvestment rates in all the preceding YTM computations have been assumed to be both constant and known. In real life, of course, you cannot know what the reinvestment rate is going to be, since you don't know where interest rates will be in the future. Consequently, you cannot know at the time you purchase a bond exactly how much you will earn in actual dollars. Moreover, for longer maturities, since the amount represented by the interest-on-interest becomes greater on a percentage basis, the yield-to-maturity estimate becomes increasingly less exact, and less reliable. That uncertainty is known as the *"reinvestment risk."*

Calling this uncertainty a "risk" is a misnomer in that there is no risk of an actual loss, either of principal or of interest. There is, of course, the risk that coupons may have to be reinvested at a lower rate. Actual return would then decline. But the reinvestment risk may work in your favor if coupons are reinvested at a higher rate: that would increase the actual return.

Reinvestment risk can be eliminated by purchasing zero coupon bonds. For most investors, however, reinvestment risk is not a major problem. Investors should simply be aware that YTM does not predict actual return accurately.

If YTM does not predict actual return, what information does it convey? The chief usefulness of YTM quotes is that they permit direct comparison between different securities, with dissimilar coupons and prices (par, premium and discount). Suppose, for example, that you are considering three different securities for purchase, the first an A-rated bond, selling at a discount, and maturing in five years; the second a AAA-bond selling

---

3. Sidney Homer and Martin Leibowitz, *Inside the Yield Book.* Englewood Cliffs: Prentice Hall, 1972), p. 24.

at a premium and maturing in five years; and the third an A rated bond selling at par and maturing in 30 years. The only measurement of return common to all three is the YTM. The YTM enables you to evaluate, for instance, how much yield you might be giving up for higher credit quality; or how much yield you are picking up as you lengthen maturities.

But overall, there is too much emphasis on yield. YTM should not be the main criterion for selecting specific bonds. More appropriate criteria would depend on your objective when you purchase bonds. If, for example, you do not intend to reinvest coupons, then you might look for bonds with high current yield. If you are primarily interested in stability of principal, that would dictate selecting bonds with intermediate (2 to 7 year) maturities. Such criteria are discussed at greater length in other sections of the book.

TOTAL RETURN

Investors in fixed-income securities sometimes make the mistake of equating interest income or advertised yield with return without taking into consideration what is happening to principal. One very useful way of measuring return includes the changing value of principal. It is called "total return." Total return consists of whatever you earn in dividends, plus or minus changes in the value of principal. To be 100 percent accurate, you would also subtract taxes and commission expenses from return.

For example, let's assume that a year ago, you invested $10,000 in a bond fund, purchasing 1,000 shares at $10.00 each. Assume also that the bond fund was advertising a yield of 10 percent, or $1.00 per share, which was maintained for the entire year. But suppose that in the meantime, interest rates have risen so that now bond funds with similar maturity and credit quality yield 11 percent. As a result, your bond fund is now selling for $9.00 per share. What have you earned on that investment for the past year?

One answer is that you have earned simple interest income (based on the dividend distributions) of 10 percent, or $1,000. But, that ignores the fact that your bond fund has now lost approximately $1 per share (10 percent of its principal value) and that your principal is now worth $9,000.

Add the dividend earnings of $1,000 to the current value of your fund ($9,000). Your investment is now worth $10,000. But it was worth that one year earlier. (For the sake of simplicity, I am ignoring interest-on-interest and commission costs). Therefore, the net return is $0, or 0 percent. That is your total return, to date, even though you have received 10 percent dividend interest.

In the trade, among professionals, that kind of calculation is done daily, and it is known as "marking-to-market." It describes to each trader exactly what his holdings are worth at the end of the day, if he had to or wanted to sell them. But you may say: I am only interested in income. I am not interested in total return. I haven't sold my bond fund. Therefore, I have not lost anything. I'll just wait until the bond matures or until the bond fund goes back to what I paid for it.

Unfortunately, that is not true. Your fund is now worth $9.00 per share and you have lost 10 percent of your principal. It is gone. The future value of each share of the fund will depend on a variety of factors, such as the future course of interest rates and the specific management practices of the fund managers. At some future date, the fund may be worth more than $9.00 per share. But it also may not. The fund's price may or may not return to what you paid for it.

This scenario can become even more depressing. Let us assume, for example, that you were charged a 5 percent commission, which was paid when you bought the fund. Subtract the commission from the above calculation and you get: total return, minus 5 percent after one year, *even though the fund has paid out* 10 percent in dividend income, and is accurately quoting its current yield at 10 percent. If, disgusted with this turn of events, you decide to sell this bond fund, your total return, which in this instance would become your actual (or realized return), would then become minus 15 percent. (Some of this could be used to generate a tax loss; but for the moment, I am leaving tax considerations aside). So even though the dividend yield of 10 percent was paid out to you, after one year, your investment is worth 16 percent less than a year earlier.

To be 100 percent precise, let's note again that if you hold individual bonds to maturity, the price will return to par. But that may take 30 years! The price of bond funds, however, does not necessarily return to par. (This is discussed in the chapters on bond funds.)

The important point to remember is that when you are evaluating fixed-income securities, you must assess potential fluctuations in the value of the principal and not just look at dividend yield. Such fluctuations are not theoretical. They affect your assets in real dollars. Even if you do not sell your bonds (or your bond fund) and do not realize the loss in principal value, you experience another loss: you are unable to take advantage of the currently higher yields (that is called an opportunity cost); and you have lost liquidity because you may be unwilling to sell a bond if it has declined significantly in value.

If you look only at the dividend yield side, bond investments look very predictable. But if you include potential changes in a bond's principal value, and you look at bonds as total return vehicles, the picture changes vastly.

But, you may be thinking, "I just want to invest in bonds for income."

Unfortunately, whether you like it or not, like Moliere's character who found out that he had been speaking in prose without realizing it, if you are buying bonds with 30-year maturities, you are making a bet on interest rates, whether you know it or not.

Investors intent on boosting yield sometimes place their principal at risk for very little gain. When purchasing bonds, the first question to ask, always, is, "how much more am I really earning?" The second is, "what kinds of risk am I assuming in order to earn that extra amount?"

For example, on May 31, 1989, a well-known family of mutual funds was quoting a current yield of 6.99 percent for its tax-free State of New Jersey money market fund, and of 6.92 percent for its hi-yield State of New Jersey bond fund. (The numbers are correct. Short-term rates at that date were above long-term rates. For a discussion of this phenomenon, see the section on the yield curve.) Now, remember that the money market fund has essentially no risk to principal, whereas the New Jersey hi-yield bond fund currently has a maturity of about 22 years, so that risk to principal, due to potential interest rate fluctuations, is high. In this instance, if your money is in the hi-yield fund, are you getting compensated for the risk to principal that you are assuming? Well, it would appear that you would have to be crazy to put your money in the long-term bond fund under these conditions, and you would be right, with one exception: if you think that interest rates are declining, you might put some of your money in the long-term bond fund, assuming that the resulting capital gain would boost your total return.

No one can quote total return to you ahead of time. Total return is actual return to you, based on your own investment experience. For any investment, you start out with a given sum. For a chosen period period of time, (say one year) add all the income streams that have accrued (whether from dividends, or interest-on-interest, or capital gains), subtract all transaction costs, and be sure to add or subtract any changes in principal value. You can also subtract taxes to obtain total return on a net-after-tax basis. For the year, calculate how much (as a percentage) your investment has grown or declined. That is your total return.

There is one further virtue to "total return." The concept is easy to understand. The exact formula for calculating total return is:

$$\frac{(\text{Ending Figure} + \text{Dividends} + \text{Distributions}) - \text{Beginning Figure}}{\text{Beginning Figure}}$$

The same formula can be used to calculate total return on any investment, whether it's stocks, gold bullion, baseball cards, or real estate. Calculating total return keeps you honest; it helps you to evaluate what your investments are really doing for you. It is, therefore, a very useful concept.

Actual Returns: A Prototypical Bond Transaction

A discussion of bond returns can appear dry as dust. So let's apply it to a prototypical bond transaction, in order to illustrate how a variety of factors affect your investments.

First, let's remember that when you buy a bond—or a bond fund—you cannot know at the time that you buy the bond how interest rates are going to behave, and you may not know how long you will hold the security. Therefore, it follows that you cannot know at what rate(s) coupons will be reinvested, and if you need to resell, at what price. Let's briefly illustrate how to calculate what you have actually earned. In order to do that, let's buy and sell a bond, include some transaction costs, and figure out actual returns.

You decide to buy a bond. Your broker shows you the 10 percent State of Bliss bonds, of 02, (that is, maturing in about 2002, about 11 years) quoted at 90 bid/92 ask. You buy the 10 bonds but you do not hold them to maturity. Instead, you sell them three years later. At that date, the bonds are still being quoted at 90 bid/92 ask (interest rates are unusually stable). At the time of purchase, what was your current yield? Your yield-to-maturity? And how much did you actually earn when you sold?

Well, first of all, since the coupon is 10 percent of par, you know that you will receive two coupon payments every year, each $500, or $1,000 annually for 10 bonds. You will pay the "ask" (or offer) price (the higher price), $920 per bond, for a total of $9,200 for the 10 bonds. The current yield will be $1,000 divided by $9,200, which equals 10.87 percent.

To calculate the yield-to-maturity, take out your financial calculator, plug in the price that you are paying for the bonds ($9,200), the par value of the bonds at maturity ($10,000); the coupons of $500 paid twice a year; and the holding period to maturity (11 years). Since you are planning to hold the bonds until maturity, you project that you will earn an additional $900 in capital gains. The yield-to-maturity therefore is going to be somewhat higher than the current yield. In fact, it is quoted at approximately 11.4 percent.

But you sell your bonds after three years for $90 per bond ($9000 for the 10 bonds). Since you paid $9,200 for the 10 bonds, you now have a capital loss of $200, and not the anticipated $900 capital gain. Because of that small capital loss, it should be clear immediately that your actual earnings were less than either the anticipated yield-to-maturity, or the current yield. In fact, the actual yield-to-maturity turns out to be 10.21 percent.

Commissions are actually included in the above example, since they are the difference between the "bid" and the "ask" price. In this instance, the commission was not very high. However, a higher commission (say 5 percent) would drop the yield-to-maturity for that three-year holding period to 8.9 percent.

Also, the difference between the sale price and the purchase price was not very high. If the bond price had declined a lot further, say to $80.00 per bond, you would now have a capital (or principal loss) of $1,200. That in turn would drop the actual yield-to-maturity to only 6.8 percent (that number includes coupon interest as well as interest-on-interest).

Using the total return formula would give you a cumulative number for the three-year holding period. For the first transaction described (buy at $9,200, earn interest income for three years of $3,000, sell at $9,000), total return for the three-year holding period would be 30.4 percent. If you increase the spread to 5 percent (and therefore buy at $9,500, earn $3,000 interest income but sell at $9,000) cumulative total return for that three-year holding period would decline to 26 percent. (Yes, that is correct.) If you buy at $9,200, earn $3,000 interest income, but sell after three years at $8,000, cumulative total return declines to 19.5 percent for the three-year period.

These examples demonstrate the dramatic impact of commissions and of changing bond prices on actual returns. That is why they are emphasized throughout the book.

Also note also that none of the preceding examples includes still another important transaction cost—taxes. In order to compare returns on fixed-income instruments with precision, any tax owed on dividends or capital gains should be subtracted from the estimated yield. The tax calculation would depend on current tax rates and your own tax bracket. This is discussed in greater detail in later sections.

DURATION

One of the newer concepts in the management of bond portfolios is "duration." Duration does not measure return. It is primarily a gauge of bond volatility; that is, it predicts how much specific bonds will go up (or down) in price if interest rates change. Duration is used heavily by professionals for the management of institutional portfolios. The term crops up, however, in newsletters or to explain the volatility of one bond fund when compared to another. It is beginning to appear in material intended for individual investors. I am including it in an appendix to this chapter for reference.

SUMMARY

This chapter discussed a number of ways of evaluating bond returns. It first showed how bond cash flows interact to compound over time and pointed out the importance of compounding (the eighth wonder of the world) in building assets. The different concepts of yield were then defined. Current yield is based on coupon and price only. It ignores all other cash flows. Yield-to-maturity takes into account all of the bond's known cash flows. It is a projection, however, and not necessarily what you will actually earn because neither the price at which you sell (if you sell before the bond matures), nor the rates at which you reinvest coupons can be predicted at the time you buy the bond.

If you want to know what you have actually earned while owning a bond, you would use the concept of total return, which includes changes in the value of your bond, commission costs, and interest income.

The prototypical bond transaction was included in order to show that commission costs and changes in the price of bonds due to interest rate fluctuations make a significant difference to your overall returns from fixed-income securities. It is important to consider them when you buy bonds, and not just to buy on the basis of the quoted yield.

APPENDIX: DURATION AND BOND PRICE VOLATILITY

Duration is based on the same cash flows as yield-to-maturity. But duration adds in as important elements the timing and the size of all the cash flows. It takes into account not just how many dollars will be received as coupons and repayment of principal, but also when those cash flows occur. These, in turn, affect interest-on-interest.

To understand duration, you have to be familiar with a concept known as "the time value of money." In its simplest form, it states that "a dollar received today is worth more than the same dollar received next year or in ten years." There are two reasons for this. The first is that the dollar you have or receive today will start earning interest today, which can be reinvested, further compounding the earnings. In addition, your dollar will be worth less in the future (it will have less purchasing power) than today because of inflation.

If you assume an inflation rate, you can calculate precisely what a dollar will be worth at some date in the future (that is, its future value). For example, if you assume an inflation rate of 5 percent, you can calculate that $10,000 will be worth $10,500 in one year, and $12,763 in five years. The formula used for calculating the future value of any sum is the same as that used for compounding interest, not for calculating simple interest. Similarly, if you know that you will receive a certain sum at a known date, such as the coupons on the bonds you own, you can extrapolate what that future dollar is worth to you today (its present value). To illustrate, assuming an inflation rate of 5 percent, you can derive the present value of a coupon payment of $10,000 received five years from today (it would be $7,835).

Calculating duration is tedious, even with a calculator, because it requires computing the present value of all cash flows. To compute duration, you plug into your calculator the exact amount and date of coupon payments, and the date when principal will be repaid (at maturity). You derive the present value of all of the bond's known cash flows: coupon payments, redeemed principal, and capital gains (or losses). And you compound them (for interest-on-interest) at the assumed reinvestment rate.

The resulting number is the bond's duration, in years. In effect, the number you have obtained readjusts the maturity date to account for coupons and interest-on-interest. The reason for this is that with a low coupon bond, since much of the return is received at maturity, you will be earning much less interest-on-interest. With a high coupon bond, you receive more money earlier and this can be reinvested earlier. In effect, a low coupon bond becomes a longer bond than a high coupon bond with the same maturity date.

With the exception of zero coupon bonds, the duration of a bond is always shorter than its term to maturity. (The duration of zero coupon bonds equals their term to maturity).

Duration explains why for a given maturity, bonds with larger coupons are less volatile. As an example, take two bonds maturing in 10 years, one with a 10 percent coupon; the other with a 4 percent coupon. The bond with the 10 percent coupon would be less volatile than the bond with the 4 percent coupon.

The reason is that the 10 percent coupon would have a higher present value than would the 4 percent coupon. The larger coupon results in a higher cash flow than the 4 percent coupon. The investor receives more cash, earlier; therefore, a larger sum can be reinvested and it will earn greater interest-on-interest. Such a bond will decline less in a down market; but it will also appreciate less in an up market than the bond with the 4 percent coupon.

Conversely, for a given maturity, the bond with a smaller coupon would be more volatile than the bond with the 10 percent coupon. In a down market, it would decline more quickly than the 10 percent coupon bond, and the percentage of the price decline would be larger. But it would appreciate more in an up market.

Duration explains why zero coupon bonds are the most volatile of all bonds. Since there are no coupon payments, no monies can be reinvested until the bond matures. As a result, in up markets, when interest rates decline, zeros absolutely soar in value; in down markets, their price plummets.

Remember that duration is a relative concept. A bond's duration is always compared to its maturity date. Bonds (or bond funds) with longer durations are more volatile. Bonds with shorter durations are less volatile. The most volatile bonds are zeros.

5

A Guide for the Perplexed: How to Read the Financial Pages

This chapter discusses

■ *the Table of Treasury Bills, Bonds and Notes*

■ *the yield curve.*

INTERPRETING THE TABLE OF TREASURY BILLS, BONDS AND NOTES

You are on the train in the morning and reading the daily newspaper. If you are currently investing in bonds, what do you want to look at? Well, before you turn to sports, or gourmet cooking, or whatever else really turns you on, your newspaper probably contains its own version of a nifty table that looks like Exhibit 5.1. Its title will be *Table of Treasury Bills, Bonds, and Notes* and it will tell you very quickly almost everything you might want to know about what is happening in the credit markets.

Exhibit 5.1
Table of Treasury Bills, Bonds and Notes

Treasury Bills

Date 1991	Bid	Ask	Chg.	Yield
Mar 28	5.97	5.94	+0.06	6.04
Apr 18	5.79	5.75	+0.12	5.87
May 9	5.88	5.84	-0.03	5.98
May 30	5.88	5.84		6.00
Jun 21	5.91	5.88	+0.02	6.06
Jul 11	5.89	5.88		6.08
Aug 1	5.92	5.88	-0.02	6.10
Aug 29	5.93	5.91	-0.02	6.16
Sep 5	5.91	5.88	-0.01	6.14
Oct 24	5.93	5.91		6.19
Dec 19	5.96	5.94	+0.01	6.25
1992				
Jan 16	6.00	5.97	+0.01	6.30
Mar 12	6.00	5.97	+0.02	6.35

Bonds and Notes

Date	Rate	Bid	Ask	Chg Yld
Mar 91 p	6¾	99.30	100.02	1.03
Apr 91 n	12	100.09	100.13	-01 4.33
May 91 p	8	100.06	100.10	5.63
Jun 91 n	7⅞	100.13	100.17	+01 5.71
Jul 91 n	13¾	102.05	102.09	-01 5.95
Aug 91 n	14	103.09	103.13	-02 5.84
Sep 91 p	9	101.12	101.16	6.10
Nov 91 p	7¾	100.01	100.05	6.23
Nov 91 p	7	100.25	100.29	-01 6.34
Jan 92 p	8	101.09	101.13	-01 6.38
Feb 92 p	8½	101.20	101.24	6.51
Mar 92 p	7⅞	101.06	101.10	-01 6.51
Apr 92 k	11¾	105	105.04	-02 6.62
May 92 n	13¾	107.14	107.18	6.70
Jun 92 p	8⅜	101.25	101.29	-01 6.76
Aug 87-92	4¼	95.17	96.19	6.86
Aug 92 p	8¼	101.20	101.24	6.90
Sep 92 p	8¾	102.14	102.18	6.93
Nov 92 p	7¾	100.31	101.03	7.02
Nov 92 p	7⅜	100.14	100.18	-01 7.00
Jan 93 p	7	99.23	99.27	-01 7.08
Feb 93	6¾	99.13	99.19	-01 6.98
Feb 93 p	8¼	101.27	101.31	-01 7.11
Mar 93 p	9⅝	104.15	104.19	-02 7.13
May 93 n	10⅛	105.19	105.23	7.18
Jul 93 p	7¼	100	100.04	7.18
Aug 93 p	8¾	103.03	103.07	7.25
Sep 93 p	8¼	102.02	102.06	7.28
Nov 93	8⅝	103	103.06	-01 7.27
Dec 93 p	7⅝	100.17	100.21	-01 7.35

Bonds and Notes

Date	Rate	Bid	Ask	Chg Yld
Feb 94	9	104	104.06	+02 7.36
Apr 94 p	7	98.25	98.29	-02 7.40
May 94 p	9½	105.14	105.18	-01 7.47
Aug 94 p	8⅝	103.01	103.05	-03 7.55
Sep 94 p	8½	102.22	102.26	-02 7.57
Nov 94 p	11⅝	112.09	112.15	-03 7.63
Jan 95 p	8½	102.31	103.03	7.67
Feb 95 p	11¼	111.17	111.23	-03 7.70
May 95 p	8½	102.17	102.21	-03 7.73
May 95	12⅝	116.24	116.30	-02 7.75
Aug 95 p	8½	102.17	102.21	-05 7.77
Nov 95 p	9½	106.08	106.12	7.83
Jan 96 p	9¼	105.11	105.15	-01 7.86
Feb 96 p	8⅞	103.30	104.02	-01 7.85
Jul 96 p	7⅞	99.22	99.26	-02 7.91
Jan 97 p	8	100	100.04	7.97
Jul 97 p	8½	102.06	102.10	8.02
Nov 97 p	8⅞	103.31	104.03	-01 8.06
May 98 p	9	104.20	104.24	-03 8.11
Nov 98	3½	94.10	95.12	-02 4.21
May 94-99	8½	101.25	102.01	-01 7.75
Nov 99 p	7⅞	98.05	98.09	+02 8.15
Feb 95-00	7⅞	98.13	98.19	+01 8.10
Aug 00 p	8¾	103.15	103.19	+01 8.19
May 01	13⅛	133.16	133.22	8.17
Nov 01	15¾	152.18	153	8.19
Feb 03	10¾	118	118.06	+01 8.31
Nov 03	11⅞	127.01	127.07	+04 8.35
Nov 04 k	11	125.24	125.30	+04 8.39
Aug 05 k	10¾	119.01	119.07	+01 8.42
Nov 02-07	7⅞	96.04	96.14	+04 8.27
May 04-09	9⅛	105.10	105.20	+05 8.41
May 05-10	10	112.15	112.25	+05 8.43
May 06-11	13⅞	145.01	145.07	+05 8.50
Aug 08-13	12	131.03	131.07	+05 8.52
Nov 09-14k	11¾	129.30	130.04	+05 8.50
Nov 15 k	9⅞	114.17	114.23	+05 8.44
Nov 16 k	7½	90.09	90.13	+06 8.42
May 18 k	9⅛	107.15	107.19	+05 8.41
Aug 19 k	8⅛	97.03	97.07	+05 8.38
Aug 20 k	8¾	104.09	104.13	+05 8.34

k = Non U.S. citizen exempt from withholding taxes.
n = Treasury note.
p = Treasury note and non U.S. citizen exempt from withholding taxes.

Exhibit 5.1 shows a partial listing of the prices that would have been published in the financial pages of major dailies on March 26, 1991. This exhibit summarizes the major price changes

that occurred the preceding day to securities issued by the U. S.
government and trading in the secondary market. It lists specific
issues, starting with the shortest maturities and goes through the
entire maturity spectrum, including bills (any security with a maturity of one year or less); notes (maturities between 2 and 10
years); and bonds, (maturities between 10 and 30 years). A similar
table is published Tuesday through Saturday. Any newspaper that
covers finance will publish some version of this table. The most
complete appears daily in the *Wall Street Journal.*

Spending one minute a day skimming this table is the most
useful thing that you can do to be a well-informed bond investor.
You will want to focus on the interest rate levels and on the price
changes.

First, let's go through a couple of sample listings in order to
demonstrate how to read this table. Exhibit 5.2 illustrates both the
column headings, and a typical listing under *Bonds and Notes.*

Exhibit 5.2
Note Listing

Date	Rate	Bid	Ask	Chg	Yield
March 1992	7 7/8	101.06	101.10	-01	6.51

Let's go through the listing, reading from left to right.

- The date is the maturity date of the note. Since this note
  matures in March of 1992 (one year approximately after the
  date on which the table appeared), it is a one-year note.

- The rate listed—7 7/8—is the coupon rate.

- Both the "bid" and "ask" prices are listed.

- The column headed "Chg" lists the change in price compared to the previous day (calculated from the bid). The
  previous day, the price of this note went down by one point
  (indicated by -01).

- The last column lists the yield-to-maturity for the note, 6.51
  percent.

Exhibit 5.3 illustrates longer dated paper.

Exhibit 5.3
Long-Term Bond Listing

Date	Rate	Bid	Ask	Chg	Yield
May 06-11	13 7/8	145.01	145.07	+05	8.50

Again, reading from left to right:

- The maturity date for this bond is May 6, 2011. It is therefore a 20-year bond.

- The bid price is 145.01 (about $1450) and the ask is 145.07 (slightly higher).

- Yesterday, the price of this bond went up by five basis points (indicated by + 05).

- Its yield-to-maturity is 8.50 percent.

These listings may be used for a variety of purposes. First, the table tells you in very precise detail the exact interest rates available on the previous day for a broad spectrum of Treasury securities, from the shortest to the longest maturities. These are the yields-to-maturity listed for individual securities. The first listing discussed (Exhibit 5.2) indicates that on March 29, 1991, one-year Treasury paper was yielding 6.52 percent. The second listing (Exhibit 5.3) shows that on the same date, twenty-year bonds had a yield-to-maturity of 8.50 percent.

Suppose you want to invest some money and would like to know what one-year Treasuries are yielding. You would look for an issue maturing one year from the date that you are reading your paper. That would be March 1992, the listing already shown in Exhibit 5.2, which shows a yield of 6.5 percent. Similarly, if you are interested in five-year paper, you would look for a security that matures five years from the date you are reading the paper. In this instance, the closest date listed on the table is February 1996; and that note yields 7.85 percent.

The *Table of Treasury Bills, Bonds, and Notes* also tells you exactly what happened to interest rates the previous day in the Treasury market, through the information conveyed by price changes, under the "Chg" (Change) heading. All you need to do is to look at plus (+) or minus (-) signs.

Remember that prices and yields (that is, interest rates) move in opposite directions. Plus (+) signs indicate that prices moved up, and therefore interest rates (yields) went down. Minus (-) signs indicate the reverse. If prices of bonds went down, interest rates (and therefore yields) went up.

On most days, all signs in the *Table of Treasury Bills, Bonds and Notes* are either (+) or (-), indicating that short rates and long rates moved in the same direction. But it is not uncommon for short rates and long rates to move in opposite directions. That was the case on March 26. This is immediately apparent when you look at the entire table (Exhibit 5.1) if you notice that there are both (+) plus and (-) signs. The (-) signs go from the beginning of the table (very short maturities) through about the eight-year notes (intermediate maturities). For those maturities, yields rose and prices declined. But from the eight-year note on, the signs are all (+). Therefore, for those maturities, prices rose and yields went down.

If you get into the habit of looking at the *Table of Bills, Bonds and Notes*, you will realize that it gives you very precise information much more quickly than any other source. It will enable you to compare the yields available on Treasury issues (the safest instruments) to those of any other fixed-income instrument you might be considering. It will also tell you exactly what is happening to both long and short interest rates. They may or they may not be moving in the same direction.

One peculiarity of Treasury bond pricing should be noted. Prices are quoted in 32nds of a point. "Minus 01" (-01) does not mean minus one cent. It means minus one thirty-second (-1/32nd) of a point. One point represents $10.00 per $1,000 par value bond. Therefore, 1/2 of 1 point would be half that amount, that is $5.00; 1/32 of a point would be $10.00 divided by 32, that is 31.25 cents. One thirty-second (1/32nd) of one point is called a "tick." Traders will say that the long bond moved up one tick, or down two ticks.

The size of the price changes also conveys useful information. On most days, prices may not change at all; or they may
move up one tick; or down three ticks. This means that interest
rates for those maturities on those days are relatively stable.
However, if prices move a full point ($10.00 per $1,000 bond), this
is a substantial price move. If prices move as much as two points
($20.00 per $1,000 bond) or more, this is a violent move; and it
indicates turbulence in the credit markets. Therefore, if you look
regularly at the *Table of Treasury Bills, Bonds and Notes,* you will
learn to distinguish between periods of relatively stable interest
rates, with relatively minor changes from day to day, and periods
of great volatility.

Finally, note also that since the *Table of Bills, Bonds and Notes*
lists both bid and ask prices for a broad spectrum of Treasury
issues trading in the secondary market, it permits you to calculate
the price of any older issue you might want to sell (or to buy)
very accurately. Since spreads between the bid and the ask prices
of Treasuries are very narrow (3/32nds or 4/32nds of 1 point, or
about $1.25 per $1,000 bond), you should be able to buy or sell
older securities at close to the price listed in the exhibit.

But why focus on this particular table?

Because the market in U. S. debt securities is considered the
key interest rate market not only for the United States, but also
for other countries worldwide. The shortest maturity paper—the
three-month bill—is considered the safest security that you can
buy. It is so short that it has virtually no interest rate risk, and its
credit quality is the highest available. In fact, it is used as a proxy
for risk-free returns by professionals. Similarly, the most recently
issued 30-year bond, referred to as the long bond, is the key bellwether security for long maturities.

Any other type of bond is deemed to be riskier than a Treasury, even if the risk is slight. Therefore, all other securities of the
same maturity will have a slightly higher (or a much higher)
yield than a Treasury of the same maturity, depending on their
credit quality. No professional buys a debt instrument of any
kind, in any maturity, without first comparing it to a U. S. government security of the same maturity, and neither should you.

The "Credit Markets" Column and Other Columns

After looking at the *Table of Treasury Bills, Bonds and Notes,* and usually on the same page, there are several other columns you should read. The first column is the one entitled "credit markets." It summarizes the previous day's developments in different sectors of the bond market:

- whether a Treasury auction took place;

- what yields resulted;

- any outstanding development in any other sector of the bond market (munis, GNMAs, corporates);

- interest rates available in those markets.

In addition, the column provides a running commentary on where professionals think the market, or interest rates, are headed, and why. It is must reading, if only because it is the best method for finding out how bond professionals view the market.

In addition, several briefer articles may be devoted to recent bond sales that appear newsworthy for a variety of reasons. Such an article might, for example, describe a very large sale of municipal bonds by an issuer whose credit is deteriorating. The article would supply a variety of details such as who were the underwriters; the yields for various maturities; whether demand was strong or weak and so forth. Again, articles such as these are useful if you want to know what is happening in various sectors of the bond markets.

Finally, the Monday issues of the *Wall Street Journal* and of the *New York Times* list specific upcoming bond sales in both the muni and the corporate market, and the date of the sale. If you want to buy bonds at issue, this will alert you to upcoming sales that may interest you.

The financial pages contain other tables and graphs relating to specific bond sectors, and these will be discussed in the appropriate chapters.

THE YIELD CURVE AND WHAT IT CAN TELL YOU

Located next to the "credit markets" column, the financial pages of the newspaper usually contain a small graph which looks like Exhibit 5.4. This graph is called a "yield curve." The yield curve graphs the key points along the *Table of Treasury Bonds, Bills, and Notes*. It plots interest rates for the 3-month, 6-month, 1-year, 2-year, 3-year, 4-year, 5-year, 7-year, 10-year and 30-year Treasury maturities.

For purposes of comparison, let's look Exhibit 5.5, which shows three very different yield curves. Pay particular attention both to the interest rate levels and to the shape of the curve.

The first graph, dated November 16, 1988, shows three-month bill rates at about 8 1/4 percent and 30-year rates at 9 percent. The spread between the three-month rate and the 30-year rate is about 80 basis points (less than 1 percent). That is considered very narrow. As a result, the curve is considered "flat."

The December 1954 graph shows bill rates at about 1.2 percent, and 30-year bonds at about 2.7 percent. The spread between the shortest three-month paper and the 30-year maturity is about 150 basis points (1 1/2 percent). That is considered a normal (or "upward sloping") yield curve, with long bonds yielding considerably more than short maturities. (The 150-basis point spread is somewhat narrow for an upward sloping curve, due to the over-

---

Exhibit 5.4
Treasury Yield Curve

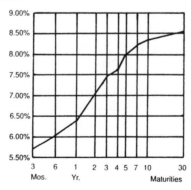

Exhibit 5.5
Three Different Treasury Yield Curves

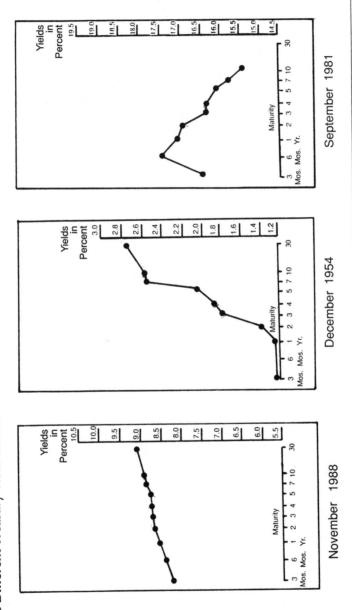

all low interest rate level. At higher interest rate levels, the spread may be as high as 250 to 300 basis points).

Finally, look at the last graph, dated September 1981. Three-month rates are close to 16 percent; six-month rates are 17 percent; 30-year rates are actually *below* six-month rates, at 15 percent. That is called an "inverted" yield curve, with long rates actually *lower* than short rates. Inverted yield curves are said, to predict recessions. Unfortunately for some would be forecasters, it is also said that postwar, inverted yield curves have predicted nine out of five recessions.

I have purposely used the December 1954 and September 1981 yield curves for shock value. The interest rate levels are so different from those of the late 1980s and early 1990s that they appear to be mistakes. These levels demonstrate "graphically" that current conditions may be no more normal, or permanent, than those of the 1950s or the early 1980s.

The Shape of the Yield Curve

The shape of the yield curve changes continually because interest rate expectations of the major users of credit (that is, large corporations and institutional investors) change constantly. If buyers expect an increase in inflation and a concurrent rise in interest rates, they seek the safety of short-term paper. As a result, short rates decline. If, on the other hand, they anticipate lower economic growth, recessionary times, and lower interest rates, they try to "lock in" high yields by buying bonds with longer maturities. This results in declines of long-term interest rates. These explanations are highly oversimplified. Anyone who follows interest rate movements soon learns that at any given time there are some "experts" who believe interest rates will go up and can make a good case for that, while other "experts" can make an equally strong case explaining why interest rates must go down.

Some professional economists argue that the shape of the yield curve contains an implicit consensus forecast of the future of interest rates and can, therefore, be used both to predict the direction of interest rates and future economic activity. This entire subject is highly technical and controversial, with little agreement among professionals. Suppose, for example, that the yield curve

is flat. The curve could return to a normal shape (upward sloping) in a number of ways. Short rates could fall, or long rates
could go up, or both could occur. Or the curve could remain flat
for another three years. Or, as happened in the early 1980s, all
interest rates might rise for an additional two or three years. The
experts are unlikely to agree about the likely outcome.

The Yield Curve and the Individual Investor

The yield curve, however, can be used by the individual investor
in a number of ways.

- It is a quick summary of current interest rate levels at all
  points of the maturity spectrum.

- It can be used to pinpoint advantageous buy points as far
  as maturity length is concerned.

- Specifically, it provides a very precise answer to the question: for the additional risk to principal incurred in going
  out further on the yield curve, how much more am I earning?

In the December 1988 yield curve, for example, there was a
difference of about 50 basis points between 1-year and 30-year
paper. Now the question is: if you can buy 1-year paper with no
risk to principal, are you getting adequately compensated if you
buy a 30-year bond with a great deal of risk to principal, for the
additional yield of only 50 basis points? Similarly, at any one
point along the curve, the investor should constantly ask how
much more yield he is getting for the increasing risk to principal
as maturities increase in length.

Recently, two- to seven-year maturities have yielded perhaps
only 30 to 50 basis points less than the 30-year bond, but with far
less risk to principal. Ten-year maturities have sometimes yielded
only a few basis points less than the 30-year bond. The twenty-
year bond has sometimes yielded *more* than the 30-year bond
(about 15 to 30 more basis points). While that seems illogical on
the basis of risk, the explanation has to do with the fact that the
30-year bond is a more frequently traded issue among profession-

als than the 20-year maturity. Since the 30-year bond is in greater
demand, it costs more to buy and yields less than the twenty-year
bond. (That, of course, could change.) Remember that the bond
market is a dealer-to-dealer market. This explains pricing anomalies which can sometimes be exploited to advantage by an individual investor.

Investors intent on boosting yield sometimes place their
principal at risk for very little extra gain. When purchasing
bonds, always ask yourself "how much more am I really earning?" And "what kinds of risk am I assuming in order to earn
that extra amount?"

The 1981 yield curve deserves an additional comment. As indicated, on that date the yield curve was steeply inverted, with
30-year paper yielding 130 basis points less than short paper. Indeed, the very shortest rate, which is an overnight rate known as
the "fed funds rate" was actually at 20 percent, making the inver-
sion even more extreme. It would appear that at that point, the
buyer of the 30-year bond was clearly not getting compensated
for the risk of buying paper with a 30-year maturity. Or was he?

Well, with the wisdom of hindsight, you now know that in
1981, you should have squirreled away every possible dollar,
hocked the house, and bought as many of those 15 percent Treasury bonds as possible, because that happened to be almost the
peak of that interest rate cycle. The actual peak occurred the following year, at 16 percent. At the time, however, many learned
pundits were predicting that long rates would continue to climb
and might possibly reach 20 percent. Mortgage rates did reach
those levels. Is there some way you might have realized that these
rates were highly advantageous, in spite of what the pundits
were saying?

One indicator would have been a knowledge of the history
of interest rates. The rates of the early 1980s were extraordinarily
high; indeed, they were at the highest level that they had reached
since the beginning of the century. To put this return into perspective, remember that historically the stock market has had an annual rate of return of about 10 percent. Therefore, a dividend
yield of 15 percent on a government guaranteed instrument, with
call protection, represented an amazing opportunity. To some, another clue was the shape of the yield curve. The yield curve was
inverted because the professionals (who dominate the bond mar-

kets) did not expect rates to continue climbing at the long end. They anticipated an end to the prevailing inflationary conditions. And they realized that with lower inflation rates, those very high interest rates would decline, as they did.

While I have discussed the yield curve for Treasuries only, a yield curve can be constructed for any other security as well; and that yield curve can be used to evaluate return vs. risk for all maturities of that security.

PART II

Individual Securities

If you have at least $50,000 to invest (less for Treasuries, since you can buy individual Treasury bonds with complete safety for as little as $1,000), you might consider purchasing individual securities.

I chose the sum of $50,000 because the first rule of investing, in bonds or anything else, is to diversify. If you do not have at least $50,000, you will be unable to buy a diversified portfolio. (Some experts place the minimum required to purchase a diversified portfolio much higher: at $100,000, or even at $250,000.) Also, your transaction costs, namely commission costs incurred in buying and selling, would be too high.

This section discusses four different types of fixed-income securities:

- Treasury debt.
- Municipal bonds.
- GNMAs and other pass-through securities.
- Corporate bonds.

They are discussed in order of their appeal for individual investors.

Treasuries are the benchmark against which all other debt instruments must be compared. They have the highest degree of safety. They are inexpensive to buy and sell. And they are easy to understand. Anyone looking for safety who does not have a great deal of time or interest in finance could very well limit himself to Treasuries alone, or for an investor in higher income brackets, to a combination of high-grade municipals and Treasuries.

Municipal bonds are perhaps the securities most widely held by individual investors. Their appeal is twofold. They are sound investments; and because of the exemptions from federal and some state and local taxes, they are among the highest yielding fixed-income securities that an individual investor can own.

GNMAs and corporates both yield more than Treasuries (on a current yield basis). Surprisingly, however, the total return for those securities may not be higher than for Treasuries. More importantly, GNMAs and corporates are more complex than either Treasuries or munis. Each requires owner involvement. They should not be purchased unless the investor has both the time and the interest to analyze specific securities in some depth before purchase and to monitor them after purchase.

6

Treasuries and Federal Agency Paper

This chapter discusses

■ *different Treasury maturities*

■ *how to buy Treasuries directly at auction, without paying commissions*

■ *zero coupon bonds*

■ *EE bonds*

■ *Federal agency debt*

I want to buy a security that is completely safe, easy to buy, easy to sell, easy to understand and high-yielding. Is there such an instrument?

Surprisingly, the answer is yes. Treasuries are that rare paradox: common and high quality. While they are not formally "insured," since Treasuries are a direct obligation of the U. S. government, which is itself the ultimate insurer, Treasuries are (if one can rate safety among issues backed by the U. S. government) safer than insured accounts. In addition, since 1985, long-dated Treasuries have not been callable before maturity, far more generous call protection than is afforded by any other debt instrument. Finally, Treasuries are the most liquid securities you can buy; they trade with lower markups than any other debt instrument.

Before buying any other fixed-income security, you should check out the yield on a Treasury with a comparable maturity. Professionals do. Every single debt instrument is priced by professionals off Treasuries. Never buy a security with a maturity comparable to a Treasury unless the additional yield (the spread to the Treasury yield) is large enough to compensate for the additional credit risk of the other security. The greater the risk, the wider should be the spread.

If you are risk averse and/or don't have much time to devote to the management of your finances, then Treasuries are for you. Even if you have a lot of time, Treasuries may still be your best option.

The only real decision that has to be made when buying a Treasury is how much interest rate risk you want to assume; that is, where on the yield curve you will find the best trade-off between return and interest rate risk. If this were a perfect world, there would be no interest rate risk. But as we know, the price of long Treasuries is as volatile as the price of any other long-dated instrument. However, if you limit your purchases to maturities of five years or less and hold securities until maturity, you can put together a portfolio that has all the characteristics people associate with bonds, namely, complete safety of principal and predictable returns.

What is surprising is that in spite of their high quality, on a total return basis, Treasuries often outperform other instruments. There are two main reasons for this. First, whenever any financial market becomes turbulent, investors sell these financial assets—stocks, for example—and put their money in Treasuries. This is referred to as a "flight to quality." And second, the significant call protection Treasuries enjoy, compared to other debt instruments, boosts the return of long-dated Treasuries whenever interest rates decline significantly.

Treasury securities are issued periodically by the Treasury and sold through auctions run by the Federal Reserve Banks. Most Treasuries are sold to so-called "primary" dealers, who in turn sell to everyone else: to banks, to brokerage firms, to large and small institutions, to money market funds or to individual investors. Individuals can purchase Treasuries from banks or from brokerage firms, but they can also purchase them directly at auction in amounts ranging from $1,000 to millions.

Treasuries are taxable at the federal level, but exempt from state taxes. As a rule, in states with high income taxes, this feature adds about 50 to 60 basis points (1/2 of 1 percent or slightly more) to the yield of a Treasury. As a result, net-after-tax-yield on Treasuries (particularly those with maturities under five years) are often competitive with tax-exempt paper.

TREASURY BILLS

A Treasury bill (called a "T-bill" for short) is technically a non-interest bearing instrument. When you purchase a T-bill, you do not receive interest in the form of a coupon. Instead, the T-bill is sold at a discount from par. When it matures, the Treasury redeems the T-bill at par. The difference between the discounted price paid and the face value of the bill when it is redeemed is its yield.

Financial pages of major newspapers list T-bill yields daily, at the top of the *Table of Bills, Bonds, and Notes.* This table is very brief. Exhibit 6.1 shows the format and most yields that appeared on April 4, 1991.

Reading from left to right, the listings show the same data as for longer dated paper:

- the maturity date of the bill (listed as date);
- the bid and ask prices;
- the change in price (calculated from the bid).
- the yield

Note that the actual yield, rather than the price, is quoted, even under the bid and ask price columns. T-bills are always priced and sold on the basis of yield. The yield changes daily, but seldom by more than a few basis points. For individuals holding T-bills to maturity, those changes do not represent a risk.

You will see the yield on T-bills quoted in two ways: at the discount at which a T-bill sells from par; and on a so-called "bond equivalent yield basis." The two are not identical. A simplified

Exhibit 6.1
Format for Treasury Bills Listing

Date 1991	Bid	Ask	Chg.	Yield
Apr 11	5.51	5.47	-0.08	5.57
Apr 18	6.10	6.06	+0.04	6.18
Apr 25	5.71	5.69		5.80
May 2	5.78	5.75	-0.03	5.87
May 9	5.78	5.75		5.88
May 16	5.76	5.72	+0.01	5.85
May 23	5.75	5.72	-0.01	5.86
May 30	5.74	5.72	-0.04	5.87
Jun 6	5.77	5.75	-0.01	5.91
Jun 13	5.75	5.72	-0.02	5.88
Jun 21	5.74	5.72	+0.02	5.89
Jun 27	5.70	5.66	-0.03	5.83
Jul 5	5.78	5.75		5.93
Jul 11	5.72	5.69	-0.05	5.87
Jul 18	5.74	5.72	-0.03	5.91
Jul 25	5.76	5.72	-0.01	5.92
Aug 1	5.81	5.78	-0.01	5.99
Aug 8	5.82	5.78	+0.01	6.00
Aug 15	5.81	5.78	-0.01	6.01
Aug 29	5.84	5.81	+0.01	6.05
Aug 22	5.83	5.81	+0.01	6.05
Sep 5	5.82	5.78	+0.02	6.03
Sep 12	5.82	5.78		6.03
Sep 19	5.81	5.78		6.04
Oct 3	5.80	5.78		6.05
Oct 24	5.82	5.78	+0.01	6.06
Nov 21	5.87	5.84	+0.02	6.13

explanation for this distinction is that the discount is quoted on the basis of the one time premium earned when a T-bill is redeemed, which is equivalent to simple interest. But when a three-month or a six-month bill is redeemed, the investor has the opportunity to reinvest that money and earn interest-on-interest. Therefore, the actual rate of return (annualized) is higher than the discounted rate. The bond-equivalent yield of T-bills is always slightly higher (by between 10 and 20 basis points) than the discount rate. The formula for converting the discount rate to a bond equivalent yield is complicated, but anyone selling a T-bill has tables quoting both rates.[1]

---

1. Several other factors go into the calculation of bond-equivalent yields. For one thing, the Treasury calculates the price of T-bills as if a year had 360 days. When the yield is annualized (to a 365-day year), the actual yield turns out to be slightly higher than the discount. Also, the bond-equivalent yield is computed on the assumption that the interest-on-interest will compound at the issue rate and for a 364 day year. (One-year bills are actually outstanding for 52 weeks, exactly 364 days).

T-bills are currently issued in three-month, six-month, and one year maturities. They are offered in minimum denominations of $10,000, with multiples of $5,000 thereafter. Individuals can purchase T-bills directly at the Fed's weekly auctions. They can also purchase T-bills trading in the secondary market for any desired maturity—from a few days to one year—from banks or brokerage firms for a small fee. T-bills may be resold any time; they are the most liquid of all instruments. T-bills are issued in book-entry form only.

Without a doubt, T-bills are the safest instruments that you can buy. They have zero credit risk. And they are so short that interest rate risk may be ignored. In fact, the yield on the shortest bills is used by investment professionals as a proxy for a risk free-rate of return, and institutions use them as cash-equivalents.

WHY TREASURY NOTES BELONG IN YOUR PORTFOLIO

Treasury notes mature in two to ten years. Currently, the Treasury is selling the following maturities:

- Two-year
- Three-year
- Five-year
- Seven-year
- Ten-year (the four-year was recently discontinued)

The price of notes fluctuates more than the price of T-bills in response to interest rate changes, as you would expect given their longer maturities. Consequently, if you need to resell a note before it matures, you can have either a capital loss or a capital gain. Price changes, you will remember, are directly tied to maturity length. They would be smallest at the two-year end, and larger closer to the five-year mark. Interest rate risk becomes significant at the seven-year mark.

Treasury notes are extremely attractive securities. They yield more than T-bills, typically 50 to 150 basis points more, depending on the shape of the yield curve. If you buy and hold to maturity, you are guaranteed to get back 100 percent of principal. In addition, because interest on notes is exempt from state and local taxes, on a net-after-tax basis (that is, after deducting the federal tax to be paid), notes may actually yield more than municipal paper of comparable maturity, even though that is exempt from state taxes. This is particularly apt to be the case in states with high tax rates. Also, whenever the yield curve is inverted (that is, when yields on shorter securities are higher than those on long dated instruments), Treasury notes maturing in two to five years may yield more than municipal bonds, on an after-tax basis, by a significant amount. This occurred most recently in 1987 and 1988.

If you think you are giving up income by purchasing notes, rather than longer term instruments, think again. Studies have shown that over long periods of time, notes have outperformed both long-dated Treasuries and T-bills. One authoritative study showed that between 1926 and 1989, average annual total return for Treasury notes was 4.9 percent, compared to 4.6 percent for long-dated governments, and 0.5 percent for T-bills. These figures are taken from the *1990 Yearbook*, by Ibbotson and Sinquefield.[3] This study is updated annually, and the 1990 results are consistent with those published in preceding *Yearbooks*.

In another study by Neuberger and Berman, total return for the period between 1951 and 1989 averaged 6 percent annually for two-year Treasuries; and 6.1 percent on five-year Treasuries. In comparison, annual return on long-term government bonds averaged only 5.1 percent annually, and on T-bills, a slightly higher 5.4 percent.[4] If these annual total return numbers seem low, remember that yields during the decade of the 1980s were significantly higher than during any prior decade.

The higher total return of two- to five-year Treasuries compared to longer dated paper is due to the lower price volatility in response to interest rate changes; and compared to shorter dated paper, to the fact that two-year paper normally yields more than T-bills (assuming an upward sloping yield curve).

---

3. Ibbotson and Sinquefield, *Stocks, Bills, Bonds and Inflation, 1990 Yearbook*, Chicago, Ibbotson Associates, 1991, pp. 10-30.
4. Neuberger and Berman Management, Inc., New York City, brochure published by the Research Department.

TREASURY BONDS

Treasury bonds are the longest dated instruments issued by the Treasury, maturing in 10 to 30 years. Currently, the Treasury sells a 10-year and a 30-year bond. (It no longer sells either 15- or 20-year bonds.) Because there is a very active secondary market in Treasury bonds, however, any maturity can be purchased.

You might expect that at any time, the 30-year bond would yield more than all other maturities. Curiously, this is not the case. The highest yield is often found somewhere near the 20-year mark. This is because this maturity is less actively traded by dealers and therefore less in demand than either shorter or longer dated bonds. The lower demand results in a higher yield.

Investors wishing to "lock in" the highest possible returns purchase the current 30-year bond because of its generous call protection. If interest rates drop, the call protection translates into higher capital gains.

BUYING TREASURIES

Treasuries can be purchased or sold through banks and brokerage firms. Fees are modest, typically $40 or $50 per transaction, regardless of the amount purchased. Nonetheless, if you roll over securities periodically, over the course of a year, those small amounts can add up. Also, the smaller the face amount of the securities purchased, the higher those fees are as a percentage of the face amount. $50 represents 1/2 of 1 percent of a $10,000 purchase; but 5 percent of a $1,000 purchase.

Treasury Direct: Buying Treasuries at Auction

It is now possible for individuals to buy Treasury securities directly at auction by establishing an account with the Federal Reserve, through its Treasury-direct program. Minimum amounts required vary with each security, but are as low as $1,000 (for the 30-year bond). This is a very attractive option:

- It eliminates all transaction costs.

- Individuals receive the same yield as institutional investors.

■ All of the individual's Treasury securities can be consolidated in one account.

The process of buying through Treasury-direct is a very simple one. You open an account by filling out a one-page form,
available by mail or by telephoning any of 37 servicing offices in
the United States. (A list of the 37 countrywide Treasury-direct
direct offices and telephone numbers is included in the appendix
at the end of the chapter.) In addition to your address and social
security number, you need to provide the number of an account
that you hold either with a commercial bank or with a major brokerage firm (such as a cash management accounts), so that the
Fed can wire interest payments and matured principal directly to
that account. Once an account is open, you can participate in any
auction held by the Fed.

To purchase a security, you submit a very brief form called a
non-competitive tender whereby you agree to purchase the maturity you select at the average yield of the auction—that is, the
average of all the competitive tenders submitted by dealers purchasing billions of dollars worth of securities. Tenders may be
submitted by mail. As long as the envelope is postmarked by
midnight of the day preceding the auction, no matter when the
post office actually delivers your envelope, your tender is good.
Tenders may also be submitted in person at any of the twelve
Federal Reserve Banks until noon on the day of any auction. All
securities are sold in book-entry form only.

Treasury-direct is a highly efficient operation. Interest payments are automatically mailed to the account that you designate,
as is matured principal. If you want to roll over any security, that
can be done automatically. T-bills can be rolled over automatically
for up to two years with one form. No matter how many different
securities are in your account, in whatever combination of maturities you desire, all are held in one central account with one account number. Information about that account is on a central
computer and may be reviewed at any of the 37 offices that service Treasury-direct.

Exhibit 6.2 shows the auction schedules and minimum
amounts required for purchase. The exact dates of the auctions
are listed in the major financial papers. They can also be obtained
from the Treasury-direct offices.

Exhibit 6.2
Auction Schedule of Treasuries and Minimum Amounts Required
for Purchase

T-Bills	Schedule	Minimum Investment
13 week	Every Monday	$10,000 initially; 5,000 increments
26 week	Every Monday	
52 week	Every Fourth Tuesday	
T Notes		
Two-year	Monthly: last Wednesday	$5,000 initially; 5,000 increments
Three-year	Quarterly: February, May, August, and November	
Five-year	Quarterly: February, May, August, and November	
Seven-year	Quarterly: January, April, July and October	
Ten-year	Quarterly: February, May, August, and November	
Treasury Bonds		
30-year	Quarterly: February, May, August, and November	$1,000 amounts

A Treasury-direct account enables you to purchase any security, from three-month to 30-year, and to put together a portfolio that is totally tailored to your needs. One possible strategy would be to stay with notes, for the reasons outlined above. Another popular strategy is to constitute a so-called stepped portfolio, buying one-year, two-year, three-year, and five-year maturities, and automatically renewing with the same maturities as the securities are redeemed. The average yield of such a portfolio would be about 100 to 150 basis points above money market fund yields and exempt from state taxes. Interest rate risk is low because average maturity would be between two and three years. And the different maturities enable you to take advantage of higher yields as they occur.

Purchasing T-bills, notes, and bonds directly is actually safer than purchasing them through a mutual fund. This is because by buying individual securities and holding them to maturity, you can be certain that you will redeem your principal in entirety. If you buy the same securities through a mutual fund, you may not. (This is discussed in greater detail in Chapters 10 and 11.)

The only inconvenience in the Treasury-direct program is that if you have to sell your Treasuries before they actually mature, you must do so through a broker (after filling out the appropriate form).

Would you like to know the probable yield before you purchase at auction? You can come fairly close by checking the *Table of Treasury Bills, Bonds and Notes* a few days before the auction for the maturities that interest you. Also, dealers actually begin trading these securities a few days before the auction on a so-called "when issued" basis—that is, in anticipation of their issue. The "when issued" yield is often mentioned in the "credit markets" column of either the *New York Times* or the *Wall Street Journal* on the days preceding the auction.

ZERO COUPON BONDS

Zero coupon bonds (zeros for short) are also colloquially known as "strips." This is not a humorous nickname. The word "strips" actually describes the process of creating zeros.

Behind every zero stands an ordinary so-called "plain vanilla" U. S. Treasury bond. In 1982, investment banks got the brilliant idea of separating the different revenue streams of government bonds (the coupons-only and the principal-only) and repackaging each separate stream as a distinct security. The zero was born.

Whether the zero is based on the interest-only or on the principal-only strip is unimportant to the buyer. In either case, the buyer of a zero (like that of a T-bill), does not receive any interest coupons. Instead, the zero is sold at a very deep discount from par, but it matures at par. The difference between the discount paid and par represents the interest earned.

You will recall that when you invest in ordinary bonds, return on the bond includes interest-on-interest earned by reinvesting the coupons. For long-term maturities, the interest-on-interest is the major source of return. Since zeros have no coupons, you might think you lose that source of income. Quite the contrary. The final lump sum payment is calculated so that it includes the interest-on-interest that would have been received if the coupons had been reinvested periodically *at the yield-to-maturity rate.* That is why zeros seem to multiply like magic. Invest $197.00 in a zero with a coupon rate of 8.3 percent; in 20 years, you will receive $1,000.

Advertising for zeros makes them look like a unique method of creating wealth. You invest a small sum. In a number of years—10 years, for example—you realize a huge profit, guaranteed. It looks magical. Actually, this is just another manifestation of the magic of compounding. The only difference between a zero and another Treasury of the same maturity is that the zero has no reinvestment risk. The actual return in dollars is known and guaranteed. With a Treasury of comparable maturity, the actual return will vary since reinvestment rates will vary. But it might actually turn out to be higher than for the zero if you are able to reinvest coupons at higher rates.

You should be aware that investing small sums in zeros can be expensive. Markups are high and vary a great deal from dealer to dealer. If the yield-to-maturity is under 8 percent, and the zero is short (under five years), the conventional coupon Treasury may actually be the better buy. Locking in a yield-to-maturity with a zero is an advantage only if the yield-to-maturity is attractive— that is, above 8 percent.

Before investing in zeros, you should carefully consider two unique aspects of these securities; namely, the tax treatment of zeros and their extreme volatility.

Even though the owner of a zero receives no interest payments prior to its maturity, the interest that is accrued (earned) is taxed annually as if it were actually paid out. (That interest is known as "imputed interest," or "phantom interest"). As a result of this feature, zeros are suitable mainly for two types of accounts: tax-sheltered accounts such as IRA's or Keoghs; or accounts taxed at low tax rates, for example, accounts of children in a low tax bracket.

The volatility of zeros is unique. Zeros are the most volatile of all bonds. This is because the volatility of a security—in response to interest rate changes—is inversely correlated to the size of its coupon. The lower the coupon, the higher the volatility. Since zeros have no coupons, they are the most volatile of all securities.

As a rule, the volatility of a zero is approximately two and one-half times higher than for bonds of comparable maturities. The exact volatility depends on both the coupon and the maturity of the securities.

To illustrate, let's look at Exhibit 6.3, which shows what would happen to the price of a zero coupon bond yielding 8 percent if interest rates were to rise modestly, to 9 percent; or more dramatically, to 10 percent.

Because zeros sell at a discount, Exhibit 6.3 lists a discounted price for the 8 percent zero, in every maturity. (The longer the maturity, the greater the discount.) Exhibit 6.3 demonstrates that the volatility of the zero increases as maturity length increases; and with the amount of the interest rate change. For instance, if interest rates rise to 9 percent, the price of the 5-year zero declines by $32.00, lesss than 5 percent. If interest rates rise to 11 percent, however, the price decline for the same zero jumps to $91.00 (over 13 percent). But those declines are small compared to those that occur to the 30-year zero with a yield of 8 percent. If interest rates rise to 9 percent, that zero declines in value by $23.00 (24 per-

---

Exhibit 6.3
What Would Happen to the Price of a Zero Coupon Bond, Yielding 8 Percent, if Interest Rates Were to Rise to 9 Percent; or to 11 Percent

	Price of the Zero at:		
	8%	*9%*	*11%*
5-Year	$676	$644	$585
10-Year	456	415	343
30-Year	95	71	40

Source: Salomon Brothers, Inc.

cent). If interest rates rise to 11 percent, the price declines from $95.00 to $40.00, that is, by over 58 percent.

The process operates in reverse. Exhibit 6.4 illustrates what would happen to the price of the same zero coupon bond, yielding 8 percent, if interest rates were to decline to 7 percent—or more dramatically, to 5 percent.

Once again, the price swings are the most dramatic for the longer maturities, and for the larger interest rate swings. A decline in interest rates to 7 percent results in a price increase of not quite 5 percent for the 5-year bond, but of almost 34 percent for the 30-year bond. A steeper decline in rates, to 5 percent, results in a price increase of approximately 16 percent for the 5-year bond and an astonishing 38 percent for the 30-year bond.

The price changes illustrated in both of the preceding tables are based on a sudden, overnight change in rates. In real life, such changes do not occur overnight. The numbers in both tables, therefore, would need to be adjusted for time. For instance, if the interest rate change were to occur five years after the bonds were initially purchased, then five years would have to be subtracted from the age of the bond. Five years after the purchase date, the 10-year bond would have become a 5-year bond; the 30-year bond, a 25-year bond. The numbers in the tables do not change, but you would look up the price of the then current bond maturity.

Bear in mind that the interest rate changes illustrated are entirely plausible. As described in Chapter 3, during the 1980s, in-

---

Exhibit 6.4
What Would Happen to the Price of a Zero Coupon Bond, Yielding 8 Percent, if Interest Rates Were to Decline to 7 Percent; or to 5 Percent

	Price of the Zero at:		
	8%	*7%*	*5%*
5-Year	$676	$709	$781
10-Year	456	503	610
30-Year	95	127	227

Source: Salomon Brothers, Inc.

terest rate swings of 100 basis points occurred sometimes within a period of a few months, and much wider interest rate swings took place between 1982 and 1985.

While there is no risk to principal if you hold a zero to maturity, if you want to resell it before it matures, you might have a very substantial capital gain or a significant capital loss.

Zeros for Investment Purposes

The peculiarities of zeros makes them ideal investments for two totally different purposes; for tax-deferred (IRA or Keogh) accounts and for leveraging interest rate bets.

Zeros are ideal investments for tax-sheltered accounts such as IRAs or Keoghs, particularly if you would like to invest small sums periodically. Suppose, for instance, that you want to invest $2,000 annually in an IRA account. Because zeros are sold at a deep discount from par, you can buy several zeros each year, choosing zeros that will mature when the money will be needed. Furthermore, buying zeros eliminates the inconvenience of having to reinvest coupons in odd sums and small amounts. Finally, purchasing zeros every year enables you to take advantage of changing levels of interest rates.

The other interesting use of zeros is based on their volatility. They can be used for speculative purposes to make interest rate bets. Zeros enable you to achieve some leverage with less risk and at a lower cost, than using the traditional tools for leverage. Leverage is a technique for speculating that works essentially by multiplying risk. If the speculator is right, using leverage magnifies profits. But it can also result in extremely high losses. To leverage, you would normally use use options, futures, or margin, any of which are expensive and potentially very risky.

The uniquely high volatility of zeros in effect constitutes a form of leverage. If interest rates appear high (say above 9 percent on the long bond), then you might consider purchasing zeros, with maturities of 10 years or longer. The longer the maturity, the higher the leverage. If interest rates drop, or when they drop, you can sell the zero and realize a substantial gain.

If interest rates continue to rise, however, your downside risk is twofold. You may have to hold the zero to maturity (or longer than you expected). Second, there is the opportunity cost of not receiving the higher interest rate. (If you purchase options or futures, on the other hand, you can lose your entire investment, and if you're really unlucky, you may lose more than your initial investment.)

With zeros, the only cost for leverage is the actual commission cost of buying the zero, which is negligible when compared to the cost of options, future, or margin. There would be no risk of loss of principal, unless you actually sell the zero at a loss. If, however, you are not prepared to hold the zero to maturity, and if you then decide to sell after interest rates rise, you can suffer a substantial loss. Therefore, it would not be advisable to purchase zeros unless you are prepared to hold them to maturity if interest rates rise.

U.S. SAVINGS BONDS: SERIES EE

Initially sold during World War II, these securities have been brought up to date and now have some very attractive features:

- Like other Treasury securities, savings bonds are not subject to state or local taxes and they have no credit risk.

- If you hold EE bonds for at least five years, you are guaranteed the higher of two rates: a minimum rate of 6 percent; or a market rate pegged to 85 percent of the rate on five-year Treasuries, which is reset every six months. If interest rates rise, so does the market rate. If they fall, you are guaranteed the minimum rate.

- Taxes on these bonds are deferred until you actually cash in the bonds, as long as you hold the bonds for at least five years. Therefore, these savings bonds are attractive for retirement monies if you have no other tax-deferred accounts.

- Because the coupon rate is reset every six months, there is little interest rate risk and, therefore, there is no risk of capital loss.

The newest feature of these bonds is that they can be used to save for a child's college education, tax-free. If the proceeds from savings bonds are used to pay college fees and tuition, no federal taxes are due. Under those conditions, EE bonds will normally yield more than munis. Note, however, that the tax exemption holds only if the bonds are bought in the parent's name (not that of the child whose tuition will be paid). That may not seem logical, but that is the way it is. Also, to be eligible for the tax exemption, the parents' income must meet certain income guidelines. These caps are reset and pegged to the inflation rate. In 1990, the full exemption applied to joint taxable incomes of $60,000 with partial exemptions to taxable incomes of $90,000.

EE bonds are purchased from banks. The minimum amount is $25.00, and the maximum amount is $5,000. These are purchase prices. The par value is exactly double the purchase price. There are no commissions of any type. The maximum that can be purchased during any one year is $15,000 purchase price ($30,000 par amount). After six months, EE bonds can be redeemed at any time for the purchase price plus any accrued interest.

FEDERAL AGENCIES

A number of agencies of the U. S. government sell bonds. Only debt sold by Federal National Mortgage Association (Fannie Mae or FNMA), Federal Land Banks, and Federal Home Loan Banks (FHLB) is exempt from state and local taxes. (Other agency paper is not exempt.) In general, debt sold by federal agencies is deemed to have some credit risk (usually slight) compared to Treasuries. As a result, agency paper yields more than Treasuries of comparable maturities by anywhere from five to 150 basis points, depending on current interest rates and supply factors.

The main agencies that would be of interest to you are the following:

The Resolution Funding Corporation Bonds (REFCORP)

These are the Savings and Loan bailout bonds issued by the Resolution Funding Corporation (also called the Resolution Trust Corporation) to pay for the cost of bailing out failed thrifts. Technically, they are not direct obligations of the United States.

But interest is guaranteed by the Treasury and principal is secured by Treasury securities. Therefore, default risk is minimal.

Refcorp initially issued 40-year bonds. These sold very poorly. As a result, Refcorp bonds yield more than Treasuries and that is their main attraction. (Remember that Treasuries are issued with 30 years as the maximum maturity.) However, because of their longer maturity, these 40-year Refcorp bonds might represent an interesting speculation if interest rates rise substantially (say above 12 or 13 percent on the long bond). Forty-year strips, backed by Refcorp bonds, exist. They are highly speculative, but would provide enormous leverage in the event of an interest rate spike.

Federal Home Loan Banks (FHLBs)

These are the twelve regional banks, which back the nation's Savings and Loans (S & Ls). They are actually owned by the private S & Ls. Bonds issued by the FHLBs are known as "consolidated" bonds because they are joint obligations of the twelve Federal Home Loan Banks. That means that if one bank experiences financial difficulties, the other eleven banks are under a legal obligation to step in and cover any payments due by the weaker bank. The credit quality of these bonds is very high.

These bonds are issued in maturities of one year or more; are not callable; and are sold in denominations of $10,000, $25,000, and above. The Federal Home Loan Banks also issue short-term securities in the form of discount notes, in minimum amounts of $50,000.

Farm Credit Agencies

These are obligations of the 37 Farm Credit Agencies. Like the FHLB, they are consolidated obligations. The Farm Credit Agencies issue a variety of short instruments that require a minimum investment of $50,000, as well as longer-term paper, in denominations of $1,000 and up.

Debt of any of these agencies can be purchased through banks or brokerage firms. Currently, agency bonds are still mainly

an institutional product, because minimums required for purchase are so high. Tables of yields of Agency bonds are published
daily in the *New York Times* and the *Wall Street Journal* and in most
major newspapers; and weekly in *Barron's*. They are read like the
Treasury Table of Bills, Bonds and Notes.

Treasuries vs. Bank CDs

Insured CDs of banks are a popular alternative to short and intermediate Treasuries. No doubt, the bank CDs owe their popularity
to the fact that they are insured. Because both are extremely safe,
let's go over some of the advantages and disadvantages of each.

Treasuries have the following features. They have no credit
risk. They are more liquid than CDs. They can be sold at any time
with no interest penalty. There is no upper limit on the amount
that is "insured." Finally, interest is exempt from state and local
taxes. Their major disadvantage compared to CDs is that if you
sell a two- to five-year note before maturity, changes in interest
rate levels may result in some loss of principal.

Interest earned on CDs is subject to state and local taxes.
During the late 1980s, some banks offered unusually high yields
on CDs in order to attract investors. Some of these banks failed.
No principal was lost if the CD was insured and if the total in
one account did not exceed $100,000. But when thrifts failed and
the Federal Deposit Insurance Corporation (FDIC) took over, interest payments were lowered.

Note that there have been proposals in Congress to limit the
amount that the government will continue to insure in thrifts or
savings and loans accounts. Although to date all of these proposals have died, they resurface from time to time and one version
might finally be adopted.

Note also that many large brokerage firms sell insured CDs.
The advantage is that these firms stand ready to buy back your
CDs if you need to resell before they mature. This feature makes
them more liquid than ordinary bank CDs. But then, of course,
the value of the principal in the CD fluctuates with interest rates.

SUMMARY

Treasury bills, notes and bonds are the safest and the most liquid securities that can be bought for any maturity. Historically, Treasury notes with maturities between two and five years have had a better total return than either T-bills or long-term bonds. They are particularly attractive investments for anyone looking for safety of principal and predictable returns.

SUMMARY: QUESTIONS TO ASK WHEN BUYING TREASURIES

How much interest rate risk am I assuming?

Where on the yield curve is the best current trade-off between yield and interest rate risk?

APPENDIX

Exhibit 6.5
List of Treasury-Direct Servicing Offices

For In-Person Visits	*For Written Correspondence*
104 Marietta Street, N.W. Atlanta, Georgia 404-521-8657 (Recording) 404-521-8653	104 Marietta Street, N.W. Atlanta, GA 30303
502 South Sharp Street Baltimore, Maryland 301-576-3300	P.O. Box 1378 Baltimore, MD 21203
FRB Birmingham 1801 Fifth Avenue, North Birmingham, Alabama 205-252-3141 Ext. 215 (Recording) 205-252-3141 Ext. 264	P.O. Box 10447 Birmingham, AL 35283
FRB Boston 600 Atlantic Avenue Boston, Massachusetts 617-973-3805 (Recording) 617-973-3810	P.O. Box 2076 Boston, MA 02106

For In-Person Visits   *For Written Correspondence*

FRB Buffalo
160 Delaware Avenue   P.O. Box 961
Buffalo, New York   Buffalo, NY
716-849-5046 (Recording)   14240-0961
716-849-5030

FRB Charlotte
401 South Tryon Street   P.O. Box 30248
Charlotte, North Carolina   Charlotte, NC
704-336-7100   28230

FRB Chicago
230 South LaSalle Street   P.O. Box 834
Chicago, ILlinois   Chicago, IL
312-786-1110 (Recording)   60690
312-322-5369

FRB Cincinnati
150 East Fourth Street   P.O. Box 999
Cincinnati, Ohio   Cincinnati, OH
513-721-4787 Ext. 334   45201

FRB Cleveland
1455 East Sixth Street   P.O. Box 6387
Cleveland, Ohio   Cleveland, OH
216-579-2490   44101

FRB Dallas
400 South Akard Street   Securities Dept. Station K
Dallas, Texas   400 South Akard Street
214-651-6362   Dallas, TX 75222

FRB Denver
1020 16th Street   P. O. Box 5228
Denver, Colorado   Terminal Annex
303-572-2475 (Recording)   Denver, CO 80217
303-572-2470 or 2473

FRB Detroit
160 West Fort Street   P.O. Box 1059
Detroit, Michigan   Detroit, MI
313-964-6153 (Recording)   48231
313-964-6157

FRB Houston
1701 San Jacinto Street   P.O. Box 2578
Houston, Texas   Houston, TX
713-659-4433   77001

For In-Person Visits	*For Written Correspondence*
FRB Jacksonville 800 West Water Street Jacksonville, Florida 904-632-1179	P.O. Box 2499 Jacksonville, FL 32231-2499
FRB Kansas City 925 Grand Avenue Kansas City, Missouri 816-881-2767 (Recording) 816-881-2409	P.O. Box 440 Kansas City, MO 64198
FRB Little Rock 325 West Capitol Avenue Little Rock, Arkansas 501-372-5451 Ext. 273	P.O. Box 1261 Little Rock, AR 72203
FRB Los Angeles 950 South Grand Avenue Los Angeles, California 213-624-7398	P.O. Box 2077 Terminal Annex Los Angeles, CA 90051
FRB Louisville 410 South Fifth Street Louisville, Kentucky 502-568-9232 (Recording) 502-568-9236 or 9238	P.O. Box 32710 Louisville, KY 40232
FRB Memphis 200 North Main Street Memphis, Tennessee 901-523-7171 Ext. 225 or 641	P.O. Box 407 Memphis, TN 38010
FRB Miami 9100 N.W. Thirty-Sixth Street Miami, Florida 305-593-9923 (Recording) 305-591-2065	P.O. Box 520847 Miami, FL 33152
FRB Minneapolis Marquette Avenue Minneapolis, Minnesota 340-2075	250 Marquette Avenue Minneapolis, MN 55480
FRB Nashville 301 Eighth Avenue, North Nashville, Tennessee 259-4006	301 Eighth Avenue, North Nashville, TN 37203
FRB New Orleans St. Charles Avenue New Orleans, Louisiana 522-1659 (Recording) 586-1505 Ext. 293	P.O. Box 61630 New Orleans, LA 70161

For In-Person Visits	*For Written Correspondence*

FRB New York
Liberty Street
New York, New York
720-5823 (Recording)
720-6619

Federal Reserve
P.O. Station
New York, NY 10045

FRB Oklahoma City
Dean A. McGee Avenue
Oklahoma City, Oklahoma
270-8660 (Recording)
270-8652

P.O. Box 25129
Oklahoma City, OK
73125

FRB Omaha
Farnam Street
Omaha, Nebraska
221-5638 (Recording)
221-5633

2201 Farnam Street
Omaha, NE
68102

FRB Philadelphia
Independence Mall
Philadelphia, Pennsylvania
574-6580 (Recording)
574-6680

P.O. Box 90
Philadelphia, PA
19105

FRB Pittsburgh
Grant Street
Pittsburgh, Pennsylvania
261-7988 (Recording)
261-7863

P.O. Box 867
Pittsburgh, PA
15230-0867

FRB Portland
S.W. Stark Street
Portland, Oregon
221-5931 (Recording)
221-5932

P.O. Box 3436
Portland, OR
97208

FRB Richmond
701 East Byrd Street
Richmond, Virginia
804-697-8000

P.O. Box 27622
Richmond, VA
23261

FRB Salt Lake City
120 South State Street
Salt Lake City, Utah
801-322-7911 (Recording)
801-355-3131

P.O. Box 30780
Salt Lake City, UT
84130

FRB San Antonio
126 East Nueva Street
San Antonio, Texas
512-224-2141 Ext. 311 (Recording)
512-224-2141 Ext. 303 or 305

P.O. Box 1471
San Antonio, TX
78295

For In-Person Visits	*For Written Correspondence*
FRB San Francisco 101 Market Street San Francisco, California 415-882-9798 (Recording) 415-974-2330	P.O. Box 7702 San Francisco, CA 94120
FRB Seattle 1015 Second Avenue Seattle, Washington 206-442-1650 (Recording) 206-442-1652	Securities Services Dept. P.O. Box 3567 Terminal Annex Seattle, WA 98124
FRB St. Louis 411 Locust Street St. Louis, Missouri 314-444-8602 (Recording) 314-444-8665	P.O. Box 14915 St. Louis, MO 63178
United States Treasury Washington, DC	Mail Inquiries to:
Bureau of the Public Debt Securities Transactions Branch 1300 C Street, S.W. Washington, DC 202-287-4113	Bureau of the Public Debt Division of Customer Services 300 13th Street, S.W. Washington, DC 20239-0001
Device for hearing impaired 202-287-4097	Mail Tenders to: Bureau of the Public Debt Department N Washington, DC 20239-1500

7

Municipal Bonds

This chapter discusses

- *unique characteristics of municipal bonds*
- *when it pays to buy municipal bonds (municipal bond arithmetic)*
- *revenue vs. general obligation bonds*
- *bond insurance and other credit enhancements*
- *municipal bonds with special features: zeros, put bonds, alternative minimum tax bonds, supersinkers*
- *municipal bond pricing and vocabulary*

WHAT IS UNIQUE ABOUT MUNICIPAL BONDS?

Municipal bonds, "munis" for short, are issued by city, county, and state governments, as well as by enterprises with a public purpose, such as certain electric utilities, universities, and hospitals. The chief attraction of municipal bonds is that they are federally tax-exempt. If you live in the state issuing the bonds, with a few exceptions, they are also exempt from state and local taxes, or, as the ads proclaim: triple tax-free.

The Tax Reform Act of 1986 transformed municipal bonds into the last genuine tax shelter available to the individual investor. This Tax Act, moreover, made munis much less attractive to former institutional buyers (mainly banks and insurance companies). As a result, the municipal market is the only sector of the bond market where the primary buyers are individual investors. This has led issuers to add features to munis that make them more attractive to individuals. It has resulted, for example, in the phenomenal growth of bond insurance.

Overwhelmingly, munis deserve their popularity among individual investors. Even though there are thousands of issues outstanding, muni securities are sound and relatively uncomplicated instruments. Nonetheless, munis require more caution than Treasuries. Interest risk should be a primary concern to the individual; but it is sometimes ignored. Credit quality is an important consideration. But ratings are not always understood. Also, in spite of the tax exemption, many investors would earn more after taxes on alternative investments. Commission costs, particularly for selling munis, are high. This almost dictates a buy-and-hold strategy for anyone investing in munis.

In addition, it is difficult to obtain accurate information concerning munis. It is usually impossible to obtain the prospectus for older issues trading in the secondary market. Coverage of munis in the daily financial press is virtually nonexistent. Some stockbrokers have little interest in this area. For this reason, investors should make a special effort to deal only with salespeople who really understand this particular market.

There is an effort under way to improve disclosure. In May of 1991, the Municipal Securities Rulemaking Board, which functions as an arbiter for the industry, together with underwriters and firms that disseminate information to major broker-dealers, approved the establishment of a centralized data bank or electronic library. This data bank would function as a central clearing house for information. It would contain, for example, copies of the prospectus (official statement) of issues trading in the secondary market, detailed information concerning call provisions, and even pricing data. However, at this point, the project is still in the preliminary planning stages, and it is anticipated that a minimum of three years will be required before it is operational.

All of this means that buyers of munis must make a special effort to understand exactly what they are buying and why. Munis are not the right product for every investor. Let's see if they belong in your portfolio.

Should I Buy Munis?

No one likes to pay taxes. But not everyone benefits from buying tax-exempt bonds. If you are in a low tax bracket, you may actually earn more by buying taxable bonds and paying the taxes. Yet, a surprising number of individuals buy tax-exempt bonds when it makes no economic sense for them. It would appear that they are suffering from a disease called "taxaphobia."

If you are considering buying munis, your first step should be to determine whether you will earn more by buying munis or by buying taxable instruments. That decision requires some arithmetic. The method used most often is to calculate how much you would have to earn on taxable investments to earn as much as you net on municipal bonds. This is called the taxable-equivalent yield.

Brokerage firms, mutual funds, and newspapers all publish tables that list both tax-exempt yields and their taxable equivalent. Exhibit 7.1 shows what some of these numbers would have been during November, 1990.

Exhibit 7.1
Tax-Exempt Yields and Taxable-Equivalent Yields

			Taxable-Equivalent Yields	
		Tax-Exempt	28%	31%
Rating	Type	Yield	Bracket	Bracket
Triple-A	General Obligation	6.95%	9.65%	10.07%
Double-A	General Obligation	7.05	9.79	10.22
Triple-A	Insured (Stronger Issuer)	7.15	9.93	10.36
Single-A	General Obligation	7.20	10.00	10.43
Triple-A	Insured (Weaker Issuer)	7.30	10.14	10.58
Single-A	Revenue (Essential Service)	7.40	10.28	10.72

If a similar table is not available, the taxable-equivalent yield is easy to calculate. The procedure is simple. The first step is to determine your exact tax bracket. The formula for computing the taxable-equivalent yield is:

$$\text{taxable–equivalent yield} = \frac{\text{tax–exempt yield}}{(1 - \text{tax bracket})}$$

For example, suppose you are in the 33 percent (federal) tax bracket and you are considering purchasing a muni yielding 7 percent (yield-to-maturity). To obtain the tax-equivalent yield, convert percentages to decimals. Your calculation looks like this:

$$\text{taxable–equivalent yield} = \frac{.07}{1 - .33} = 10.45$$

That means that you would have to earn 10.45 percent in a taxable security in order to earn an equivalent yield.

If you are in the 15 percent tax bracket, the taxable-equivalent yield on the same 7-percent muni drops to 8.23 percent. You might actually earn more by buying a taxable instrument.

Similarly, many buyers in states with high taxes such as New York, California, Massachusetts, or Minnesota prefer to buy munis free of state and local taxes. But again, demand for such paper may drop the yield to a point where you may earn more on out-of-state munis (federally tax-exempt, but not exempt from taxes in your own state) than on munis from your own state.

To determine whether in-state bonds are more attractive than out-of-state bonds, a simpler procedure is to compute the net-after-tax yield—that is, what you are left with after paying the tax). Suppose, for example, that you are considering two tax-exempt securities: one in-state and one out-of-state. The out-of-state bond yields 7 percent. The in-state bond yields 6 percent. Which will earn more? To compute, subtract the state tax from 100 percent and multiply the out-of-state interest by that amount. This tells you what you would keep after paying the state tax. For the preceding example, if you assume an 8 percent state tax, the calculation is as follows

- Subtract 8 percent from 100 percent, to get 92 percent.
- Convert to decimals, and multiply the out-of-state yield of 7 percent by .92.
- The net-after-tax yield is 6.44 percent, which is higher than the yield on the in-state bond.

There are some fine points to remember when comparing taxable-equivalent yields. First, remember that Treasuries and some federal agency paper are both exempt from state taxes. Particularly in high tax states, either Treasuries or paper of certain agencies can net you more, net-after-taxes, than municipals. Also, if you are considering purchasing munis at a discount, remember that the yield-to-maturity for those bonds includes a capital gains component, which is federally taxable. Particularly if the discount is substantial, you may want to determine how much the capital gains taxes would decrease the total yield-to-maturity. Finally, make sure that you are comparing the same yield. Usually, it will be the yield-to-maturity.

As a rule, taxpayers in the highest tax brackets benefit from buying tax-exempt bonds; those in the lowest do not. Whether tax-exempts make economic sense for investors in the middle depends on the relationship between taxable and tax-exempt yields at the time of purchase (these change continually) as well as on current tax laws and of course on your income. Whenever any of these change, by all means, recompute.

GENERAL OBLIGATION AND REVENUE BONDS

Much of what has been previously published concerning municipal bonds is devoted to elaborate guidelines for analyzing individual municipal credits. Unfortunately, this information may not be particularly useful. In real life, the average investor does not have the time or the access to information to perform extensive credit analyses. First, the investor would need a prospectus. For new issues, the prospectus may be unavailable for several days until after the bond sale. For issues trading in the secondary market, the prospectus may not be available at all. Second, when your broker "shows" you a bond, you may have only a few hours to decide whether to buy. So what is a poor investor going to do?

In practice, most individual investors rely on the ratings assigned by the rating agencies. (See Chapter 3.) But there is so much confusion concerning municipal ratings that I would like to clear up some common misconceptions and to describe the essentials that any investor should understand.

Municipal bonds come in two varieties: general obligation and revenue. General obligation bonds (also called GOs) are issued by states, cities, or counties to raise money for schools, sewers, road improvements, and the like. Monies to pay interest to bondholders are raised through taxes and some user fees. Revenue bonds are issued by a variety of enterprises that perform a public function such as electric utilities, toll roads, airports, hospitals, universities, and other specially created "authorities." Money to pay interest to bondholders is generated by the enterprise of the issuer. Electric utilities depend on the fees paid by users of electricity; hospitals depend on patient revenues; toll roads depend on tolls, and so on.

One important misconception concerning municipal bonds is that GOs are much safer than revenues. There are strong and weak credits in each bond sector. The supposed safety of GOs is ascribed to the fact that they are backed by the taxing power of the issuer. Theoretically, that power is "unlimited." That is because bond indentures state that general obligation bonds are backed by the unlimited taxing power of the issuer. In the real world, however, the power to tax is limited by political and economic considerations. The classic question any analyst has to ask is: if there is an economic crunch, who will the issuer pay, its teachers, police and fire department, or the bondholders? If municipalities could tax at will, all GOs would be AAA, and as we know, this is not the case.

Similarly, the supposed lower safety of revenue bonds is based on the fact that issuers run businesses whose revenues cannot be predicted with certainty. Again, that bears no relationship to what goes on in the real world. Most electric utilities and toll roads can, and do, raise rates to pay for increasing costs. Consequently, many revenue bonds, particularly those issued for essential services such as electric power, sewer, or water are high quality credits. So are many toll roads or state "authorities."

How much importance should you ascribe to differences in rating among sound quality credits (A or A+, or higher)? Not as much as you might have thought. It's more important to understand what is behind the rating. Ratings of GOs are determined by the overall economic strength of the tax base, compared to debt service requirements. AAA issuers have flourishing tax bases, a strong and diversified economy not dependent on a single industry, low levels of overall debt, and/or a strong tradition of prudent fiscal management. But factors other than the economy are also critical to GO ratings. One of them is size. Small cities or counties which come infrequently to market, even those with prudent fiscal management, are generally not rated higher than A. They may nonetheless be strong credits, particularly if you know the communities and are purchasing intermediate maturities. (Some wealthy communities have issued so little debt that they do not even have a rating!)

Ratings of revenue bonds revolve around an analysis of revenues generated by sales, compared to money needed to cover interest payments (debt service). In practice, the rating is determined mainly by a key ratio known as the debt service coverage ratio. That is defined as the amount of money specifically available for payment of debt service divided by the amount of debt service to be paid. This ratio is calculated for the past: how much money was actually available for debt service last year, or for the past five years? It is also estimated for the future: how much money is going to be available next year, and the year after, and so on, for debt service? The past ratio is called "the historical debt service ratio."

An historical debt service ratio of at least two is generally required for an "A" rating. That ratio indicates that monies reserved for payment of debt service were equal to twice the amount needed for debt service. An historical ratio of five or six times debt service is considered fantastic. An historical ratio below one—indicating there wasn't enough money in the till to cover debt service—would almost guarantee a below investment grade rating. Nonetheless, no matter how sound their management or how strong debt service coverage has been, revenue bonds are almost never rated AAA on their own merit. This does not make them unattractive investments—just the opposite. They yield more than GOs.

In the late 1980s, hospitals were viewed as particularly risky because of the stresses on the medical system. But even in this area, there were some very strong credits; for example, teaching hospitals affiliated with outstanding universities, such as Massachusetts General, which is affiliated with Harvard University, or strong chains such as the Sisters of Charity hospitals in the Midwest.

Also, in practice, the boundary lines between revenue and general obligation bonds are sometimes fuzzy. For example, some counties and cities own hospitals and/or electric revenue plants, sometimes both. Therefore, the revenue bonds they issue have both general obligation and revenue backing. These bonds are sometimes called "double barreled" credits.

Among GOs, the weakest credits are found in two groups: GOs of large cities with deteriorating downtown cores, and large social outlays; and older, smaller cities or districts with shrinking populations, a shrinking tax base, and deteriorating economies. Among revenue bonds, the riskiest bonds have been hospitals with strong dependence on government reimbursement (government programs do not cover hospital expenses in full); bonds issued by developers of nursing homes (many of these are highly speculative); and so-called private purpose bonds (also called industrial development bonds, or IDBs). These are issued by specially constituted authorities on behalf of private businesses.

When you buy a municipal bond, it's important to get a very clear sense of the factors underlying its rating. Who exactly is the issuer? Where does money to pay debt service come from? These factors should be extremely specific. For example, in 1990, both the Port of Authority of New York and New Jersey and the Denver Airport issued private purpose bonds on behalf of Continental Airlines, which then went into bankruptcy proceedings. It is probable that some buyers of those bonds did not realize that Continental, whose financial troubles were well publicized, was responsible for debt service, and not the Port Authority or the Denver Airport.

Therefore, it's important to ask very specific questions.

- Who pays debt service?

- How adequate are sources of revenue?

- For a utility bond, what is the historical debt service coverage ratio?

- For a housing bond, where will the development be located, and how is real estate doing in that area? (If nothing has been built, the bonds may be very speculative).

- If the bond is a GO, does the locality normally run a balanced budget, or does a deficit threaten continually?

- Finally, find out the rating history and not just the current rating. Has the rating been stable? Has it gone up and down a lot? Is the credit quality improving or deteriorating?

Even if a prospectus is not available, a knowledgeable broker should be familiar with the outstanding credit features of specific bonds and should be able to answer these questions. If she can't, find another broker!

Note also that the AAA rating of many bonds is based on insurance. Some brokers do not differentiate between bonds rated AAA on their own, and those that are rated AAA because of the insurance feature. Bonds rated AAA on their own are stronger. The bond market differentiates between the two, and you should do the same.

Finally, remember that the rating is only one of many factors to consider when buying munis. As always, maturity length and potential total return should be equally important considerations.

CREDIT ENHANCEMENTS

Municipal Bond Insurance

Bond insurance is fairly recent. While one bond insurance firm was started in the early 1970s, the current popularity of bond insurance owes its existence primarily to the shocks created by the WPPSS and New York City defaults. Since 1985, approximately 25 percent of all municipal bonds have come to market with insurance. Insurance, however, does not remove all of the risks of buying bonds. And it comes at a cost. Let's see why.

Insurance is purchased by an issuer when bonds are brought to market. The insurance guarantees that if the issuer experiences financial problems, the insurer will step in and take over payment of both interest and principal. Generally, an entire bond issue is insured. Occasionally, only part of an issue is covered; perhaps only specific maturities (the longest term bonds); or perhaps the reserve fund only.

At the beginning of 1991, there were three major bond insurance firms: Municipal Bond Insurance Association (MBIA); Financial Guaranty Insurance Company (FGIC); and American Municipal Bond Assurance Co. (AMBAC). A fourth bond insurance firm, Bond Insurance Guaranty (BIG), the last to enter the industry, and the smallest, sold its portfolio to MBIA. Its bonds are now insured by MBIA. All bonds insured by these three bond insurance firms are rated AAA by both Moody's and Standard & Poor's. This is because in the opinion of these rating agencies, the insurers have sufficient reserves to back up their guarantee even under a simulated severe depression scenario.

Issuers who have a strong credit history (A+ or better) generally come to market without insurance. Issuers who need "enhancements" in order to attract buyers are most likely to insure their bonds. These would include credits that are marginally investment grade, that are not well known, or that may be undergoing temporary difficulties. In effect, bond insurance transforms a potential lemon into lemonade. Instead of coming to market with a rating that may be barely investment grade, the bond comes to market as a AAA bond, based on the rating of the insurance firm.

For insurance companies, municipal bond insurance has proved a dream product. These three insurers screen bonds very carefully. Only issuers deemed unlikely to default are granted insurance. To date, none of the three major bond insurance firms has suffered a major default.

For purchasers of insured bonds, the benefits are less clear-cut. The main cost is that insurance lowers yield. Bond insurance, furthermore, protects only against default risk. It does not protect against fluctuations in the price of a bond due to changes in interest rates.

Nor is there any guarantee that the rating of the bond insurance firms will not be downgraded. Insurance companies are businesses, and they are subject to the same vagaries as other business enterprises. They may continue to prosper; and they may not. In the event any of the bond insurance firms is downgraded (certainly a possibility), then all the bonds guaranteed by that firm would be downgraded as well to reflect the new rating of the insurer. This, in turn, would result in a price decline for those bonds because at that point, the bonds would trade based on the lower rating of the insurer. The rating of the issuer might also become more important to pricing.

There are, on the other hand, positive aspects to bond insurance. Bond insurance makes it somewhat easier—and therefore cheaper—to resell bonds. Also, when New York City and Philadelphia bonds were downgraded, the insured bonds of those cities declined less in price than the uninsured bonds of those cities. This may turn out to be a precedent. Finally, bond insurance functions as a second opinion on credit quality. Someone other than the rating agencies—and who moreover has money on the line—has carefully screened a possibly marginal issuer for credit quality.

As a group, investment professionals (presumably the experts) avoid insured bonds. As a result, insured bonds trade like AA credits, and not, as their rating would suggest, like AAA credits. To an individual investor, this means that insured bonds yield somewhat more than AAA bonds. The yield (and, therefore, the price) of an insured bond is actually based both on the insurance and on the underlying credit of the issuer. For that reason, you should find out how the bonds would be rated if they were not insured. To check the rating of the issuer, find out, if you can, how uninsured issues of the same issuer are rated.

For the individual investor, bond insurance makes a lot of sense in situations where it adds a layer of protection against totally unforeseeable risks. This applies to bonds with maturities longer than ten years; or if you are buying riskier credits such as hospitals; or if you have a relatively undiversified portfolio (not necessarily a small portfolio, but one consisting of a few individual issues).

Before leaving the topic of bond insurance, let's briefly mention two recent episodes that involved bonds insured by Executive Life Insurance Co. and by Mutual Benefit Life Insurance Co. As this is being written (October of 1991), both of these insurance companies are in very deep financial difficulty and may not survive. Executive Life had insured a number of taxable housing issues, that were initially rated AAA because of the insurance; and that were subsequently downgraded. Mutual Benefit Life had insured a variety of municipal bonds. All of these bonds are currently trading at very low prices (perhaps 20 cents on the dollar) and some of the bonds are in danger of default.

Both of these situations are extremely complicated, and this summary is vastly oversimplified. It is mentioned here because of its relevance to the topic of bond insurance. These episodes should not alarm anyone holding bonds insured by MBIA, FGIC or AMBAC. These three bond insurance firms are monoline insurers. Their only business is to insure bonds. To date, these three firms are in sound financial condition. Both Mutual Benefit Life and Executive Life had more general and very different lines of business. Nonetheless, these episodes should be viewed as a reminder that bond insurance does not confer any absolute guarantees and that before purchasing insured bonds, investors should investigate the credit quality of the issuer and the current rating of the firm insuring the bonds.

Letters of Credit

Letters of credit (LOCs) are issued by banks and insurance companies as a form of credit "enhancement." They are similar to bond insurance, but they do not confer the same degree of protection.

A LOC does not obligate the bank to actually take over interest payments. Rather, a letter of credit is a line of credit. It obligates the bank issuing the LOC to lend money to the issuer, if the issuer does not have enough cash on hand to cover interest payments. But LOCs differ in the degree of "obligation" imposed on the bank. Some are irrevocable. Others obligate the bank to make the loan only under certain stipulated conditions.

Because the degree of protection afforded by LOC backing varies for each individual issue, the rating of LOC backed bonds also varies, from A to AAA, depending on the strength of the obligation, the financial condition of the bank, and the underlying credit quality of the issuer. Since the entire banking sector is under pressure, it would be prudent to check the rating of the bank before purchasing any bond with LOC backing. It might be more prudent to stay away from LOCs altogether since the probability of downgrade is strong and you would be paying for a rating that is unlikely to be sustained.

Other Strong Credit Features

If credit quality is an important consideration for you, there are many possibilities other than insured bonds.

Bonds rated A+ to AAA on their own are sound investments. As of October 1991, the following states were rated AAA by Standard and Poor's: California, Maryland, Missouri, North Carolina, South Carolina, Utah and Virginia. At the same date, Moody's rated the same states Aaa as well as Tennessee, New Jersey and Georgia.

The strongest credits are those of "refunded" bonds. These are high coupon bonds, possibly selling at a premium, which are backed by U. S. Treasury bonds held in escrow. How can that be? Well, suppose a municipality issued bonds five years ago when interest rates were 12 percent. Further suppose that interest rates decline, say to 9 percent. Call provisions prevent the municipality from just recalling the 12 percent bonds.

The municipality may "refinance," however, by issuing new bonds at the 9 percent coupon rate. These 9 percent bonds are known as "refunding" bonds. The municipality issues an amount of 9 percent bonds sufficient to cover interest payments and to redeem principal of the 12 percent bonds at the first call date. The proceeds from the sale of the 9 percent bonds (the refunding bonds) are used to purchase U. S. Treasury securities, which are then placed in an escrow account. The Treasuries are used to pay the coupon payments on the 12 percent bonds, now called the "refunded" bonds. At the first call date, the remaining Treasuries in the escrow account are used to redeem the refunded bonds.

The refunded bonds are totally free of default risk since monies to pay the bondholders are held in escrow and invested in Treasuries. Whatever the initial rating of the bonds, it now jumps to AAA. This is not automatic, however. Technically, the issuer has to apply for a new rating—because the rating agencies want their fee. If the refunded bonds are not re-rated, they will generally trade like AAA bonds anyhow. The refunding bonds, on the other hand, trade with the rating of the issuer.

Note that another advantage of "refunded" bonds is that maturities for such bonds are short to intermediate. Therefore, interest rate risk is low.

A number of states, such as Maine and Virginia, issue bonds for small localities through very well-run and highly rated "bond banks." Other states (including New York and New Jersey) add a layer of protection to the bonds of local school districts by reserving state aid payments for debt service if the school district is in financial difficulty.

Many other possibilities will no doubt continue to turn up as the markets and economic conditions change. This is one reason for dealing with a knowledgeable specialist who can assist you in uncovering new opportunities.

MUNICIPAL BONDS WITH SPECIAL FEATURES

This is a partial listing of features that may be of interest to individual investors.

Notes

Municipal issuers issue debt with maturities under three years, with names such as "revenue anticipation notes" (RANs), "tax anticipation notes" (TANs), or "bond anticipation notes" (BANs). As these names suggest, these securities are issued in anticipation of revenues from one of two sources, from taxes or from bonds. Notes are rated. But their ratings differ from those of long-term bonds. The higher quality ratings are: "MIG 1" and "MIG 2" by Moody's; and "SP 1+" or "SP" by Standard and Poor's.

Notes are purchased mainly by institutional investors. But they can be purchased in amounts as low as $10,000. And if the yield curve is normal (that is, upwardly sloping), these securities yield more than tax-exempt money market funds by perhaps 50 to 100 basis points.

The yields of tax-exempt notes are comparatively low. For individual investors, they are most appropriate for short-term investments, that is; when the money will be needed within a short period of time. They would be attractive alternatives to tax-exempt money market funds. But individuals should limit their purchases of notes only to those with impeccable credit quality.

Municipal Zeros

Muni "zeros" are sold under a variety of names: "municipal multipliers," "principal appreciation bonds," "capital appreciation bonds," or zeros. Whatever their name, they have similar investment characteristics. They are issued at a deep discount from par. At maturity, they are redeemed at par. The difference between the issue price and par represents a specified compounded annual yield.

The price behavior of municipal zeros is comparable to Treasury zeros. The volatility is about 2 1/2 times as high as that of other bonds with similar maturities. But since muni zeros are federally tax-exempt, no tax needs to be paid annually on "phantom" interest.

Another similarity between Treasury zeros and muni zeros is that there is no reinvestment risk. The final dollar amount is known. This is not an advantage unless the yield-to-maturity is particularly attractive. Also, since no interest is paid until the maturity date, muni zeros should not be purchased by anyone relying on interest payments for income.

There are some major differences, however, between muni zeros and Treasury zeros. The credit quality of muni zeros varies with the issuer. For muni zeros, credit quality is critical because no interest is paid until the final maturity date. If the zero defaults after several years, you would not have had the consolation of a single interest payment. (This is one instance where bond insurance would make a lot of sense).

In addition, muni zeros are subject to call. Muni zeros are called at stipulated *discounts* from par, and not, as some investors assume, at par.

At one time, muni zeros had the reputation of being expensive to resell. There is now a much more active secondary market for zeros. And markups are comparable to those of other munis. Remember, however, that the costs of selling munis are high and that the volatility of zeros makes them high risk investments if you plan to resell. Because of this, they are appropriate purchases mainly if you plan to hold them to maturity.

Muni zeros are most appropriate for funding future known expenses, for high tax bracket investors. They might be used, for example, to coincide with an early retirement date or to fund a child's college education. Some states now issue tax-exempt bonds, called "college bonds," that are basically muni zeros tailored to the needs of individuals saving for a child's college education.

Alternative Minimum Tax Bonds

The *Tax Reform Bill of 1986* provides for direct federal taxation of certain categories of municipal bonds. Only bonds specifically designated as "nonessential" bonds, issued after August 7, 1986, are subject to this tax; and then only if the individual investor's tax bracket makes him subject to the alternative minimum tax.

Because of the possibility of a tax, however, these bonds yield somewhat more than other municipal bonds. Therefore, for those individuals not subject to the alternative minimum tax (and that's almost everyone), these bonds will result in a somewhat higher yield.

Bonds with Put Provisions

A "put" is the exact opposite of a call. A put feature gives the purchaser the option of tendering (or "putting") a bond back to the issuer at stipulated intervals or dates at par. This is a form of protection for the bondholder, since if interest rates rise, she can redeem her bond without incurring any loss of principal; and she can then reinvest the proceeds at a more attractive rate. Because of this feature, "put" bonds are less volatile than other long-term bonds and they normally trade at or close to par. But since there is no free lunch, there are a couple of disadvantages. First, the coupon interest is usually lower than that of bonds with a similar maturity (total return may therefore be lower). And second, if interest rates decline, "put" bonds appreciate in value much less than other long-term bonds.

"Supersinkers"

"Supersinkers" are a variety of housing bonds with specifically designated maturities singled out for early retirement if mortgages are prepaid. This means that some of the bonds may be called early. The name "supersinker" derives from the fact that monies to retire the bonds accumulate in a "sinking fund." The retirement date is uncertain because prepayments are unpredictable.

The potential early call feature of "supersinkers" is considered attractive because, since there is not a specific call date, the yield of the bond—and its price—are determined by the maturity date, and not by the uncertain call date. Supersinkers normally mature well before their maturity date. In effect, the purchaser earns a long-term yield on a short-term security.

Be very cautious, however, if a supersinker is selling at a high premium. An early call would result in a loss of principal.

BUYING MUNICIPAL BONDS

Call Risk

Munis—mainly those with long-term maturities—are subject to call. You will remember that means that the issuer may choose to redeem a bond before its maturity date.

Call provisions on most munis are straightforward. Typical call provisions stipulate an initial call date 10 years after issue, at a price slightly above par (typically 101); and several additional consecutive call dates (in 15 years at 102, and so on). Housing revenue bonds, however, may have unusual call features allowing the issuer to call bonds. This can happen, for example, if the money raised by the bonds is not needed for actual mortgages. The difference between those call provisions and ordinary call provisions is that no date is mentioned. The bonds may be called as early as a few months after issue, and this has happened.

Under normal circumstances, issuers are likely to call munis only if interest rates drop substantially. The higher and the more attractive the yield to the investor, the more expensive the interest for the issuer, and the more likely it is that a bond will be called. As explained earlier, be particularly careful to investigate call provisions for any bond selling at a premium. Be doubly careful for housing bonds selling at a premium. A broker should quote both the yield-to-maturity; and the yield to the first call date (that will usually be lower than the yield-to-maturity). If the bond is called, the yield-to-call becomes the actual return.

"Dollar" Bonds and "Basis" Bonds

Some munis are called "dollar bonds" because the price of these bonds is quoted in dollars. Other bonds are priced "to the basis." Instead of a dollar amount, the yield-to-maturity is quoted. Therefore, the buyer has to work backwards from the quoted yield to compute the price (the broker will pull out his trusty calculator).

"The Dated Date"

This is the date on which the bond begins accruing (earning) interest.

Markups

The author of a recent book on municipal bonds characterized pricing in the muni market as "let the buyer beware" or "what the market will bear."[1] For an individual investor, commission costs vary from under one point ($100 per $10,000 par value bonds) for actively traded issues with short maturities and high credit quality to about 4 points ($400 per $10,000 par value bonds) for inactively traded bonds with long maturities.

---

1. James Cooner, *Investing in Municipal Bonds*. New York: John Wiley, 1987, p. 44.

Small lots (under $25,000 par value) are considered a pain by brokers and they are marked up accordingly. This makes them particularly expensive to sell. Brokers, in fact, have an expression for the pricing of these lots, which is that they "punish the coupon." Translation: the commission costs for selling such a lot are extremely high. Dealers who buy a small lot from you do so with the understanding that they are doing you a special favor. Inevitably, however, the dealer will be anxious to get rid of small lots and will price them attractively for resale. Paradoxically, this may then translate into lower transaction costs and higher yield for the buyer of small lots.

Pricing of munis is a quagmire. It is almost impossible to generalize about commissions in the muni retail (i. e., individual investor) market. The chief characteristic of municipal pricing (and as a result, of municipal yields) is its inconsistency from dealer to dealer. In order to research pricing inconsistencies, I pretended to be selling a number of retail sized lots of munis that I had inherited. I called seven different firms to see what prices they would offer. Among the lots was a high quality, widely traded New Jersey Turnpike bond; one very controversial credit, Philadelphia—its financial difficulties were highly publicized at the time; and some infrequently traded issues.

I was offered prices all over the lot. The prices were closest on the New Jersey Turnpike bonds. This was not unexpected since I live in New Jersey and New Jersey Turnpike bonds are actively traded. Nonetheless, even on this lot, offers varied by 150 basis points on a price of 98. Since I was "selling" a $40,000 par value lot, that translates into a price difference of $612.00 between the highest and the lowest offer. The largest difference occurred on an out-of-state housing bond (375 basis points, almost 4 percent, or $1500 on a $40,000 lot). A number of the dealers refused to bid on some of the lesser known names.

The moral of the story is that it is absolutely essential to shop around if you are either buying or selling munis. As a rule, individual municipal bonds should be purchased only if you do not plan to resell your bonds. Otherwise, commission costs (which are paid both when you buy and when you sell) seriously reduce overall returns. Remember also that commission costs are particularly high if you need to sell.

Exhibit 7.2
Cover Page of a Sample Issue of "The Blue List"

The Blue List
of Current Municipal and Corporate Offerings
A Division of Standard & Poor's Corporation

Published every weekday except Saturdays and Holidays by
The Blue List Publishing Company, 65 Broadway, New York, N.Y. 10006
Telephone 212 770-4300 FAX 212 425-6864

Reg. U.S. Patent Office · Printed in U.S.A.

INDEX

New Housing Authority Bonds.. 45	Corporate Bonds.. 53A
Taxable Municipals.. 46	Bank Qualified.. 54
Industrial Development and Pollution Control Bonds.. 47	AMT Bonds.. 59A
Notes.. 49	Zero Coupon Bonds.. 61
Unit Investment Trusts..	Offerings Wanted.. 63A
New Issue Delivery Dates.. 49A	Insured Bonds.. 64
Pre-refunded Bonds.. 50	List of Advertisers..
Federally Sponsored Bonds.. 53	Late Breaking CUSIP's..

The bonds set forth in this list were offered at the close of business on the day before the date of this issue by the houses mentioned, subject to prior sale and change in price. Every effort is made by The Blue List Publishing Company and the houses whose offerings are shown in The Blue List to avoid mistakes and inaccuracies, but due to the fact that many offerings come in late and that the list is published after the offering houses have closed for the day, occasional errors are unavoidable. Neither The Blue List Publishing Company nor the offering houses take responsibility for the accuracy of the offerings listed herein.

+ Items so marked did not appear in the previous issue of The Blue List
# Prices so marked are changed from the previous issue.
o Items so marked are reported to have call or option features. Consult offering house for full details.

ANNUAL SUBSCRIPTION RATE (approximately 250 issues) : Hand Delivery (Wall Street Area) $635.00 ; First Class Mail $810.00

ALABAMA

AMT. M	SECURITY	PURPOSE	RATE	MATURITY	YIELD OR PRICE	OFFERED BY
1200	ALABAMA ST	CA @ 103	8.000	03/01/95 C93	5.35	FBC
620	ALABAMA ST		4.500	05/01/97	5.80	BARBRBROS
100	BIRMINGHAM ALA HSG FIN AUTH SINGLE	GNMA	7.550	10/01/16	7.30	PORTER
145	BIRMINGHAM ALA MED CLINIC BRD	BAPTIST MED	8.300	07/01/08 ETM	6.25	SOTRBALA
	(S/F 7/11/00@100)(YTM 8.67)					
15	BIRMINGHAM ALA NEW PUB HSG		3.750	05/01/93	6.20	WACHOVIA
65	BIRMINGHAM ALA NEW PUB HSG		3.375	01/01/99	6.25	SEASONGD
85	CHEROKEE CNTY ALA BRD ED CAP	BK. QD	7.000	02/01/02	6.65	FIRALINV
80			7.000	02/01/03	6.75	
120	CHEROKEE CNTY ALA BRD ED CAP	"B/E"	7.100	02/01/11	7.10	PORTER
25	COURTLAND ALA INDL DEV BRD		5.750	11/01/97	90 1/2	BARBRBROS
1000	EAST ALA HEALTH CARE AUTH	MBIA	6.875	09/01/11	100	HOUGHWMC
500	EAST ALA HEALTH CARE AUTH	MBIA	6.875	09/01/21	100	TOWNESCO
500	EAST ALA HEALTH CARE AUTH	MBIA	7.000	09/01/21	99 5/8	WHEATFST
100	FAIRFIELD ALA INDL DEV BRD	U.S.X.	6.800	12/01/08	7.25	PORTER
200	HOOVER ALA	BK. QD	6.500	09/01/08	6.80	PORTER
10	HOUSTON CNTY ALA HOSP BRD		8.000	04/01/98	5.80	HOMEBARN

ALABAMA - CONTINUED

AMT. M	SECURITY	PURPOSE	RATE	MATURITY	YIELD OR PRICE	OFFERED BY
30	HUNTSVILLE ALA NAT GAS REV	BK. QD	6.400	04/01/03	100	AGEDWRFL
100	JACKSON CNTY ALA HEALTH CARE		7.300	02/01/11	100	CENTBGM
65	LEE CNTY ALA HOSP BRD REV		6.750	10/01/08 ETM	6.50	EQUITSEC
300	MARENGO CNTY ALA PORT AUTH		0.000	07/01/11 N/C	7.50	VICKMS
315	MARENGO CNTY ALA PORT AUTH		0.000	03/01/19 N/C	7.75	RICKEL
500	MARENGO CNTY ALA PORT AUTH		0.000	03/01/19 N/C	7.50	VICKMS
500	MOBILE ALA	BKG	0.000	08/15/00 C86	5.50	PORTER
	(P/C @ 66.289)					
100	MOBILE ALA INDL DEV BRD DOCK &	IDEAL BASIC	6.750	08/01/04	8.25	GPICT
200	MOBILE ALA INDL DEV BRD DOCK &	IDEAL BASIC	6.750	08/01/04	8.25	PRUBANY
400	MOBILE CNTY ALA		7.100	02/01/05 C97	6.80	BYN.4295
	(L.T._KCA @ 103.50 @ 100)					
	AGEDWRFL LEGGMANO					
450	NORTH ALA ENVIRONMENTAL IMPT REYNOLDS METALS		6.125	06/01/93	100 1/4	TUCKERNY
100	ORANGE BEACH ALA INDL DEV BRD		10.500	04/01/16	98	SMITHB

Buying at Issue

Both the *New York Times* and the *Wall Street Journal* list upcoming sales of municipal bonds every Monday. If a bond interests you, let your broker know that you would like to buy at the issue price.

There are definite advantages to buying at issue. For a few days, the bonds are priced at par (or at a uniform price) by all the dealers in the syndicate, until the bonds "break syndicate" and are allowed to trade at what the market will bear. During that time, moreover, prices—and therefore yields—are usually attractive because dealers are anxious to sell the bonds. The buyer also receives the longest possible call provisions.

Buying in the Secondary Market—the Blue List

To become better informed about both prices and yields available in the secondary market, you might want to find a "Blue List." The Blue List is a brochure about 60–75 pages long, which is published daily by Standard and Poor's, on blue paper, in blue ink (no, I am not pulling your leg.) It lists some of the "floating supply" of bonds that dealers currently own and would like to sell and the price at which the dealers would like to sell these bonds. (The total "floating supply" varies between $1.5 billion and $3.0 billion per list.) Exhibit 7.2 shows the front page of a Blue List, dated May 6, 1991.

Listings in the Blue List follow the usual pattern of bond listing. Reading from left to right, the first listing on the right contains the following data:

- the number of bonds offered for sale (30);
- the issuer (Huntsville, Alabama, gas revenue bond);
- the coupon rate (6.4 percent);
- the maturity date of the bonds (04/01/03);
- the yield or price (in this instance, a price of 100—as a percentage of par—which is equivalent to par);
- the name of the dealer offering the bonds for sale.

Note that the column in the middle, headed *purpose* lists a variety of data for different bonds such as the name of the insurer if the bond is an insured bond (MBIA); or the call price. Note also that under "yield or price," for many bonds, the yield is listed rather than the price. Those bonds are priced "to the basis."

There are some important caveats in reading the Blue List. The Blue List does not tell you the price at which the bonds actually sell. Also, if you owned one of the bonds on the list and wanted to sell it, you would get a lower price (Remember the bid/ask spread. You always sell at a lower price than you buy). Furthermore, by the time you get your Blue List, it is likely to be several days old. Many bonds will have been sold. And many prices will be stale. Nonetheless, the Blue List represents the single best source of information about pricing and yield available to retail investors in the secondary market. Almost any firm that sells bonds will have a copy of the Blue List, and it should make it available to you.

Newspaper Listings

Another source of information which is easily available but less satisfactory than the Blue List, are the tables published daily by the *Wall Street Journal* and *Investor's Daily*, and on the weekend, by *Barron's*. Exhibit 7.3 shows the format of a partial listing. (These yields were published October 10, 1991).

Reading from left to right, for the first bond listed, the table specifies:

- the name of the issuer (Beaver County);
- the coupon rate (7.00);
- the maturity date (06/01/21);
- the bid price as a percentage of par (101 1/2);
- the change from the bid since the previous day (-1/8); and,
- the yield-to-maturity (6.89 percent).

Remember that prices and yields move in opposite directions. If prices go up, yields go down. The actual prices on the list

Exhibit 7.3
Format for Tax-Exempt Bond Listings

Representative prices for several active tax-exempt revenue and refunding bonds. Changes rounded to the nearest one-eighth. Yield is to maturity.

Issue	Coupon	Mat.	Price	Chg.	Bid Yld.
Beaver Co. IDA Pa.	7.000	06-01-21	101½	− ⅛	6.89
Charlte NC Part Conv	6.750	12-01-21	100½	− ⅛	6.71
Cook Co IL GO 91	6.750	11-01-18	99	− ⅛	6.83
Fulton-Dekalb Hos Au	6.900	01-0120	100½	− ¼	6.86
Ill. Set N Build	7.000	06-15-20	105⅝	− ⅛	6.95
L.A. Dept Wtr & Pwr	6.625	10-01-31	99½	− ⅜	6.66
Metro Seattle Swr	6.875	01-01-31	99⅜	− ¼	6.92
NC Mun Pwr #1	6.500	01-01-10	99⅝	− ⅛	6.54
NYC Muni Wtr Auth	7.100	06-15-12	99⅝	− ¼	7.14
NYS Muni Wtr Auth	7.000	06-15-15	99⅛	− ⅜	7.08
P.R. Elec Pwr Auth	7.000	07-01-21	105⅝	− ⅛	6.95
Portland Ore.	6.700	05-01-21	99⅞	− ¼	6.71
Trib Brdg & Tun Auth	6.875	01-01-15	99⅞	− ¼	6.95
WPPSS Refunding	6.875	07-01-17	99¼	− ¼	6.94

Source: *The Bond Buyer.*

are available to institutional buyers only, on very large lots, but they give some indication of yields. Note, however, that this table (and others like it) covers only a tiny fraction of all issues traded. It is not highly representative because it does not list yields of short or of intermediate issues (maturity dates range from 2010 to 2031); and it lists very few bonds rated lower than AA. But no other source in the general financial press is more complete.

Discount vs. Premium Bonds

Your broker telephones. She has just gotten some terrific bonds in inventory: one a discount and the other a premium. Both yield 7 1/2 percent to maturity. Which should you buy?

Well, you reason, I should buy the discount bond because if I buy the premium bond, at maturity, I will lose for each bond the amount of the premium over par.

Wrong, but a common misconception. If you are looking primarily for income—all other factors such as credit quality and maturity being equal—you should buy the premium bond. Premium bonds generally yield more than discounts. Here is why.

It is a common error to think that one "loses" the difference in price between par and the amount of the premium. The yield quoted for the premium bond is based on the net price, including the premium. The premium is not lost. Even if the yield quoted for the premium and the discount bond are exactly the same, the discount bond yield includes anticipated capital gains. That capital gain is taxable, whereas the entire dividend yield of the premium bond is tax-free. Hence, the net yield of the discount bond will be lower than the quoted yield-to-maturity, whereas for the premium bond, it will be the same.

The yield advantage is amplified by several additional factors. First, the premium bond has higher coupons. This results in larger amounts to reinvest every year and, therefore, more interest-on-interest. More importantly, because many investors avoid premium bonds, they are usually offered with higher yields than comparable maturity discount bonds. Finally, premium bonds are less volatile than discount bonds, which protects principal if interest rates rise.

Therefore, if your style of investing is to buy and hold, muni premium bonds have two advantages: higher yield and lower volatility. On the other hand, if you are a trader, or want to speculate on interest rates, then you might want to consider discount bonds, since those will appreciate more quickly in response to a decline in interest rates.

Overall Strategy

You have decided to invest in munis. If you are seeking maximum income and safety, what should you buy?

That question is often answered: "buy bonds rated AAA (for safety) with 30-year maturities (for maximum income). But that strategy buys neither. The 30-year maturity exposes the buyer to maximum interest rate risk. And AAA paper has low yields when compared to bonds with lower ratings.

A better strategy would be to buy intermediates, that is, bonds with five- to ten-year maturities and buy A to AA credits. Exhibit 7.4 shows why. This table lists yields available the week of September 23, 1991, for a broad spectrum of issues. It shows that the yields available at the five-year or at the ten-year mark, on

Exhibit 7.4
Yields of Municipal Bonds for Different Maturities and Ratings

	1	5	10	15	20	30
			Years			
AAA	4.50	5.40	6.00	6.40	6.70	6.65
AA	4.75	5.70	6.20	6.60	6.80	6.95
A	4.90	6.00	6.30	6.70	7.00	7.30
B	5.25	6.20	6.65	7.00	7.25	7.05

Source: *Muni Week*, published by the *Bond Buyer*, New York, September 23, 1991, p. 17.

paper rated A or AA, are approximately 90 percent (or higher) of the highest yield available on 30-year, AAA-rated bonds. Note that this is the case even though the yield curve at that point was rather steep, with 30-year paper yielding between 210 and 240 basis points more than paper with a one-year maturity. But of course, interest rate risk at either the five-year or the ten-year mark would be significantly lower than at the 30-year mark. Under those circumstances, the buyer is not being paid for the risk of buying bonds with a 30-year maturity. This strategy has the further advantage of minimizing credit risk and commission costs.

Diversification increases safety. If you do not have sufficient funds to buy a diversified portfolio of individual issues (that is, at least $50,000, preferably more) you can enhance credit safety by buying a mutual fund (but then it is best to stick to mutual funds with short maturities). Below that amount, you would be buying very small lots of individual issues, and incurring high transaction costs. If you have less to invest, consider intermediate Treasuries.

SUMMARY: QUESTIONS TO ASK BEFORE BUYING MUNICIPAL BONDS

When does the bond mature?

Who is the issuer?

What is the rating?

If the bond is rated AAA, is it insured or AAA on its own?

If the bond is insured: Who is the insurer? How is the bond rated without insurance?

Who is the issuer and where does revenue from debt service come from?

For a revenue bond, what is the debt service coverage ratio?

What is the yield-to-maturity?

When is the bond callable? At what price? What is the yield-to-call?

What is the price?

What is the coupon?

ADDITIONAL REFERENCES

For additional information on municipal bonds, there are several excellent books. A recent, very clear and readable book is *Investing in Municipal Bonds,* by James Cooner, New York: Wiley, 1987. For a totally different viewpoint, see Wilson White, *The Municipal Bond Investment Advisor,* Chicago, IL: Probus Publishing Co., 1991.

The standard reference text on munis is *The Municipal Bond Handbook,* Volumes 1 and 2, Feldstein, S. G. et al (editors), Homewood, IL: Dow Jones Irwin, 1983.

For current information, some bond firms publish excellent newsletters on municipal and other bonds. Most firms that sell to individual investors publish their own newsletters, and many are extremely informative. One that is particularly well done is published by the New York firm of Gabriele, Hueglin and Cashman (1-800-422-7435). It is free to customers.

The *Lynch Municipal Bond Advisory* is a newsletter devoted entirely to municipal bonds. It is published monthly and targeted to individual investors with large municipal portfolios. The annual subscription rate is $250. Mr. Lynch is a veteran professional with strong views about every aspect of the municipal market. For a sample copy, write to: P. O. Box 1086, Lenox Hill Station, New York 10021.

Finally, the bible of the municipal bond market is *The Bond Buyer,* One State Street Plaza, New York, New York, 10004. Subscription to this daily publication costs about $1,750 per year. A weekly summary, called *MuniWeek* can be purchased for about $600 per year. A subscription to *MuniWeek* should be considered by anyone with a very large municipal bond portfolio ($500,000 or more).

APPENDIX: THE NEW YORK CITY DEFAULT

Let's briefly look at the highly publicized default that happened to New York City, in the 1970s. While no two defaults are exactly alike, analyzing a default illustrates how a default can take place. In addition, defaults may create attractive speculative opportunities, as this one did. Therefore, it is instructive to examine how the default developed.

In April 1975, New York City found itself in a cash crunch. As a result, the City deferred an interest payment on a short-term note. (Long-term bonds were never involved). Technically, this delay constituted a default and it was highly publicized. But the interest payment was ultimately made, and no investor lost money unless he sold bonds that had dropped in value because of the publicity surrounding the default. (Note: to this day, some New York City officials insist that there was never a real default.)

In September, the state passed the Financial Emergency Act, putting the city under the authority of the Emergency Financial Control Board. The crisis was resolved through cooperation between three sectors: the unions, which agreed to use its pension funds for assistance, the state, which extended cash advances, and the banking community. Ultimately, the crisis was resolved through the creation of the Municipal Assistance Corporation (MAC), which was empowered to issue bonds on behalf of the city. Bear in mind that even though they were issued for the city, MAC bonds were not obligations of the city of New York. The revenues to pay debt service were backed, not by the taxing power of the city, but rather, by the state of New York, and by a special lien on the city's sales tax (there were distinctions between the first and subsequent liens), and on a stock transfer tax.

In retrospect, New York City's default was not at all that surprising. The city's financial problems had been widely reported in the press. They included revenue shortfalls due to economic decline; inability to contain spending within revenues, and poor fiscal management (for example, funding long-term expenditures through short-term borrowing). Under these circumstances, a downgrade should have been anticipated.

Because of the publicity surrounding the city's financial woes, and despite the fact that MAC bonds were not obligations of the city, the MAC bonds came to market with yields well above then current market rates: 10 percent as compared to 8 percent for securities with comparable maturity and credit. From the beginning, MAC bonds represented a very solid investment. The bonds were secured by strong revenue sources. Debt service coverage was predicted to be strong and turned out to be even stronger than anticipated. In 1990, it reached 11 times on first lien bonds, and between 4 and 5 times on second lien bonds. MAC bonds were initially rated A, but because of the excellent historic debt service coverage ratio, by 1990, they were rated AA.

What can be learned from this episode? First, that defaults can and do occur and will continue to occur. Can they always be anticipated? In this case, yes. The city's financial troubles were well publicized and the default was preceded by several downgrades.

Finally, this episode demonstrates why it pays, literally, to be very precise about exactly which revenue streams back debt service. In this instance, MAC bonds were tarred by the woes of New York city, even though they were not obligations of the city, and rated higher than direct obligations of the city. And that is the main reason why even though MAC bonds represented a very solid investment from the start, their yields were so high.

8

Government National Mortgage Association (GNMAs) and Other Pass-Through Securities

This chapter discusses

■ *the unique nature of GNMA cash flows*

■ *the vocabulary of GNMA securities: average life, remaining term, payment history, factor, and cash flow yield.*

■ *par, discount, and premium GNMAs*

■ *Sons of GNMA: CMO's, Freddie Mac, FNMA*

Government National Mortgage Securities (GNMAs) were initially issued in the middle 1970s. Since that time, GNMAs and similar instruments have become one of the largest segments of the bond market. Currently, a staggering $800 billion are estimated to have been issued.

GNMAs are very much an institutional product. The minimum required to purchase a new GNMA is $25,000, although older GNMAs can be purchased for less. Banks, insurance companies and pension funds are the primary buyers of GNMAs.

The appeal of GNMAs to individual investors is based on a number of factors: impeccable credit quality (GNMAs have the unconditional backing of the U. S. government); high cash flow (unlike other bonds, interest is paid monthly); and higher current yield than Treasury securities. But there is never a free lunch. If GNMAs yield more than Treasuries, then they must have features which make them less desirable than Treasuries. And this, of course, is the case.

In reality, GNMAs are extremely complex. Anyone who tries to tell you GNMAs are simple does not understand the product. While they have no credit risk whatsoever, they are not riskless. Like other bonds, they expose the buyer to interest rate (and price) risk. More importantly, because of the particular nature of GNMA cash flows, the buyer of a GNMA cannot tell with certainty how much money he will earn, or when principal will be returned. Finally, each GNMA is unique. Two GNMAs with similar coupons and quoted maturities may ultimately perform very differently.

Analysis of a GNMA is totally different from that of any other fixed-income instrument. Analysis of a GNMA focuses on two elements: the probable longevity of the security; that is, how long payments are likely to continue; and its total return. Both are highly uncertain. Professional investors rely on extensive statistical analysis in their decision process. Individuals usually do not have access to these models.

For institutional investors, GNMAs are attractive investments, because the performance of large numbers of GNMAs, owned in portfolios totalling one billion or more, conforms to the complex statistical models they use. For individuals, the situation is very different because one single GNMA (or even a few) may behave very differently from statistical models. When you see statistics about total return of GNMAs, remember that these are aggregate statistics, which apply only to groups of GNMAs. As this chapter will demonstrate, when you buy one GNMA security (or even several), you are taking a chance. There is really no way to know what you are going to earn.

Analyzing GNMA cash flows is tedious, time consuming, and boring. It requires mastering a whole new set of conceptual tools and vocabulary. But you should not purchase GNMAs unless you are prepared to spend some time mastering the peculiarities of these securities. Within the scope of this chapter, I can only begin to describe what you need to know.

Note also that GNMAs are taxable both at the federal and the state level. Since Treasuries are exempt from state taxes, this erases some of the yield advantage that GNMAs have compared to Treasuries, particularly in states with high tax rates.

GNMAs were the first and remain the prototypes of so-called pass-through obligations. They remain the easiest to trade; that is, the most liquid, or the cheapest to buy and resell. While new types of pass-throughs are constantly being created, if you understand GNMAs, you are well on your way to understanding any of the other pass-throughs. So, let's first look at the simplest prototype, a GNMA pool on single family houses. CMOs and newer pass-throughs will briefly be analyzed towards the end of the chapter.

WHY GNMAs ARE UNIQUE

The easiest way to start is to describe how a GNMA security is created. GNMA stands for Government National Mortgage Association, which is an agency of the U. S. government, within the Department of Housing and Urban Development (HUD). That agency does not issue bonds. Rather, its role is that of an insurer and facilitator.

The process of creating GNMA pools begins when a builder or a developer puts up a development. At the point where the builder has obtained financing and sold a number of houses to individual homebuyers (who have obtained individual mortgages), the builder—or more precisely, the mortgage originator—applies to the GNMA for a pool number and GNMA backing. Only mortgages insured by the Veterans Administration (VA) or Federal Housing Administration (FHA) are accepted. Because these mortgage payments are insured by government agencies, GNMA is able to unconditionally guarantee payment of interest and repayment of principal. The mortgages are then bundled together by a servicer into one pool totaling a minimum of $1 million. Pieces of this pool are then sold to investors. You might think of this pool as similar to a mutual fund. Only in this case, the fund is made up entirely of mortgage payments.

When you buy a GNMA security (colloquially known as "Ginnie Mae" or "Ginnie" for short), you are buying a percentage amount of a bunch of mortgage payments, which have been repackaged (the Wall Street word is "securitized") in order to create a debt instrument with a fixed coupon. Through the magic of investment banking, individual mortgages have been transformed into debt instruments. The cash flows of these instruments are exactly those of the underlying individual mortgages "passed through" from the original homeowners to the purchaser of the GNMA security.

All mortgages in one pool share certain characteristics. They are fixed rate; they are issued for 20 to 30 years; and they are issued at the same interest rate, based on prevailing interest levels. (There are also adjustable rate pass-throughs, but that's another topic). The servicer acts as middleman. He receives the mortgage payments made by homeowners and sends them to the purchasers of GNMA securities, charging 1/2 of 1 percent for his services. As a result, the coupon rate of GNMA securities is 1/2 of 1 percent lower than the homeowner's interest cost. For example, 10 percent mortgages are bundled together into GNMAs with a 9 1/2 percent coupon.

The payments received by holders of GNMAs are percentage amounts of those sent by homeowners to the bank. The homeowner sends a fixed monthly amount to his bank that includes interest as well as principal. On a 30-year mortgage, during the first few years, a small fraction of the monthly payment pays down principal. That percentage gradually increases through the life of the mortgage based on an amortization schedule, and correspondingly, the amount of interest declines. Exhibit 8.1 shows is what the amortization of principal would look like.

This is the first important aspect of GNMA monthly cash flows, which differentiates them from those of other fixed-income instruments. Every month, the holder of a GNMA receives some principal and some interest. When the last payment has been made by the homeowner, the entire principal has been paid back. (There is not a large sum remaining to be to be redeemed as there is when other bonds mature).

Exhibit 8.1
Monthly Mortgage Payments—Interest/Principal
(30-Year 10 Percent Conventional Loan)

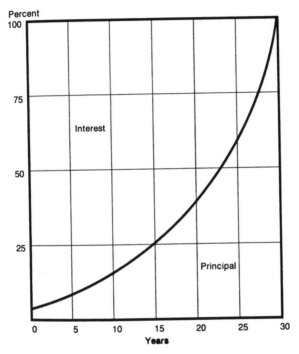

Source: *The Handbook of Mortgage Backed Securities*, Frank Fabozzi, Editor, Chicago, IL: Probus

You should also realize that the principal payments are not income. Any principal returned is your own money. If that is not immediately obvious, consider the following analogy. Suppose you lend someone $100 to be repaid in ten monthly installments with interest. Each month, you would receive $10.00 worth of principal, in addition to the interest payment. At the end of the 10 months, your entire principal would have been repaid; no more would be forthcoming.

However, there is another complication. Remember that your GNMA is made up of small pieces of many mortgages. Few homeowners hold mortgages for 30 years. Whenever a home is sold, its mortgage is prepaid in full. Homes may be sold for many different reasons. Homeowners may buy a larger house. They may retire, or divorce. Or they may have to move because of a job change or a birth or a death in the family. If interest rates decline, homeowners may refinance their mortgage in order to reduce monthly payments.

Whatever the reason, whenever a mortgage is prepaid, the prepayments are passed through directly to the holders of GNMAs. This radically complicates GNMA cash flows for two different reasons. First, while the mortgages and the GNMAs both mature in 30 years, payments usually cease well before that. Indeed, nationally, on a statistical basis, mortgages are prepaid on the average in twelve years. As a result, GNMAs with 30-year mortgages are sold with the presumption that on average, they will be paid down in 12 years. Also, remember that your interest payments continue only on the remaining principal. As principal comes back to you, your interest income decreases.

But the second problem is that no pool behaves exactly like the average. Because of this, holders of GNMAs cannot predict either the timing or the speed of principal prepayments. They also cannot predict the final date when all payments cease. This, in turn, means that all yield calculations are, at best, only estimates.

Let's sum up the differences between GNMA cash flows and those of other bonds. When you buy a bond, you receive interest payments in the form of coupons, usually twice a year. At the bond's maturity, you receive a much larger sum, the principal, which is redeemed in full in what is in effect a large balloon payment. You know at the outset exactly how much you will receive for each coupon and the dates of these coupon payments, as well as the date of repayment of the principal balloon.

Payment schedules for GNMAs, however, differ totally from the above. You receive a check each month that consists of some principal and some interest, based on the amortization schedule. The bulk of principal, however, is paid off not in one balloon at the bond's maturity, but carved up into little monthly increments which are sent back to you in unpredictable amounts that can increase sharply whenever mortgages are prepaid. As a result, a GNMA has no preset maturity date. GNMA payments continue until the last mortgage in the pool is paid down. At that point, all payments cease. No one, not the servicer, not the builder, and not the GNMA can predict with certainty either how long it will take before all mortgages are prepaid; or the timing and size of prepayments. So when you buy a GNMA security, you cannot know how much you will receive each month; or how long it will take before that particular GNMA is paid down.

HOW INTEREST RATE CHANGES AFFECT GNMAs

GNMAs, like any debt instrument with a fixed coupon, react to changes in interest rate levels. But, again, they do so in their own unique way. Once again, prepayments are the complicating element. Elsewhere, I emphasized that when interest rates decline, the value of your bonds goes up. On the other hand, when interest rates rise, bond prices decline. That volatility is directly tied to maturity length. But for GNMAs, that relationship is modified. Here is why.

Suppose, for example, that interest rates decline substantially. In that event, homeowners are likely to rush to refinance their mortgages. This will have two results. First, prepayments are likely to speed up; the entire GNMA pool may be paid down far earlier than you anticipated. And second, you get lots of principal back, just when rates are lower. Now, you have to reinvest at lower rates. The result is: not only won't your GNMA appreciate in price as much as other bonds with similar maturities; but in some cases, it might actually decline. Also, your actual—or realized—return is likely to be substantially lower than you anticipated, since you will be reinvesting large amounts of money at much lower rates than those initially anticipated. As a result, in rising markets, the upside potential of GNMAs is more limited than that of other bonds with similar maturities.

Now suppose interest rates rise. This also has a number of undesirable consequences for holders of GNMAs. First, prepayments slow so that the life of the pool is likely to lengthen. You will have to hold on to your GNMA security longer than you anticipated. But, the coupon of your GNMA is now lower than what is currently available. Therefore, you guessed it: the price of your GNMA is likely to decline more steeply than that of other intermediate securities.

Both of the preceding scenarios are simplified. Premium, discount and par GNMAs react differently to interest rate changes.

Also, volatility in the face of interest rate fluctuations is cush-
ioned for GNMAs by the fact that the market treats them as intermediate, rather than long-term, instruments. But often, interest
rate fluctuations create a kinds of "heads I win, tails you lose"
situation. In rising markets, GNMAs underperform other bonds.
In declining markets, they may decline somewhat less, but not
much less than other bonds. So while GNMAs yield more than
Treasuries on a current yield basis, when total return is considered, it is not clear that they outperform significantly over long
periods of time.

THE VOCABULARY OF GNMA RETURNS

If you are purchasing a GNMA from a firm that knows these securities, and does a good business in them, you will be shown an
offering sheet or printout that will contain all of the terms shown
in the same offering sheet illustrated in Exhibit 8.2. (This sample
offering sheet is for a GNMA pool originally issued in 1979, with
a coupon of 9.5 percent, and being offered in 1988).

Let's define the terms on this sheet which are not self-ex-
planatory, starting on the top line, on the left-hand side.

Face Amount

That is the initial amount of mortgage principal outstanding for
this GNMA pool.

Factor

Expressed as a decimal, the factor is the percentage of the mortgages in the pool that has not been paid down. (Factors are published by the GNMA for all outstanding GNMA mortgage pools).

Balance

The balance is the principal amount of the original mortgages that
has not been paid down, in dollars. The balance is calculated by
multiplying the face amount by the factor. The balance is identical

Exhibit 8.2
Sample GNMA Offering Sheet*

Face amount	$40,000	**Pool #** 16007	Coupon 11%
Current factor	.75		
Balance	$30,000	Minimum **Principal:**	$ 17.26
		Minimum **Interest:**	$275.00
		Total P&I next month:	292.26
Current offering price	100		
Amount of Investment	$30,000		
+ Accrued interest	128		
Amount due	$30,128		

Payment history	2 yr. 50% FHA	1 yr. 75% FHA	Since issued: 70%
	300% FHA	**100% FHA**	**0% FHA**
Cash flow yield	10.86%	10.92%	10.94%
Bond equivalent yield	11.12%	11.17%	11.19%
Remaining term:	27 years		
Average life:	11 years		

*Note: Highlighted terms are explained in the text.

Source: *Stoever Glass Securities.* Material given to the author.

to *the amount of the investment.* It is, in a sense, the current par value of this particular pool.

Current Offering Price

This particular GNMA is being offered at 100 percent, that is, at par. That is somewhat unusual for an older GNMA. Because the price of a GNMA changes in reaction to interest rate changes,

GNMAs trading in the secondary market usually sell either at a premium or at a discount, depending on the original coupon and interest rates at the time of sale. Because this particular GNMA is being offered at par, the current offering price equals the balance, plus the accrued interest due to the seller of the security.

Payment History

The payment history is included in order to describe past prepayments and to formulate assumptions concerning future prepayments.

The basic method used has been to compare the prepayment history of each pool to a benchmark. The benchmark most often used by brokers who sell GNMAs to individual investors is based the data compiled by the the Federal Housing Administration (FHA). Periodically, the FHA publishes updates of past prepayment patterns, based on the latest nationwide figures.

The GNMA maintains statistics for each pool, expressed as a percentage of current published FHA experience; that is, the latest FHA data. If prepayments are an exact match of FHA experience, the pool is said to prepay at 100 percent FHA experience. If at twice the speed, it is said to pay at 200 percent. For the pool in the example above, after two years, prepayments were 75 percent; that is, slower than FHA experience (three-quarters the FHA speed).

Using FHA experience as a yardstick, however, is not without its problems. The main problem is that, whenever data is updated, FHA experience is revised. In other words, the yardstick (FHA experience) keeps on changing. Another model, known as CPR, (Constant Prepayment Rate), is gaining acceptance within the dealer community. CPR, as the name implies, is a constant. Prepayment patterns, which change constantly, are expressed as multiples of CPR. Individual investors are more likely to encounter FHA experience as the yardstick, but that may change if CPR becomes more widely accepted.

Currently, FHA experience shows that after 12 years, only 17 percent of 30-year mortgages are still outstanding. As a result, GNMA returns and yields are often compared to those of 12-year bonds. But it should be understood that the speed and timing of prepayments of any particular GNMA will, in all likelihood, vary considerably from that average.

Let's return to the sample offering sheet, left-hand side.

Cash Flow Yield

I'm sure that by now you are thinking: I thought we'd never get to yield. Well, here it is: The cash flow yield is comparable to what is known for other bonds as yield-to-maturity. It takes into account interest earned (total interest payments for the year); the price paid, and the interest-on-interest earned on reinvested interest.

The "cash flow yield" is always tied to specific prepayment assumptions—that is, either FHA speed, or CPR—and it is meaningless unless those assumptions are spelled out. Most brokers formulate two or three scenarios for prepayments (one fast, one slow, and one average). These are spelled out, as they are in the offering sheet above: at 100 percent FHA speed (equal to FHA speed), 300 percent FHA speed (three times FHA speed), 0 percent FHA speed (much slower than FHA speed). None of them is a prediction of the actual return, but formulating a number of assumptions enables the buyer to compare potential rates of return. To be safe, assume you will earn the lowest amount possible. You may do better, but at least you know the risks.

Don't worry about how to calculate the cash flow yield. Brokers use numbers prepared by their research departments, based on standard calculation methods agreed to by the Securities Industry Association (SIA). What is important, however, is that a difference in quoted yields may be based on different prepayment assumptions. Never buy a GNMA on the basis of a quoted yield without checking the underlying prepayment assumptions.

In the preceding example, the cash flow yield is about the same for widely different prepayment assumptions. But that is because this is a par GNMA. For discount GNMAs and for premium GNMAs, the cash flow yield under different prepayment assumptions may vary by as much as 200 basis points.

Bond-Equivalent Yield

GNMAs pay interest monthly, rather than twice a year as is the case with bonds. If that money is reinvested, as a result of the more frequent compounding, GNMAs yield slightly more than bonds with the same coupon rate. The bond-equivalent yield is the cash flow yield, readjusted upwards to account for the effect of monthly compounding. As a rule, for most GNMAs, the bond-equivalent yield is about 20 to 30 basis points higher than the cash flow yield.

The two terms at the bottom on the left-hand side describe how long the mortgages still have to run.

Remaining Term

That is the number of years left before the mortgages in the pool are fully paid off, in the absence of any prepayments.

Average Life

This term (together with another term, *half-life*), pinpoints the approximate point in a GNMA's life when half of the principal will have been paid back. The market prices GNMAs based on these midpoint measurements, and not on the maturity date of the mortgages.

The term "average life" is somewhat confusing. It does not denote the anticipated longevity of the security. Average life is a technical term that describes the average number of years that each principal dollar will be outstanding. Average life is weighted for time and is related to speed of prepayments. The higher the prepayment rate, the shorter the average life.

Half-life is the time it will take before half of the principal amount of a GNMA is returned. Because it is not weighted for time, half-life is usually one to two years shorter than average life.

Remember that average life and half-life both describe the approximate midpoints in the paydown process, not its conclusion. They are not a proxy for final maturity dates. In spite of this, however, if you were comparing the yield of a GNMA to other securities (Treasuries, for example), you would compare the yield of the GNMA to that of a Treasury whose final maturity was about the same as the average or half-life of the GNMA. For example, compare a GNMA with an estimated half-life of two years to a two-year Treasury; one with an estimated half-life of twelve years, to a 12-year Treasury.

Now let's move to the top line on the right-hand side.

Pool Number

The pool number is assigned by GNMA when the developer obtains GNMA backing. GNMA maintains data concerning payments and prepayments on all pools, and any dealer should make that data available to anyone considering purchasing a GNMA.

Principal and Interest

Those are the scheduled payments, based on the underlying mortgages. This amount does not include prepayments. It is the minimum amount you would receive each month. Remember that only the interest represents income. The principal is your own money being returned to you.

Incidentally, the only yield measurement that is computed for GNMAs exactly like that of other bonds is current yield, which as you will remember is coupon divided by price. For the preceding example, dividing $275.00 (the minimum interest payment) by the price ($30,000) gives you a current yield of .092 percent a month—or 11 percent a year.

Before proceeding further, a few important caveats are in order.

1. You are unlikely to actually earn the cash flow yield.

GNMAs are often purchased because the quoted yields appear high, when compared to Treasuries or sometimes, when compared to corporates. So, let's review the assumptions underlying the cash flow yield. This will make clear why it is highly unlikely that yield will actually be earned.

The assumptions underlying the cash flow yield are:

- That all interest received will be reinvested rather than spent. Spending monthly payments will lower return.

- That interest payments will be reinvested at the cash flow yield rate. This is highly unlikely for individual investors, particularly if the quoted yield is high. If, for example, the cash flow yield is 9 percent, and monthly checks are swept into a money market account, which yields less, or if they are not reinvested, then that will lower the actual return.

- That principal is also reinvested at the cash flow yield rate. Again, this is equally unlikely.

- The cash flow yield is tied to specific prepayment assumptions. If prepayments speed up substantially, or if they slow down substantially, the yield will differ considerably from the stated cash flow yield. Prepaid principal may be returned at a lower—or higher—price than your cost, resulting in capital gains or losses. Also, both principal and interest will then be reinvested at rates differing from the cash flow yield.

In other words, anyone buying a GNMA should assume that actual return (or total return) is likely to differ enormously from the quoted cash flow yield. In fact, reinvestment risk is higher for GNMAs than for any other fixed-income instrument.

2. Don't confuse cash flow yield and monthly cash flow.

Cash flow yield measures only interest payments. Cash flow is the total monthly check you will receive, which includes regular principal payments and principal prepayments, as well as interest. Some dealers (or mutual funds) lump together both interest and principal and call it monthly income. That results in inflated yields. Remember that the principal is your own money that is being returned to you. It is not income.

3. Don't confuse factor and price.

The factor is simply the percentage of the mortgage balance that remains outstanding. The price is determined by the relationship of the coupon rate to current interest rate levels.

For example, if rates were lower at the time of purchase than when the GNMA was originally issued, the GNMA would probably be trading at a premium, say 120. That would change the cost of purchasing the GNMA to:

$$\text{balance outstanding} \quad \times \quad \text{factor} \quad \times \quad \text{price}$$
$$\$40,000 \quad \times \quad .75 \quad \times \quad 1.20$$

which equals $36,000. Similarly, if the GNMA were trading at a discount, say 80, the price would then become

$$\$40,000 \quad \times \quad .75 \quad \times \quad .80$$

which equals $24,000.

You would have to add accrued interest to these totals, as always.

4. Don't assume that future prepayments will match the past prepayment history of any pool.

Generally, prepayments occur most rapidly in the early years and slow thereafter. Also, prepayments are often related to interest rate changes (for example, owner refinancings accelerate if interest rates decline) or to overall economic conditions in an area. But homeowners often behave in ways that may not appear to make economic sense. They may, for example, not refinance if interest rates drop. They may also pay off existing mortgages that are cheap, just for the satisfaction of knowing they own their home free and clear. They may move for any number of reasons. All of this makes prepayment patterns of any one pool impossible to predict accurately.

DIFFERENCES BETWEEN PAR, DISCOUNT AND PREMIUM GNMAs

Because GNMAs have been issued since the mid-1970s, GNMA coupons range from about 6 percent to 17 percent. New GNMAs are constantly coming to market. Consequently, you can purchase GNMAs trading at a discount; at a premium; or at par. Each has advantages and disadvantages.

The *par GNMA* is the easiest to understand. GNMAs normally trade at par only when they are issued. They would therefore have no prepayment history, and would be priced based on average expectations. This means that for GNMAs with underlying mortgages of 30 years, average life would be quoted as about 14 years; and half-life, about 12 years. Actual prepayment and total return may, of course, differ completely from the quotes. Since none of the mortgages in par pools have yet been prepaid, par GNMAs are likely to run longer than either discount or premium GNMAs.

Discount GNMAs have coupons lower than current interest rates. They are all older pools. If interest rates remain stable, prepayments are less likely to speed up since coupon rates are lower than current rates. Mortgages would be prepaid mainly for considerations other than interest rates. Therefore, cash flow is a little more predictable than for par GNMAs.

Discount GNMAs are more interest rate sensitive than either par or premium GNMAs. This translates into steeper price increases or declines as interest rates fluctuate. Again, the reason for this is to be found in prepayment patterns. If interest rates decline, prepayments occur faster than anticipated. This boosts yields significantly because GNMAs purchased at a discount are returned at par. Also, the higher coupon becomes more valuable. But if interest rates rise, prepayments slow. Average life becomes longer and the longer maturities cause price declines to accelerate. Discount GNMAs then plummet in price.

Discount GNMAs are said to have higher cash flows than either pars or premiums. Because the pools are older, the percentage of your monthly check that is principal tends to be larger than the interest component.

Premium GNMAs were issued at a time when interest rates were higher than current rates. They, too, are older pools. If interest rates rise, the high coupon acts as a brake, and cushions against declines in price. Therefore, premium GNMAs are a hedge against rising rates.

But the high coupon can be a disadvantage if interest rates decline, particularly if the decline is steep. In that event, prepayments can speed up significantly. You will then have to reinvest both principal and interest at lower rates. In all likelihood, you will hold the GNMA for less time than you initially expected. Ultimate total return will then be far lower than initially anticipated.

Also, steep declines in interest rates constitute a particular risk to anyone who purchases a GNMA at a premium. That is because GNMAs purchased at a premium are refunded at par. If the prepayments occur shortly after purchase, this translates into a significant loss.

VARIETIES OF GNMAs

While GNMAs on single family homes were the initial prototype, the market has expanded to include a greater variety of mortgage assets. Cash flows for these are analyzed exactly like the preceding. But since the terms often are used without being defined, let's briefly look at the different types of pools.

GNMA I pools.   Those are the "plain vanilla" GNMAs, such as the prototype just analyzed. They are comprised of 12, or more, fixed-rate 20- to 30-year mortgages total at least $1 million face value, all issued at the same interest rate.

Midgets.   Those are the same as the preceding but the underlying mortgages are issued for 15 years. That would cut the half-life to an average of seven years, for purposes of quoting yields.

Because of this maturity difference, GNMA midgets trade at a premium to regular GNMAs with the same coupons.

GNMA II pools. These have been issued only since 1983. They differ from GNMA I pools in a number of ways.

- They are larger than GNMA I pools.
- They are based on multiple rather than single issuer pools.
- They have a wider range of interest rates than the original.

The larger size of the pool serves to even out prepayments somewhat. But because of the varieties of coupons and maturities, they are more difficult to analyze than GNMA I pools. They generally yield a bit more for that reason.

GNMA GPMs. These are based, not on fixed rate, but on graduated mortgage payments. The cash flows are even more complex than for ordinary GNMAs. Also, the market for these is smaller and less liquid than for ordinary GNMAs.

GNMA mobile homes. These are based on mortgages for mobile homes. They have a shorter history than other GNMAs and have not been as exhaustively analyzed.

WHO SHOULD BUY GNMAs?

The attraction of GNMAs is the monthly cash flow, the higher current yield than Treasuries, and the credit safety.

However, there is a down side. GNMAs are taxable, both at the state and federal level. Their cash flows are unpredictable. Their ultimate total return is uncertain. In addition, their price fluctuates with interest rate changes.

Despite these flaws, GNMAs are particularly attractive to an individual investor looking for very high cash flow, and who prefers not to wait until a final maturity to recover principal. In a sense, a GNMA functions somewhat like an annuity. For that reason, GNMAs might appeal to retirees. But remember that principal prepayments are not predictable. Moreover, if monthly income is spent, rather than reinvested, then you are spending down principal.

Financial planners sometimes advise purchasing GNMAs for retirement accounts. Unless the account is very substantial, however, investing in individual GNMAs for retirement accounts would be cumbersome because monthly payments—including principal prepayments—would in all likelihood have to be reinvested through a money market fund. This would reduce total return considerably. If you want to invest in GNMAs for retirement accounts, do so through a mutual fund.

HOW TO PROTECT PRINCIPAL WHEN PURCHASING A GNMA

First, buy GNMAs only if they yield significantly more than Treasuries. In the past, GNMAs have been a good buy when the spread was at least 150 basis points above Treasuries. Remember to compare GNMAs to Treasuries on the basis of the estimated half life or average life and not the stated final maturity. If GNMAs yield less than 150 basis points above Treasuries, they are a poor buy.

Second, ask to see cash flow yield based on a variety of prepayment assumptions. Make sure those assumptions are spelled out in terms of prepayment speeds. Brokers may quote you yields that differ for the same securities, because they are basing their quotes on different assumptions and not because of any real difference in the securities themselves.

In a sense, too much emphasis is placed on yield. The quoted cash flow yield is unlikely to be earned. Rather, individuals should purchase GNMAs if the cash flow patterns of these securities matches a need.

Also, be sure that you understand how faster or slower prepayments would affect the particular security you are considering. Would it mean a capital gain or a capital loss? Would it boost or lower total return? Would it mean you would hold the security longer or less time?

Also, purchasing only one or a few GNMA pools constitutes a risk since it is not possible to diversify properly. GNMAs should only be purchased as part of a much larger portfolio. Individuals with lower amounts to invest, who would like to invest in GNMAs, should do so through a mutual fund.

Exhibit 8.3
Format for GNMA Listings

	Remain-ing Term (Years)	WTD-Avg. Life (Years)	Price (OCT) (Pts.-32ds)	Price Change (32ds)	Cash Flow Yield*	Yield Change (Basis pts.)
30-year						
GNMA 8.0%	27.5	9.8	98-24	−19	8.30%	+11
GNMA 10.0%	28.7	4.8	107-00	−8	8.03	+11
GNMA 12.0%	24.6	3.4	114-12	−4	6.71	+7
15-year						
GNMA 9.5%	13.0	4.9	105-30	−6	7.94%	+7

*Based on projections from Salomon's prepayment model, assuming interest rates remain unchanged from current levels.

Finally, because these instruments are comparatively new, some of the brokers selling them absolutely don't know what they are doing. Be particularly leary of anyone who spells out that in a specified number of years—say 10 years—your initial investment will have become a specific sum. This is a dead giveaway. People who predict exact amounts for GNMAs don't know what they are selling and don't care. Only buy GNMAs from someone who has experience with them and can help you to analyze potential pitfalls.

Information on GNMAs is extraordinarily scanty. The *Wall Street Journal* and *Investor's Daily* publish very brief listings of a few representative issues. A typical listing would include the information contained in Exhibit 8.3. (These yields were available October 10, 1991).

Reading from left to right, the listing includes the following information:

- the length of the mortgages (30-year or 15-year);

- the remaining term of the security (that is, the number of years left before the mortgages in the GNMA pool are fully paid off, if there are no prepayments);

- its weighted average life (the approximate point in the life of the GNMA when one half of the principal will be paid back);
- the price of the security on the previous day, as a percentage of par;
- the price change since the previous day (like that of Treasuries, in 32nds);
- the cash flow yield;
- the change in yield compared to the preceding day (in basis points).

The usefulness of this, or similar listings, is reduced by a number of factors. The prices and yields quoted are valid only for institutional investors, who benefit both from lower transaction costs and from the ability to reinvest monthly payments at higher yields than individual investors. Also, the quoted yields will be realized only if interest rates do not change. Finally, the rates of return quoted are for weighted averages; that is, for statistical averages compiled on a nationwide basis for these coupons and maturities. What any individual GNMA pool will actually earn cannot be predicted.

SONS OF GNMA

GNMAs were the first pass-throughs. Their success led to innumerable clones. The variations are of three basic kinds:

- Who backs the mortgages.
- Restructured cash flows.
- Pass-throughs based on payment streams other than mortgages.

Let's briefly look at each category.

Pass-Throughs Backed by Agencies Other Than GNMA

Agencies other than GNMA now back pass-through securities. The cash flows of these securities are very similar to those of GNMAs, but their credit quality and liquidity may be somewhat lower. As a result, they usually yield more than GNMAs, by a small amount.

Freddie Mac   The second largest group of pass-throughs is guaranteed by the Federal Home Loan Mortgage Corporation (FHLMC), known colloquially as Freddie Mac. Like GNMA, Freddie Mac also guarantees timely payment of both interest and principal, but its guarantee is not a direct obligation of the U. S. government. (Technically, Freddie Mac is a corporate entity of the United States owned by the Federal Home Loan Banks). Like Treasuries and GNMAs, credit quality is considered so high that Freddie Mac securities are unrated. But because of the slight difference in credit quality, Freddie Macs trade with slightly higher yields than GNMAs. In other respects, they are very much like GNMAs. They are based on mortgages with 30-year and 15-year maturities, and they have average lives of 12 and 7, years respectively.

Federal National Mortgage Association   The Federal National Mortgage Association is known colloquially as FNMA, or Fannie Mae. Its securities were initially issued in 1981. FNMA is in effect a quasi-private corporation whose stock is traded on the New York Stock Exchange. Its ties to the government are looser than those of either GNMA or Freddie Mac. Hence, FNMA securities generally yield more than either. FNMA securities are, nevertheless, sound credits, guaranteed by FNMA, based on pool insurance. FNMA securities are based on both 30-year and 15-year mortgages.

Private issuer backing   Finally, mortgage pass-throughs are also issued by private issuers such as banks and thrifts. These are not guaranteed by any government agency. These securities provide a secondary market for conventional loans that do not qualify for any of the other government programs. They are rated by the rating agencies and generally based on credit enhancements such as private insurance, letters of credit, and so forth. Currently, this is still a very small market (perhaps two percent of the total pass-through market). But many predict it will be an expanding market, which will include not only mortgages on single-family homes, but also, mortgages on commercial real estate, shopping centers, and the like. Hence, there is potential for substantial growth.

Currently, all of these pass-throughs are still mainly institutional products. They are traded in larger sums than GNMAs. Their credit quality is slightly lower. They are less liquid. But as the market continues to evolve, this may change.

Restructured Cash Flows: CMOs

In 1983, after GNMAs came Collateralized Mortgage Obligations (CMOs).

CMOs are the newest and hottest pass-throughs. They are the latest creations of the so-called "rocket scientists," or "quants," who revolutionized investment banking. Creative Wall Street minds thought up an elegant way of redividing (or, in Wall Street terms, "restructuring") GNMA cash flows in order to eliminate some of the prepayment and longevity uncertainties of GNMAs.

CMOs are based on much larger pools than GNMAs. CMO pools range in size from $50 million to $1 billion. The key difference between GNMAs and CMOs is that CMO payment streams are redistributed sequentially to a number of different "tranches." "Tranche" is a French word meaning slice or portion. A CMO may have as few as three or as many as seventeen (or more) different tranches.

To see how that works, let us assume that we have a pool made up of three tranches. Each tranche receives interest payments. But unscheduled prepayments are sent sequentially to different tranches. The first tranche (or slice) receives all unscheduled prepayments made, say, during the first three years. Thereafter, that tranche is actually retired. In effect, it has become

ith an approximate three-year maturity. Unscheduled
nts made during the next three years then go to the second tranche. That tranche is then retired, say in eight years.

The last tranche is called the "accrual" (or the "Z-tranche").
This tranche receives no payments of any kind—either interest or
principal—until all earlier tranches are retired. But during that
time, interest accrues at the coupon rate on the principal to be
paid. When payments begin, the holder receives both principal
and interest. Z-tranches have very long average lives: typically,
15 to 20 years. This is due to the fact that, while statistically only
17 percent of all mortgages remain outstanding after twelve years,
all of those will be in the Z-tranche. Some mortgages may not be
paid down until the final maturity date of the underlying mortgage, which could be 30 or 35 years.

Z-tranches are extremely complicated. They are sometimes
compared to zeros because, as with zeros, interest is deferred and
accrues until the final payment is made. But unlike zeros, Z-
tranches have no definite maturity. They are extremely volatile
both because they are very long-term; and because all interest
coupons are deferred until the final payment. For reasons too
complicated to go into, their upside potential in rising markets is
very limited. But downside risk is high.

In part because they are so new and so complicated, the
stated yield on Z-tranches is high compared to Treasuries and to
anything else.

CMOs are a structure compatible with any guarantor. There
have been CMOs backed by GNMA, by FHLB, and by private
corporations. New features are constantly added, and will continue to be added to CMOs. One recent innovation is: guaranteed
minimum "sinking funds" meaning that some bonds are guaranteed to be retired. Another is guaranteed minimum reinvestment
rates.

Advantages of the CMO Structure

The CMO structure lessens some of the cash flow uncertainties
inherent in GNMAs, especially for the earlier tranches. The early
tranches are comparable to short maturity bonds. They afford the
buyer a measure of protection against both interest rate risk and

prepayment risk. As a result, they yield less than GNMAs with short average lives.

The buyer of later tranches is probably looking to lock in a higher yield for a longer period of time. That buyer benefits by enjoying, in effect, a kind of call protection, since the later tranches cannot receive any principal repayments until earlier tranches are retired.

The so-called accrual or Z-tranche is the most complex and the least predictable. Therefore, it has the highest stated yield. Accrual tranches may yield more than GNMAs and zeros by as much as 200 basis points, thereby entrancing the "yield junkie." But always keep in mind that where there is higher yield, there is higher risk. That yield is high only because the likelihood is also high that it will not be realized.

Disadvantages of CMOs

While CMOs have features that are attractive compared to GNMAs, it is very difficult to compare CMOs to GNMAs or to anything else, for that matter. CMO deals are extremely large and each deal structures CMOs in a unique way. Each deal has features unique and specific to that particular CMO. Because CMOs are overwhelmingly designed to appeal to institutional investors, they are less liquid than GNMAs. Also, CMO tranches are not totally devoid of prepayment risk. Faster or slower prepayments will alter anticipated longevity, with uncertainty rippling from earlier to later tranches and increasing progressively for each tranche. The later the tranche, the higher the uncertainty.

As this is being written, brokers are beginning to sell CMOs to individual investors. Minimums required for purchase are all over the lot: from $10,000 to $50,000, depending on the house and the deal. Be sure to find out the anticipated date when the first principal payments will be made (called the first payment date), as well as which tranche is being sold, and the number of tranches in the deal.

Be particularly cautious if you are offered an "accrual," or Z-tranche. Because of the longevity and the uncertainties of these tranches, brokers are able to quote very enticing yields. But be aware that these securities are going to be extraordinarily volatile.

If you need to resell at any time before maturity, they should be considered high-risk investments, whatever their rating. Note also that many CMOs are "private label." This may limit your ability to sell if you change brokers. Before you buy, find out if you can sell the securities back and to whom.

At this time, there is no information in the daily financial press on CMO's that could be used in any meaningful way by individual investors.

Pass-Throughs Backed by Cash Flows of Non-Mortgage Securities

Mortgages are financial assets. There is no reason to limit asset backing to mortgages. Therefore, Wall Street minds are busy creating securities out of assets such as credit card payments, car loans, and the like. Mercifully, to date, this remains an institutional market. But I have no doubt that in the near future, your friendly broker will tout the latest new instrument, based on car loans, boat loans, credit card loans, or what have you. Unless you know something I don't, I suggest you send him packing, or be prepared to do a lot of homework.

Tax Considerations

Taxes on GNMAs are a bit of a nightmare. Interest on GNMAs and all other pass-throughs is subject to federal and state taxes. Return of principal is not taxable. Therefore, make sure that you know how much of your cash flow is interest, and how much is principal. Otherwise, you will overpay your taxes.

In addition, if you sell your pass-through security before final payments cease, you may incur a capital gain or a capital loss (depending on the difference between the price you paid and the price at which you are selling). And finally, when prepayments occur, they too may subject you to a capital gain or a capital loss.

You may also need to await tax information until close to your required April 15 filing date. The *1986 Tax Reform Act* complicated the reporting requirements for your broker, so be prepared for a late 1099 on pass-throughs.

Clearly, if you intend to buy individual GNMAs, you need both good records and a good accountant.

SUMMARY

GNMAs—and other pass-throughs—offer the buyer certain advantages such as credit safety, monthly payments and a high cash flow. The main disadvantage is that cash flows are unpredictable, and so is total return. You cannot know how much you will earn. Moreover, GNMAs are subject to prepayment risk and to interest rate risk, either of which may cause loss of principal.

The market for GNMAs and similar securities is still changing. Initially, for example, prepayment risk was poorly understood—even by the dealer community. This resulted in major losses in the early 1980s. Current pricing and yield histories reflect the enhanced understanding of this security. For newer and still evolving instruments such as CMOs, unanticipated risks may still lie ahead which are not fully reflected in present pricing and yield.

SUMMARY: QUESTIONS TO ASK BEFORE PURCHASING GNMAs

What will minimum monthly principal and interest payments be?

What is the remaining term (and the average life) of this pool?

What kind of yield is being quoted (current yield, cash flow yield)?

What are the prepayment assumptions?

How would different prepayment assumptions affect cash flow yield?

Whose research data is being used?

If prepayments speed up (or slow down), how will this affect this security? Will it mean a principal loss? Will it mean a principal gain?

What effect will higher (or lower) interest rates have on the life of this pool?

QUESTIONS TO ASK BEFORE PURCHASING CMOs

Who is backing this deal?

What is the first payment date?

Which tranche is being offered? How many tranches are there in the deal?

How will prepayments affect this tranche?

To whom could I sell this security if I need to resell? Do you make a market in this CMO?

ADDITIONAL REFERENCES

If you want to find out more about these securities, the definitive book is the *Handbook of Mortgage-Backed Securities*, Frank Fabozzi, editor, Chicago: Probus Publishing, 1988.

9

Corporate Bonds

This chapter discusses

■ *the classification of corporate bonds*

■ *risk factors of corporate bonds*

■ *floating rate notes and bonds*

■ *bonds of U. S. corporations issued in foreign currencies*

■ *junk bonds*

WHAT IS UNIQUE ABOUT CORPORATE BONDS?

Corporate bonds are generally issued by major corporations. They are commonly classified into four major groups. The first group, the utilities, consists of both electric and telephone companies. These are highly regulated and include some of the safest corporate bonds. Many of these are rated AA or AAA. The second group, transportations, includes the bonds of airlines and rail-roads. The third group, the industrials, is the largest and most heterogenous of the four groups. It contains bonds of some of the premier corporations in the country, such as General Motors, Exxon and International Business Machines. It also contains so-called "junk" bonds. The fourth group consists of finance compa-nies such as banks and insurance companies.

Corporates are also classified on the basis of the security being pledged by the issuer as collateral for the bonds. The collat-eral may consist of mortgages (mortgage bonds); financial obliga-tions (collateral trust bonds); or railway rolling stock (equipment trust certificates). Corporates that are not secured by any collat-eral are known as debentures or notes.

If you were to consider yield only, corporate paper would appear attractive. As a group, corporate bonds always yield more than Treasuries. However, for individual investors, the higher yield is partly offset by the fact that income from corporate paper is fully taxable at every level: federal, state and local.

Moreover, corporate paper is far trickier to evaluate than ei-ther Treasuries or even munis. Credit quality varies from very high to extremely poor, and credit risk is a genuine concern. There is a lot more uncertainty concerning the future economic fortunes of corporations than there is concerning issuers of most munis. Call provisions are more complex for corporates than they are for munis. Also, in the 1980s, corporate bonds developed a unique set of risk factors, described under the rubric: event risk. Finally, whereas current yield is always higher for corporate paper than for Treasuries, over time, total return, particularly for lower quality corporates, may be far lower.

As a result of all these factors, the appeal of corporate bonds for individual investors has declined significantly over the last decade. As this chapter will make clear, for individual investors, corporate bonds make sense in limited situations, for instance, in tax-sheltered accounts. This chapter will first discuss the risk fac-tors that are unique to corporate bonds. It will then discuss cor-porate bonds that would interest individual investors because of specific features.

RISK FACTORS OF CORPORATE BONDS

Event Risk: How the Market Changed in the 1980s

The market for corporate bonds changed radically during the 1980s. This was due mainly to the emergence of the junk bond market and to the wave of takeovers, restructurings and leveraged buy-outs that swept corporate America in the 1980s, with devastating results to some bondholders. The phrase "event risk" entered the lexicon, to designate the uncertainty created for holders of corporate debt by the takeover phenomenon. This wave of takeovers and restructurings resulted in massive downgradings, sometimes overnight. As a result of these events, the price of many corporate bonds dropped like a stone, sometimes also overnight.

As the 1980s progressed, and as takeovers involved ever larger companies, event risk loomed as an increasing menace. This uncertainty was compounded by the fact that takeovers were impossible to predict.

As a direct result of this turmoil, and in order to sell new debt, corporations found it necessary to add a variety of inducements—sometimes called "bells and whistles." Some, such as so-called "poison pill provisions," were intended to prevent takeovers by making takeovers more expensive to the potential acquirer. Other innovations such as floating-rate notes and put bonds, were intended to protect the bondholders against interest rate risk (see below). Many of these "bells and whistles" have become permanent features of the corporate bond market.

Another result of the increased uncertainties in this market is that maturities have become shorter. As recently as the late 1970s, telephone bonds were issued with 40-year maturities. While some corporations are continuing to issue debt maturing in 20 to 30 years, maturities for corporate debt now average about 10 years overall. Debt in the lower rating ranges typically is issued for no longer than five to seven years.

Credit Risk

The credit quality of corporate issuers varies enormously. It ranges from AAA for some of the premier corporations in the country, to highly speculative junk, rated as low as C.

Evaluating credit quality for corporates is a more complex process than for munis. The analyst must look at a variety of factors:

- Overall economic trends.

- Trends within each industry.

- The relative ranking of the individual corporation within its industry.

- The quality of its management.

There is, in addition, one major difference between corporate bond ratings and those of munis. Ratings are assigned to each individual issue, not to the issuer. Separate bond issues of a single issuer often have different ratings because bonds are ranked in order of priority for payment in the event of default. Senior debt is paid first. Less senior debt—either "subordinated" or "junior"—would be paid after the claims of senior issuers had been satisfied and so on. Senior debt generally has a higher rating than junior debt.

Rating symbols for corporates are identical to those of municipals. But rating changes among corporates occur more frequently than years ago, partly as a result of event risk; and partly also due to generally declining credit reassessments. Moody's evaluates the bond indentures of corporate bonds for protection against takeover risk and incorporates those factors in its ratings. Two senior debt issues, for example, may have different ratings, based on event risk protection. Standard and Poor's rates corporate bonds for event risk under a special rating system, called "event risk covenant rankings." Bonds are rated from E1 to E5, E1 representing the highest degree of protection, and E5 the lowest.

It should be stressed that although event risk appears dormant at the present time, it could spring back to life at any time. Event risk should not be ignored.

Very short-term corporate paper (that is, commercial paper) has its own set of ratings. Standard and Poor's has the most categories, from A (highest quality) to D (lowest quality, and in default). "A" paper is further subdivided into A1, (strongest of the A group) to A3 (weakest). Moody's has three ratings: P-1 (strongest) to P-3 (weakest).

Call Risk

Like municipals, corporates are subject to call risk. But call features are more complex for corporates than for munis and there is more risk of capital loss. Here's why.

With some exceptions, call provisions for munis are governed by interest rate considerations. Munis are callable if interest rates decline, at a price stipulated in the indenture.

Corporate bonds, on the other hand, may be called under a variety of circumstances. Like munis, corporate bonds may be called if interest rates drop, at a price and time stipulated in the indenture. But corporate bonds may also be called under a number of contingencies designated as refundings. If a corporation obtains sources of capital cheaper than the interest it pays on its bonds, it may use these proceeds to redeem (that is, to call) its bonds. These sources of cheaper capital include retained earnings, monies raised by selling assets, or proceeds from a stock offering. Finally, some bond indentures require a sinking fund, which means that a certain percentage of bonds have to be retired every year regardless of interest rate levels or refunding contingencies.

Sinking fund redemptions sometimes work to the advantage of the bondholders because some bonds are retired at par when interest rates have gone up, and when the price of the bonds would normally decline. The lucky investor can then take his principal and reinvest it at higher interest rates. However, calls or refundings always protect the issuer and not the bondholders. Although bonds are called (or refunded) at par, that generally occurs at a time when interest rates have dropped, and when principal has to be reinvested at lower interest rates.

Particularly onerous to bondholders are calls that occur when bonds are trading at a premium to the call price. This can result in a substantial loss of capital to anyone who purchased the bonds at the premium price.

Call protection is more "absolute" than refunding protection because call protection includes protection against refundings. Short- to intermediate-bonds are generally callable in three to seven years. Many long-term bonds have 10 years of refunding protection, but are callable at any time. Unfortunately, call and refunding provisions are sometimes obscure; and the broker selling the bonds may not be aware of them.

To protect against unwelcome calls, always investigate the call and refunding features of any bond that you are considering for purchase. Another strategy is to purchase only discount bonds. They are less likely to be called than either premium or par bonds. In the event discount bonds are called, the buyer is protected against a loss of principal (compared to premium bonds) by the lower purchase price.

CORPORATE BONDS WITH SPECIAL FEATURES

Put Bonds

A put feature gives the purchaser the opportunity to "tender" (that is, to resell) a bond back to its issuer at par, before the bond matures, at time periods specified in the indenture (typically, every six months).

While a call protects the issuer, a put protects the bondholder. If interest rates go up, the bondholder can "put" the bond back to the issuer, resell his bonds to the issuer at par, and reinvest the entire principal at a higher rate. Put features in a bond are designed to protect principal against interest rate risk. The ability to resell the bond to the issuer at par is intended to keep the bond trading at or close to par (assuming no credit deterioration). Effectively, the put feature periodically turns the bond into short maturity paper.

In practice, while put features have provided some protection against interest rate risk, they have not proved to be a panacea. Whenever major sudden changes occur in the interest rate environment, the put provision may not take place rapidly enough to prevent a price decline. There are also some undesirable features to put bonds. Typically, interest rates on put bonds are lower than on bonds with similar ratings and maturities—as one would expect given their effectively shorter maturity. Moreover, put bonds trade like shorter paper and this limits their upside potential in rising markets, when interest rates decline (compared to bonds with similar maturities but without the put features).

Floating-Rate Notes and Bonds

Like puts, floating rates are intended to provide protection against interest rate risk by maintaining bond prices close to par. Floating interest rates are far more prevalent in foreign markets than in the United States. They were introduced to the United States during the early 1970s.

The main feature of floaters is that the coupon rate is reset periodically, usually every six months, based on a stipulated benchmark. The benchmark used to reset the coupon is usually a short-term Treasury (the floater rate might be 3/4 of a point higher). It may also be LIBOR (the London Interbank Offer Rate) which is a key rate for European investors. Sometimes, floaters also have a floor; that is, a rate below which the coupon will not fall. Some floaters give the bondholder the option of exchanging the floater against a long-term bond, at specified intervals, though at rates which may not be as attractive as those of the long-term bonds.

The rationale for floaters is that as interest rates change, resetting the coupon rate at periodic intervals will tend to keep the price of the bond close to par. In practice, this has tended not to work out quite as well as had been anticipated, for a number of reasons. First, during times of extreme interest rate volatility, rates are not reset quickly enough to prevent price fluctuations. Second, the coupon rates of floaters are usually well below those of long-term bonds and often not very attractive when compared to shorter maturity bonds.

Floaters are issued chiefly by major banks, such as the Chase Manhattan Bank and Citicorp.

Convertible Bonds

As the name implies, convertible bonds are issued by corporations with the proviso (in the indenture) that they can be exchanged for stocks at a specified price. The buyer has the advantage of a fixed coupon and the potential to share in the possible appreciation of the stock.

If the stock price does not appreciate, as long as there is no default, the downside risk is limited, since the buyer will continue to receive coupon payments and can redeem principal at maturity. In theory, convertibles are somewhat less risky than the stock. But they have the potential of capital appreciation if the stock does well.

Because of this feature, the price of a convertible bond will fluctuate mainly in tandem with the price of the stock, and not in response to interest rate changes. Analysis of convertible bonds is, therefore, more closely related to equity analysis than to bonds, but with its own unique twists. Convertibles are regarded as a very specialized form of investment. That kind of analysis, however, is not within the scope of this book.

Bonds of U. S. Corporations Issued in Foreign Currencies

In the late 1980s, a number of corporations including Anheuser Busch, Bankers Trust, Bank of Boston, General Electric, Sallie Mae (Student Loan Association—an agency of the U. S. government), Eastman Kodak, and Procter & Gamble issued bonds in New Zealand or Australian dollars, at interest rates of 14 percent to 17 percent, typically maturing in three years or less. Those bonds were available to U. S. investors, in the United States. And they were obligations of corporations that were highly rated at issuance.

These bonds had a number of attractive features. Yields were very high compared to those available for the same corporations in the United States at the same time (the spread was between 500 to 700 basis points). And interest rate risk was low since the securities were relatively short-term, maturing between two and three years.

The greatest risk incurred in buying such obligations is the currency risk. Before purchasing the bonds, the U. S. investor converts U. S. dollars into the foreign currency and reconverts into U.S. dollars at maturity. The coupon is received in the foreign currency. So to the usual sources of income from bonds (these are potential price changes, interest, and interest-on-interest), the investor must add capital gain or capital loss due to currency fluctuations.

If the dollar falls against the foreign currency, the investor actually reaps a capital gain in addition to the interest coupons. However, if the dollar rises against the foreign currency, the investor incurs a capital loss. For the bonds mentioned above, a 5 to 6 percent rise in the U. S. dollar against the foreign currency would be sufficient to wipe out the interest advantage. This represents a substantial risk since currency exchange rates are even more volatile than interest rates and even less predictable.

Currently, such bonds are still relatively rare. But if the dollar were to decline further against foreign currencies, similar bonds might represent very attractive opportunities. Conditions that would make such bonds attractive would include: interest rates substantially higher than those available in the U.S. on bonds of similar quality and maturity; and issuance in currencies considered particularly strong, in countries with low inflation rates.

Such bonds would also be advantageous to anyone who spends considerable time, or does business, in the country whose currency is being purchased. These bonds would in effect constitute a hedge against currency fluctuations.

Junk Bonds

"Junk" bonds have been so controversial and so significant since the 1980s that they deserve a more detailed discussion. They are unique because risk is almost entirely related to credit quality. Maturities of junk bonds have been in the 5- to 10-year range, so that interest rate risk is relatively low.

There have been speculative bonds as long as bonds have existed. Prior to the 1980s, the term junk, or speculative, bond was used to describe bonds of companies that suddenly found themselves in financial difficulty. These companies may have been about to go bankrupt or they may have been trying to emerge from bankruptcy. Their bonds were also known as "fallen angels." They were considered attractive speculations for any investor who could figure out which of those companies would ultimately survive and pay off, since they could be purchased at very deep discounts from par—sometimes as little as ten cents on the dollar.

But as everyone who reads a newspaper knows, in the 1980s, a new kind of junk bond was created: bonds that were used to finance takeovers. These were very different from the fallen angels of the past. Debt service for these takeovers often exceeded the company's total cash flow, before taxes. How then was debt service to be repaid? Not to worry: generally, through the sale of assets, usually businesses of the companies that were taken over.

During the mid-1980s, junk bonds flourished. They initially sold at a spread to Treasuries of about 400 basis points. A body of thought developed (among institutional investors and among academics) which maintained that junk bonds would continue to provide very high returns compared to Treasuries because too many people did not understand them and refused to own them. As a result (or so the theory went), investors sophisticated enough to understand the theory and buy the bonds, would be handsomely rewarded. Institutions, including banks (mainly thrifts) and insurance companies, flocked to buy junk bonds. So did individual investors, mainly through the purchase of mutual funds. As a result of all this buying, at one point, the spread between junk bonds and Treasuries narrowed to about 200 basis points.

The key to total return of junk bonds is their ultimate default rate. The theoretical underpinnings of the 1980s were the default histories of speculative bonds prior to the 1980s, that is, the so-called fallen angels. Those default rates were pegged at around three percent. Prevailing thought held that as long as default rates of junk bonds were three percent or less, the spread of junk bonds to Treasuries was sufficiently wide for junk to provide a total return higher than Treasuries, even including defaults, assuming a well-diversified portfolio. Apparently, neither the buyers nor the sellers of junk bonds worried too much about whether the default histories of fallen angels were appropriate benchmarks for the very different junk bonds created during the 1980s. In addition, the 1980s were a time of economic boom. Again, no one seemed to worry about how the massive debt of corporations would fare during a recession.

In 1989 and 1990, junk bonds began to plummet in value. Drops were horrendous. When spreads between junk and Treasuries widened to about 700 basis points, some investors saw this as a compelling buying opportunity. Junk bonds (and junk bond funds) rallied briefly, only to decline in value again as the fear of an approaching recession spread. This time, the declines in price were even more horrendous.

In November 1990, spreads between junk and Treasuries reached an unbelievable 1200 basis points, on an aggregate basis. Many junk bonds could be purchased for 30 to 40 cents on the dollar. As a direct result of the steep price declines, junk bonds were quoting a yield-to-maturity of 20 percent to 40 percent. But of course, that yield-to-maturity would only be realized if the bonds did not default.

These extraordinary price declines were due to a number of factors. Hanging over the market was a major liquidity crunch, which began with the exit of Drexel Burnham Lambert, Inc., the primary market maker in the junk bond sector, from this market. Suddenly, the junk bond market seemed to have only sellers and no buyers. In addition, individual investors were bailing out of junk bond funds and forcing these funds to sell into the already illiquid market. Even worse, government regulators ordered thrifts and banks to get rid of any junk bonds they owned. (Insurance companies may soon be in a similar position). Finally, default rates on junk bonds reached 5.6 percent in 1989 and almost 8 percent in 1990. There was increasing worry that default rates would go even higher if a recession occurred.

Much of this section was initially written at the end of 1990. At that time, it seemed evident that at some point, junk bonds would appear to represent a very attractive speculation, and that a rally would follow the debacle. Such a rally occurred at the beginning of 1991. Since the initial rally and through most of 1991, prices of junk bonds remained relatively stable. The interesting question now is what will happen next. A related issue is whether junk bonds are now "safe" for individual investors.

The answer to both of these questions is that junk bonds remain highly speculative. At this point, the story of junk bonds still contains many unanswered questions. Ugly allegations have been made about Michael Milken, who almost single-handedly created the junk bond market, and about Drexel. According to these allegations, Michael Milken and Drexel together manipulated the junk bond market extensively and perhaps fraudulently.[1] Even if these allegations turn out to be false, individual investors should realize that predicting the fortunes of any individual junk bond requires genuine expertise.

Other factors continue to be red flags. Many of the initial concerns that prompted the horrendous declines in junk bond prices remain in place. Individual junk bonds continue to remain highly illiquid. In addition, the junk bond sector may at some point face even larger liquidity problems if banks and insurance firms are forced to sell a large number of the junk bonds they still hold in their portfolios. Ultimate default rates of junk bonds continue to remain a major unknown. Finally, the recent rally should be placed in perspective. Prices have stabilized at a level well below their peak. The recent rally represented a nice speculative opportunity for traders. Over the last five years, most investors in junk bonds probably would have had higher total returns from Treasuries.

Most individual investors should continue to regard junk bonds primarily as speculative. Moreover, because it would be utter folly to purchase junk bonds without diversifying, it would be best for anyone interested in speculating in junk bonds to do so through a mutual fund. Regardless of how well or poorly managed any mutual fund investing in junk might be, at least, a mutual fund will provide diversification.

BUYING CORPORATE BONDS

Corporates are purchased mainly by institutions such as pension funds and insurance companies. Inherently, this works to the disadvantage of the individual investor who purchases smaller lots.

---

1. Benjamin Stein, "The Biggest Scam Ever?" *Barron's*, February 19, 1990.

Exhibit 9.1
Table of Listed (Corporate) Bonds

New York Stock Exchange Bond Trading,
Wednesday, April 3, 1991

Bonds	Current Yield	Sales in $1000	Last	Chge	
AlaP 8½s01	8.7	15	97⅝	+	⅝
AlaP 8⅞03	9.0	5	99	−	⅛
AlskAr 6⅞14	cv	5	94		...
AlegCp 6½14	cv	5	90		...
AlldC zr2000	...	25	41⅞	−	⅛
Amax 9.23s95	9.7	90	95¼		...
ATT 7⅛03	8.1	15	88		...
ATT 8.80s05	8.8	119	100¼	+	¼
viAmes 7½14f	cv	57	12¼	+	⅛
Amoco 8⅝16	8.8	20	98½	+	½
Andarko 6¼14	6.3	20	98½	+	½
Citicp 5¾00	cv	25	85	−	2
Citicp 8.45s07	9.6	40	87¾	+	1⅛
ClevEl 8⅜11	9.4	40	89	−	¼
Coastl 11⅛98	10.7	37	103½	+	⅛
CmwE 8s03	8.6	3	92½	−	½
CmwE 10⅝95	10.1	5	105	−	1¼
ConEd 9⅜00	9.1	45	102¾	+	¼
CnPw 8⅝00	9.0	10	95½		...
CumE zr05	...	6	28¼		...
DataDes 8½08	cv	7	42		...

Inevitably, he will buy at lower yields and at higher spreads than institutional investors.

Listed Bonds

Most corporate bonds are bought and sold like munis, over-the-counter. But bonds of a number of corporate issuers trade on the New York Stock Exchange (NYSE). A very few trade on the American Exchange. These are called listed bonds. Tables of listed bonds appear daily in the major financial papers. Exhibit 9.1 shows the format and some of the listings that would would have appeared on April 4, 1991:

Reading from left to right, for the first bond listed, the table specifies:

- the name of the issuer (Alabama Power);
- the coupon (8 1/2);

- the maturity date (01, that is, 2001);
- the current yield (8.7 percent);
- how many bonds were traded (15);
- the closing price on the preceding day, as a percentage of par (97 5/8);
- the price change compared to the previous trade (in fractions of a point—+5/8).

Note two peculiarities of this table. Unlike other bond tables, this table lists the current yield of the bonds, and not the yield-to-maturity. Also, only one price is given rather than the usual bid/ask spread. That should not be taken to mean there is no bid/ask spread.

Some experts suggest that individual investors should confine their purchases of corporate bonds only to listed bonds. Others feel that an informed investor may obtain a better deal by shopping around for unlisted bonds. The chief advantage of listed bonds is that they afford the individual investor a measure of protection because price quotes can be checked against actual trades. This is not possible for corporate bonds that trade over-the-counter.

When to Buy Corporate Bonds

The advantage of corporate bonds compared to Treasuries is that they yield more, sometimes as much as 100 to 150 basis points more for high quality (AA or better) corporate bonds. Lower quality issues, which include rating grades all the way down through junk, yield more than Treasuries by considerably wider spreads, depending on the rating.

On a total return basis, however, the yield advantage of corporate bonds is less compelling. According to Ibbotson and Sinquefield, during the 1980s, long-term Treasuries had average annual total returns of 12.6 percent. Average annual total return of long term corporate bonds for the same period was only slightly higher, at 13 percent.[2] During some years, moreover, the total return of corporate bonds actually lagged that of Treasuries.

Bear in mind, moreover, that the total return of the corporate bond sector is boosted by the fact that it includes lower rated corporate bonds, which yield more than higher quality debt. Indeed, some professionals feel that for individual investors, really high grade corporates do not yield more than Treasuries by enough (not enough spread) to be attractive investments. These professionals reason, moreover, that lower grade corporate bonds are not worth the uncertainty.

As a group, corporate bonds are somewhat less predictable than munis, for all the reasons described above. The yield advantage over Treasuries is further diminished by the fact that Treasuries are exempt from state tax. As a rule, this is worth about 50 to 60 basis points.

For individuals in the higher tax brackets, corporate bonds are most appropriate for purchase in tax-sheltered or tax-deferred accounts (IRAs, Keoghs). Corporate bonds would also be appropriate investments for someone in a lower tax bracket. On a net-after-tax basis, they would yield more than Treasuries.

For those of you who want to buy corporate bonds, here is a list of appropriate precautions:

- Buy bonds rated A+ or better. This group includes utilities—electric and telephone—and such corporations as IBM, Exxon, and Amoco.

- Monitor the ratings.

- Buy only if the spread to Treasuries of comparable maturity is at least 100 basis points.

- Stick to maturities of 10 years or less.

- Investigate call provisions before you buy.

- Buy only listed bonds (preferably those listed on the New York Stock Exchange (NYSE) if you want to be able to check price quotes in the newspaper.

---

2. *Stocks, Bonds, Bills & Inflation, 1990 Yearbook,* Ibbotson Associates, Chicago, 1991, p. 16.

Corporates vs. GNMAs

Since corporates and GNMAs have similar uses, a brief comparison of the two may be useful. Both expose the buyer to interest rate risk. GNMAs have no credit risk; but cash flow and total return are unpredictable. With high quality corporates, credit risk is small and cash flow is more predictable. Ultimate total return is unpredictable for both. Lower quality corporates expose the buyer to considerable credit risk.

SUMMARY: QUESTIONS TO ASK BEFORE BUYING CORPORATE BONDS

What is the credit rating?

What protection is there against event risk?

What are the call provisions?

What are the refunding provisions?

Is the bond a listed bond?

On which exchange does the bond trade?

What is the spread to Treasuries of a similar maturity?

ADDITIONAL REFERENCES

The best book on corporate bonds is *The New Corporate Bond Market*, by Richard Wilson and Frank Fabozzi, Chicago: Probus Publishing, 1990.

PART III

Investing Through Funds

If you are investing in mutual funds, chances are that at least one is either a money market fund or a bond fund. At the beginning of 1991, approximately 75 percent of all the assets in mutual funds were in money market or in bond funds. By contrast, only 25 percent were in equity funds. This is particularly striking in light of the fact that the explosive growth of these funds is a relatively recent phenomenon. A large percentage had their inception in the early 1980s. Since that time, bond and money market funds have been the fastest growing segment of the mutual fund industry. Demand from individual investors has been—and continues to be—extraordinarily strong.

Advertising of bond funds focuses on two themes: high yield and safe, predictable income. Reality, however, differs a good deal from this perception. All bond funds are not equally low risk. Moreover, studies have shown that returns for certain types of bond funds are almost as variable and as difficult to predict as those of equities.[1] Many investors come to this realization only when their investments have declined in value. A fund's stated objective: "the goal of this fund is to provide high yields with stability of principal" is only that—an objective. Like any objective, it may not be realized.

The purpose of this part of the book is to enable you to evaluate both potential total return and potential risks of bond funds

---

1. Markese, the *AAII Journal*, August-Sept. 1990, pp. 5-6.

in a more informed manner. These chapters will tell you which funds are most volatile (go up and down in price the most) and why; which can provide safe predictable income; and which might provide higher total return, but at what risk.

Most of this section is devoted to open end funds—ordinary mutual funds—that are by far the largest segment of the industry. Chapter 10 discusses the essential aspects of investing in fixed-income mutual funds. Chapter 11 classifies bond funds by type and risk factors. It should enable you to predict total return under a variety of market scenarios. Chapter 11 also includes money market funds. Chapter 12 briefly discusses two additional types of bond funds: unit investment trusts and closed-end bond funds.

10

Mutual Funds: An Overview

This chapter discusses

■ *characteristics of bond mutual funds*

■ *differences between bond funds and individual instruments*

■ *risk factors of buying bond funds*

■ *what happens to your money if a bond fund goes belly up*

■ *load vs. no-load funds*

■ *bond fund expenses*

■ *measuring return for bond funds*

■ *how to read a prospectus*

■ *how taxes are computed when you sell a bond fund.*

WHAT IS A FIXED-INCOME MUTUAL FUND?

Mutual funds are technically known as open-end funds, as opposed to unit investment trusts (UITs) and closed-end bond funds. Each fund is comprised of a portfolio of securities that is managed by an investment advisor—technically known as the management company—usually as one of a number of funds managed by the same management company. These management companies are probably better known to individual investors as mutual fund "families" or groups.

The mutual fund's price per share, also called its net asset value (NAV), varies daily. The main characteristics of a mutual fund are that an investor can buy or sell shares in that fund on any business day at the closing share price on that day; and that the portfolio changes continually both because investors buy and sell shares and because the manager buys and sells securities.

MAJOR TYPES OF BOND FUNDS AND HOW THEY DIFFER

Because of the extraordinary popularity of bond funds, there are now literally hundreds of bond funds available to individual investors. New ones are constantly coming to market. For any sector of the fixed-income market, you can buy either a fund, or an individual security.

Funds differ from each other in significant ways. The most obvious difference is that they invest in different sectors of the bond market. There are municipal bond funds, funds investing in Treasuries, funds investing in corporates, and so on. Second, only money market funds have a constant share price. The price per share of all other bond funds should be expected to go up and down; and with it, the value of your assets in the fund will go up and down.

As a result, funds differ both in degree of riskiness and potential total return. Generally, the higher the risk, the higher the potential total return, but also, the higher the unpredictability of return. Riskiness is determined by several factors. The most important is the average maturity of the securities in a fund's portfolio. Most funds invest in a specific segment of the yield curve. The average maturity of all the securities in the fund is the key determinant of interest rate risk. Technically, the average is weighted by the size of each issue in the portfolio. For that reason, you may see the term "average weighted maturity" used to describe maturity length of a bond fund portfolio.

As average maturity length of bond funds increases, so does risk. Money market funds are required to have an average maturity of no more than 90 days. The share price of money market funds remains at a constant $1.00 per share. As a result, the value of principal in a money market fund does not go up or down. That is the reason money funds are considered the safest funds. "Short-intermediate" funds usually have an average maturity of three years or less. Price fluctuations for that maturity range are low. Long-term funds have average maturities in the 20-year range. Share price goes up and down a lot. Note also that the average maturity of a bond fund is not fixed. It can change as the portfolio changes.

The average maturity of a bond fund determines both how much share price goes up and down in response to interest rate changes and the dividend yield. Normally, longer term funds have higher dividends than shorter term funds; but price per share goes up and down more. The price per share of shorter term funds is more stable (goes up and down less); but dividend yield is lower.

Finally, funds differ in credit quality. Again, this influences both yield and riskiness. The lower the rating, the higher the yield; but also, the higher the risk. Some funds charge commissions; others do not. Some are efficiently managed; that is, have low expense ratios. Others have high management expenses. All of these differences will be discussed at greater length in this chapter and in the next.

What are some of the major differences between individual bonds and bond funds?

There are some major differences between individual bonds and mutual funds.

For starters, a bond has a definite maturity; a fund does not. If you hold a bond to maturity, on that date it will be redeemed at par, regardless of the level of interest rates prevailing on the bond's maturity date. Assuming a default has not occurred, you get back 100 percent of your principal. You have also earned a minimum income for the period that you have held the bond, consisting of the interest coupons.

This is not the case with a bond fund. Mutual funds are comprised of a great many issues. While a number of individual issues may remain in the portfolio until they mature, there is no single date at which the entire portfolio of the fund will mature. As a consequence, the price of a fund does not automatically return to par on a specified date. Except for money market funds, the price at which you will be able to sell shares in a fixed-income fund cannot be known ahead of time. It will be determined by conditions prevailing in that sector of the bond market when you sell your fund. This price may be more than your initial investment in the fund, or less, depending on what has happened to its share price. The fact that you can sell fund shares any time you wish does not guarantee that you can sell at the price you paid. There is one exception to this rule. This is a small group of funds that are structured to mature on a specific date known as "target funds."

To illustrate this basic difference, let us assume that you are considering buying either an intermediate general municipal bond fund or a five-year New York State bond. If you buy the New York State bond, you can be reasonably certain that—barring the unlikely occurrence of default—in five years, your bond will be redeemed at par, and you will have earned the coupons. If you buy the bond fund, however, you cannot know ahead of time what the price per share will be in five years. The price will depend on conditions prevailing in the bond market at that time.

Also, since the portfolio of a fund changes continually, the yields quoted by bond funds are not directly comparable to those quoted for individual bonds. As a result, any comparison between the potential return of an individual bond and a bond fund is imprecise. You are comparing apples and oranges.

Should I buy a fund or individual bonds?

There is no clear-cut answer to this question. Some individuals feel more comfortable buying individual bonds. Others prefer mutual funds. Each has advantages and disadvantages. Direct comparison between funds and individual securities is at best, imprecise.

For example, let us suppose that you would like to find out which will result in higher returns, an individual bond or a bond fund made up of securities with similar maturities and credit characteristics (say, intermediate munis or an intermediate muni fund).

If you ask your broker whether you earn more in individual securities or in a fund, you will most likely be told that you earn more in individual bonds. In all likelihood, the broker will be able to quote a higher yield for the intermediate municipal bond than for an intermediate muni bond fund. But remember that those yields are not directly comparable. Your broker will also explain that a fund's management expenses come directly out of your return. This is true, but incomplete. Whether you buy a fund or individual instruments, your actual total return will be determined by many variables:

- The size of the commission.
- The maturity length of the securities.
- Their credit quality.
- Reinvestment rates.
- Whether you buy and hold or trade.
- The length of the holding period.
- The price at which you redeem.

On a total return basis, for investors who buy and hold over long periods of time (more than five years), and who reinvest dividends, certain features of funds boost their return when compared to individual securities. Any large fund can buy securities more cheaply than any individual. Also, a mutual fund distributes dividends monthly rather than semi-annually, as do most individual bonds. This is an advantage both if you rely on dividend checks for income; and if you reinvest. More frequent compounding also boosts return. So does reinvesting at higher than money market rates. The higher reinvestment rate and the monthly compounding may boost total return over long holding periods. On the other hand, if you buy a fund with a large expense ratio, or high commission costs, then this reduces total return.

Funds offer a number of advantages compared to individual securities. They enable an investor to buy a diversified portfolio cheaply and efficiently. They are convenient. They simplify collecting and reinvesting dividends as well as record keeping. They offer liquidity. If you want to resell, you always have a ready buyer.

Let's address the issue of safety. Which would be safer, funds or individual securities? If preservation of capital and a minimum level of income are your paramount concerns in purchasing bonds (in other words, if you are unwilling to lose any part of principal, and want to be certain to at least earn the coupon) then you should buy individual instruments. Specifically, you should buy intermediate (two to seven years) high quality bonds. If you want the highest degree of safety, whether you are investing $10,000 or 1 million dollars, put that money in 2- to 5-year Treasuries. This is as safe as anything can be in this world. The main advantage of buying the individual securities—rather than a fund investing in those securities—is that, as noted above, you are guaranteed return of your entire principal at maturity. And in addition, if you hold to maturity, you will have earned the coupons.

As a rule, if you are investing less than $50,000 (total) in bonds, and if you are buying securities other than Treasuries, then you might feel more comfortable buying mutual funds rather than individual securities. If your portfolio is larger, and if you are able to buy individual securities at a good price (without excessive commissions), then individual securities may be a better option, particularly if your style of investing is to buy and to hold rather than to trade.

Even if you feel comfortable buying some individual securities, you may want to include some mutual funds in your portfolio in order to diversify core holdings. Also, if you would like to buy securities that are complicated and require a lot of expertise, then you might prefer to invest in those through funds. As a rule, the greater the expertise required to navigate within certain sectors of the bond market, the better off you would be choosing a fund, as opposed to individual securities. Instruments that come most readily to mind as fitting that description are GNMAs; junk bonds; international bonds; and to a lesser extent zero coupon and corporate bonds.

These, however, are suggestions. There are really no best choices. Funds and individual securities are different enough so that your choice can be governed by what feels most comfortable for you.

Finally, one important caveat. Don't expect bond funds to outperform significantly their sector of the bond market. They generally don't. This, however, is not meant as a criticism of funds. Nor does it lessen their usefulness to individual investors. It means only that individuals should realize that performance of bond funds will in all likelihood track that of the sector of the bond market in which they invest.

What are the risk factors in buying bond funds?

The chief risk is that the fund's NAV will go down in price, resulting in capital losses. Declines of 5 percent to 10 percent (that is, $500 to $1,000 per $10,000 investment) should be anticipated, particularly for long-term funds. Larger ones have occurred. The chief cause of these declines is interest rate exposure (read: average maturity). Remember the other face of risk, however. If interest rates decline, the fund's NAV will go up. This, in turn, boosts total return.

Occasionally, particular sectors of the bond market experience massive sell-offs, which result in steep price declines. Such a sell-off occurred in the junk bond market in 1989 and in 1990. During that period, the value of some junk bond funds declined by as much as 50 percent (that is, $5,000 per $10,000 investment) within a six-month period. Similar—though briefer—waves of selling hit municipal, corporate and Treasury bond funds prior to the stock market crash of 1987, and GNMA bond funds in 1981 and 1982. During these episodes, the value of funds in those sectors declined by between 10 percent to as much as 30 percent (that is, $1,500 to $3,000 per $10,000 investment) within a period of less than a year. (Note: these percentages represent declines in the price per share; they do not include dividend interest).

With the exception of junk bond funds, or funds investing primarily in securities that are below investment grade, credit risk is not as significant a consideration for holders of bond funds as it is for holders of individual securities. This is because funds are, by their very nature, diversified. The larger the fund, the more diversified it is. Most very large funds hold dozens of different issues. Particularly if those securities are investment grade or better, diversification becomes an important safety factor.

Credit safety is further enhanced by a number of factors. No one issue comprises more than a small percentage of total assets in a fund's portfolio (usually less than 2 percent). In addition, many funds are monitored for credit quality by in-house credit analysts. Deteriorating credits are often sold before the problem becomes too significant.

Note, however, that management companies differ in their attitude towards credit quality. Lower credit quality translates into higher yields. A management company emphasizing credit quality may sacrifice yield; one emphasizing yield would sacrifice credit quality. Remember also that funds holding primarily lower quality credits will be somewhat riskier than those holding more highly rated bonds. For instance, a fund holding nothing but junk is riskier than one holding nothing but Treasuries. A significant deterioration in credit quality would result in price declines for a fund made up chiefly of lower rated bonds.

What would happen to my investments if my mutual fund were to go belly up? Is there any fund insurance?

No, there is not any kind of insurance. Nonetheless, even if if your mutual fund group goes belly up (a very unlikely occurrence), your investments would probably not be damaged by the financial misfortunes of the mutual fund group.

In order to explain why, it is helpful to look at the structure of a typical mutual fund group. While there are differences among groups, the typical structure consists of a management company (the mutual fund group) that oversees a group of funds. The two—that is, the individual mutual funds and the management company—are separate entities. The management company functions as an investment advisor. It manages the assets in individual funds. But it does not actually hold the assets of these funds. Also, each fund is actually incorporated as an individual corporation. The assets of the individual funds are kept entirely segregated from those of the management company. The securities in those funds are held in trust by a custodian such as a bank—again, not by the management company. The custodian also usually maintains and administers the individual accounts.

If the management company (the mutual fund group) was in financial trouble, the assets of the individual funds would continue to be held by the custodian and would remain segregated from those of the management company. All of this is very strictly regulated by the SEC. It is, therefore, unlikely that the financial misfortunes of a management company would adversely affect assets held in mutual funds.

Remember also that the greatest asset of mutual funds is the confidence of the investing public. Most management companies exercise very tight controls to prevent malfeasance or fraud on the part of employees. In addition, most management companies carry insurance in the form of a fidelity bond to protect assets under management against possible fraud or malfeasance on the part of employees.

How do I measure return in a mutual bond fund?

The important numbers are Yield, Net Asset Value (NAV), and Total Return. Each will be defined in turn.

Yield

When you invest in a fund, you receive dividends, which are usually posted each month. You may choose to receive these in cash or to reinvest them to buy additional shares. Occasionally, the funds distribute capital gains. These can also be reinvested or received in cash. The dividends constitute the income portion of the fund, and the basic measure of the fund's yield.

Money market funds generally quote a seven-day yield, which is the average dividend yield for the past seven days (annualized). Long-term bond funds usually quote the average yield for the past 30 days (also annualized).

In addition, the SEC requires any fund whose average maturity is longer than that of a money market fund to quote a yield known as the *SEC standardized yield*. This yield is complex.

The standardized SEC yield is a snapshot of the actual returns of the fund for the past 30 days. By far the greatest portion of that yield consists of the dividends accrued by the funds for the past 30 days. In addition, however, like the yield-to-maturity quoted for individual bonds, the 30-day SEC yield includes slight increases in the price of bonds in the portfolio as they rise towards par (this would be the case for discount bonds); or (for premium bonds) slight declines as the price of these bonds falls towards par.

This SEC yield formula has created some confusion because it differs by a small amount—usually not more than 20 basis points—from the fund's actual dividend payout. If you want to know the actual dividend payout, based entirely on dividends, ask for the 30-day dividend yield. Some fund groups call this number the distribution rate.

The main purpose of the 30-day SEC yield is to enable a purchaser to accurately compare the yields of mutual funds to those of similar funds. The use of the standardized formula insures that the yields are calculated in exactly the same way. Prior to the imposition of the SEC standardized rule in 1988, it was not uncommon for some funds to play games in order to inflate yield quotes. Now, if you are comparing two GNMA funds, or two muni bond funds, and you ask for the SEC yield for the same 30-day period, you know the quotes are exactly comparable for the past 30 days.

Remember also, that the 30-day SEC yield is not directly comparable to the yield-to-maturity quoted for individual securities. It would be misleading to use it as a basis for comparing individual securities to bond funds. This is because the yield-to-maturity of an individual bond is based on the assumption that the bond will be redeemed at par. And there is no date at which the entire portfolio of a fund "matures" and returns to par. The 30-day SEC yield is accurate only for the past 30 days. It should not be viewed as a prediction of future returns.

Net Asset Value (NAV)

Net asset value (NAV) is calculated daily. The value of all the assets of the fund is tabulated at the end of each trading day. The total value is then divided by the total number of shares. Expenses, of course, are deducted from the value of assets. The NAV is the market worth of one share.

The NAV of many of the larger mutual funds is printed daily in the financial pages of major newspapers. Investors can monitor

Exhibit 10.1
Format of Mutual Fund Listings

	NAV	Buy	Chg.		NAV	Buy	Chg.
Smith Barney:				**Wright Funds:**			
Equity p	15.80	16.76	+ .04	GvOb	12.08	NL	− .02
IncGro	11.68	12.39	+ .02	JrBICh	14.34	NL	+ .24
Mu Cal	11.62	12.10		SIBICh	16.07	NL	+ .03
Utlty x	12.14	12.71	− .07	TotRef	11.74	NL	− .01
SoundSh	13.86	NL	+ .03	**Zweig Funds:**			
SAM Val	13.04	NL	+ .10	ZS Gv p	9.51	9.98	− .01
Steadman Funds:				Straf	12.20	12.91	+ .03
Am Ind	1.62	NL	...				
Assoc	.63	NL	...				
Invest	1.29	NL	...	**Mutual Fund Table Explained**			
Ocean	2.52	NL	− .01	Because of the complexity of mutual fund			
Voyageur Fds:				commissions, dividends and fees, the As-			
CO TF	10.07	10.48		sociated Press uses a system of footnotes			
GrStk p	19.94	21.16	+ .27	with the fund litings. They are: **E**—Ex-capi-			
MNTF	11.71	12.29	...	tal gains distribution. **S**—Stock Dividend or			
Weiss Peck Greer:				split. **X**—Ex-cash dividend. **F**—Previous			
Tudor	22.33	NL	+ .26	day's quotation. **(NL)n**—No front-end load			
Govt	10.27	NL	− .02	or contingent deferred sales load. **P**—Fund			
Gwth	124.18	NL	+1.42	assets are used to pay for distribution			
Grinc	22.62	NL	+ .21	costs—12(b)1 plan. **R**—Redemption fee or			
WallSt	7.44	7.87	+ .05	contingent deferred sales load may apply.			
Westcore:				**T**—Both P and R apply.			
STBd	9.81	10.01	...				
Bas VI	19.53	20.45	− .01				
Midco	13.50	14.14	+ .15				

the value of their funds as often as they care to. Exhibit 10.1 shows the format and some of the prices that would have been published April 4, 1991.

The listing includes both bond funds and stock funds and includes only relatively large funds. Note that the listing includes a good deal of information in addition to price. Whenever two prices are quoted for a fund, one under "NAV" (Net Asset Value) and the other under "Buy," the fund is sold on a commission basis. The spread between the "NAV" and the "Buy" is the amount of the commission charged by the fund. You would buy fund shares at the "buy" price and sell at the NAV. If the fund is sold without commission, only one price is quoted, and the letters NL (for No Load) appear after the fund name. An "r" after the fund's name indicates that a redemption fee is charged. Funds with a 12b-1 plan are marked with a "p". A "t" indicates both redemption and 12b-1 plan fees.

Total Return

The yield quoted by bond funds—whether the dividend yield or the 30-day SEC yield—is primarily a measure of the fund's dividend distributions. It is valid only for the past thirty days. It cannot be used as an accurate projection of future returns. More importantly, the quoted yield does not enable you to estimate potential declines or potential increases in the Net Asset Value (NAV) of fund shares over future holding periods, which translate directly into capital gains or capital losses. Over long holding periods, the only measurement that accurately measures a fund's actual return to you is total return.

Total return consists of:

- Dividends + capital gains distributions, if any;
- Interest-on-interest on reinvested dividends; and
- Plus or minus any changes in NAV.

Changes in NAV have a substantial impact on total return. Suppose, for instance, that your fund's dividend yield is 10 percent for a one-year period. Further suppose that during that year, the value of your shares declines by 10 percent. This will translate directly into a 10 percent decline in the value of your principal. Such a decline will offset a dividend distribution of 10 percent and result in a total return of approximately zero for that one-year period. On the other hand, suppose that for the same period, the fund's NAV goes up by 10 percent. Then the total return jumps to 20 percent. This is equivalent (approximately) to earning an extra 10 percent in dividends. Note that in either case, the advertised dividend yield is the same.

Mutual funds will quote total return information to you if you ask. That information may also be included in some fund brochures. Interest-on-interest is automatically included since the normal procedure is to assume that dividends and capital gains distributions are reinvested.

Mutual funds differentiate between three types of total return. Suppose you ask a fund group for the total return of a fund over the past five years. The fund will quote the *cumulative* total return for the past five years. That is the total return you would have earned if you had held the fund for the past five years and reinvested dividends. The fund will also quote the *average annual total return*. That is the average return for the past five years. Finally, the fund can also quote the *actual* total return for any one year period. That would simply be called the annual total return for that year.

What is a load?

There was a time when the answer to this question could be stated in a few words: a load is a sales commission. A no-load fund charges no commission. A load fund does. Commissions, however, are no longer that simple.

Sales commissions represent a percentage of the money invested. They are paid at the time of purchase. Standard commissions are between 4 percent to 5 percent. Some so-called "low-load" funds charge less, between 1 1/2 percent and 3 1/2 percent. A very few funds charge as much as 7 to 9 percent and this is almost unconscionable.

Some funds charge graduated amounts. For instance, the commission might be 4 percent if you invest less than $100,000. It may decline to 3 1/4 percent for up to $250,000, and to 2 1/2 percent if you invest more than $250,000. Some load funds, incidentally, deduct commissions not just from the initial sum you invest; but also from every amount invested subsequently including reinvested dividends.

But the matter does not end there. Some funds that do not charge a commission at the time of purchase, do charge a fee levied when you sell the shares, called either an "exit fee" or a "back-load." These fees are usually higher for shorter holding periods. They decline if you hold a fund for longer periods of time. For example, you might pay a stiff 6 percent exit fee if you hold the fund for only one year. The back-load might drop to 5 percent after two years; to 4 percent after three years, and so on until it disappears if you hold long enough.

In addition, many funds have added a variety of charges that are really also commissions. These are more insidious because the shareholder may not be aware of either their existence or of their true cost. Some funds which advertise themselves as no-load (or low load) now charge shareholders about 1 percent to

1 1/2 percent per year for the cost of advertising and selling new shares. These fees, known as 12b-1 fees, are imposed *in addition* to usual annual fund expenses.

What is the effect of fund loads on total return?

Any commission reduces total return. Suppose you pay 4 percent in commission. That 4 percent is deducted from the monies that you invest. Only 96 percent of principal is actually invested. If you earn 8 percent in dividends during the first year, and if the fund's NAV does not change, total return for that year would be approximately 4 percent even though the dividend yield is quoted—accurately—as 8 percent.

The ultimate effect of commissions on total return depends partly on how long the fund is held. If you plan to hold a fund for less than one year, a 4 percent to 5 percent load may eat up half (or more) of the year's dividends. So would a back-load of 4 percent to 6 percent. But if you plan to hold a fund for five years or more, an initial commission of 4 percent may be cheaper in the long run than an equivalent percentage as an exit fee. It will be 4 percent of a larger amount if the fund does well.

Surprisingly, if you plan to hold a fund for over five years, the most expensive form of commission is likely to be the 12b-1 fee. Consider, as an example, that you have invested in a fund that levies an annual 12b-1 fee of 1 1/2 percent. If you hold the fund for 10 years, and multiply the 1 1/2 percent annual fee by 10 times, this results in the equivalent of a commission of 15 percent. Actually, that number understates the true cost of such a plan because if the fund does well, each year, you are charged 1 percent of a larger amount. In addition, that 1   percent eats into compounding and lowers income from interest-on-interest. Because of this, the SEC is considering a proposal to cap the total amount of 12b-1 fees that can be assessed.

In protest against these proliferating expenses, a small group of funds have formed an association that they are calling the 100 percent no-load fund association. Many of these groups are well-established, well-managed funds with impeccable reputations. But these funds are not sold by brokers who can't earn any commission by selling them, and they have to be purchased by mail.

If you own a bond mutual fund, have already paid a commission, and are happy with the fund, it makes little sense to sell it because of the commission. But if you own a so-called no-load fund with 12b-1 fees, you might investigate truly no-load, low expense fund alternatives. For new money, it is best to look for a no-load fund, with no exit or back-load fee, and no 12b-1 expenses.

What are average expenses for bond funds?

Expenses, as a percentage of assets, should be below 1 percent per year. The low cost leader is Vanguard. Some Vanguard bond funds have expense ratios of about 30 basis points (less than 1/3 of 1 percent). For a bond fund, annual expenses of 50 to 60 basis points (1/2 of 1 percent) are low; above 1 percent, they are high.

Bear in mind that expenses come directly out of yield, and reduce total return. Lower expense ratios translate into higher yield and higher total return. While annual differences in expense ratios of 30 to 50 basis points may not appear significant, particularly if you hold a fund for long periods of time (five years or more), such differences make an important difference in total return (because of compounding).

Are there any advantages to buying load funds?

The only benefit would be the advice that you may get if you are dealing with an experienced broker.

There is no evidence that load funds have performed better than no-load funds. (I am discussing bond funds, and not stock funds). Not only don't you get what you pay for (that is, better performance because you have paid a commission). The opposite is true. The load and expenses reduce total return. Many of the most efficiently managed, best funds in the industry are no-load, and have no 12b-1 fees and low expense ratios.

What are contractual plans?

Under a contractual plan, the investor contracts to invest a fixed sum (say $50 or $100) per month for a specified number of years, perhaps 10 or 15 years. Commissions are almost 9 percent for the life of the contract. These commissions, however, are paid up front. Over 50 percent of the total invested during the first year consists of commissions. That money may be lost if an investor chooses to withdraw from the plan. Contractual plans were prevalent in the 1960s. Most have been phased out with one exception: the funds sold by First Investors.

The sales practices of First Investors have been described as misleading and high pressure in a number of articles in *Barron's* (Feb. 13, 1989 and Nov. 12, 1990). In addition, two of their funds, *Hi-yield* and *Fund for Income* have been among the worst performing junk bond funds. A number of states (New York, Maine, Massachusetts among others) have brought civil lawsuits against First Investors to recover some of the sums lost by investors in these two junk bond funds, and to make it easier for shareholders to exit from the contractual plans without incurring heavy penalties. As a result of this litigation, First Investors has suspended sales of both junk bond funds.

While this is still an ongoing situation, a number of observations ought to be made. The first is that the litigation does not adversely affect the assets held by First Investors in any of their mutual funds. Remember that individual funds each constitute independent corporations, and that the assets held by the funds are segregated from the assets of the parent company. Also, it would not be prudent for anyone who has money invested in any fund managed by First Investors to panic sell. Whether or not to continue holding should be determined on an individual basis; and should depend partly on how much commission has already been paid; partly on the performance of specific funds; and partly on how much money an investor would lose if he withdraws from the contractual plan (this would vary from state to state).

At the same time, I would strongly urge anyone who wants to invest in a bond fund not to do so through a contractual plan, particularly one with commissions as high as those of First Investors. The pitch of this group is that the initial load ultimately benefits the shareholders by discouraging frequent switching and by encouraging saving. Even if you feel the need for a forced savings plan, however, one can be developed in far less onerous ways, for instance, through payroll deductions or through a profit sharing plan.

How can I buy no-load funds?

These are purchased mainly by mail. Brokers do not sell them because they do not earn commission. At least one discount brokerage firm (Schwab) sells no-load funds, but it imposes a commission.

Here is a list (in alphabetical order) of some of the larger mutual funds that you might want to contact along with the toll-free number that you can call to obtain information. All of these have a variety of well-managed, no-load bond funds. Except as noted, none of them has any exit or redemption fees; and they do not charge 12b-1 expenses.

- Benham (800) 321-8321.

- Dreyfus (800) 829-3733. Note that Dreyfus sells some load funds through brokers, and that their GNMA bond fund has 12b-1 expenses.

- Fidelity (800) 544-8888. Fidelity charges a 1/2 of 1 percent redemption fee on a few bond funds if you sell those before six months.

- Price, T. Rowe (800) 638-5660.

- Scudder (800) 225-2470.

- Stein Roe (800) 338-2550.

- Vanguard (800) 662-7447. The expense ratios of the Vanguard funds are consistently among the lowest in the industry.

If you are interested in buying a bond fund, telephone and ask for information. You will be sent a prospectus and usually additional information concerning the funds. If after reading this information you still have questions, then telephone the information number listed above, and ask questions. But be aware that the quality of information that comes over the telephone varies enormously, depending on who is at the other end of the line. This in fact is one good reason for reading the printed material.

I tried to read a prospectus and found it poorly written and confusing. Why is it important?

The fund's prospectus contains some absolutely essential information, which is really quite easy to understand. Ignore the legalese and focus on the essentials. The prospectus is clearly labelled: the word "prospectus" appears on the cover.

In addition to the prospectus, there are two additional brochures that you can request. One is the latest annual or semi-annual report issued by the fund. That usually contains information on the total return of the fund for a number of years, as well current investment policies of the fund manager. Also, in order to make the prospectus easier to understand, the mutual fund industry obtained permission to omit certain details from the prospectus. Those are contained in a brochure known as a "statement of additional information." That should be requested separately.

What do I really need to read in a prospectus?

The key information is contained in a table entitled *Selected per share data and ratios*. This table summarizes the fund's performance over time on a per share basis. These data will help you assess the fund's potential volatility and total return.

The key information to look at is in the lines entitled:

- Net asset value at the beginning of the period: price per share at the beginning of each year.
- Net asset value at the end of the period: price per share at the end of each year.

The format of this table varies from fund to fund. But the information will be the same. When you look at this table, compare NAV over time and from year to year. If NAV hardly budges, then volatility is low. If NAV changes a lot, then volatility is high. To judge the amount of volatility, I find it helpful to translate price changes into percentages.

Exhibit 10.2 shows what such a table looks like. Reading columns of numbers is not most people's idea of fun. So I have deliberately selected one that would yield a real *horror story*, as an

Exhibit 10.2
Sample Table of Selected Per Share Data and Ratios

U.S. Govt. Securities Series	1988	1987	1986	1985	1984	1983	1982	1981	1980	1979
							(Not covered by Accountant's Current Report)			
INCOME AND EXPENSES										
Income	$.728	$.737	$.830	$.920	$.980	$.890	$.730	$.800	$.905	$.750
Operating expenses	.037	.039	.040	.040	.050	.070	.065	.070	.075	.100
Net income	.691	.698	.790	.880	.930	.820	.665	.730	.830	.650
Dividends from net income	(.696)	(.724)	(.875)	(.900)	(.900)	(.905)	(.770)	(.760)	(.680)	(.660)
CAPITAL CHANGES										
Net realized and unrealized gains (losses) on securities	.115	(.500)	.165	.500	(.390)	.345	1.305	(1.350)	(1.830)	(.400)
Distributions from realized capital gains	—	(.014)	—	—	—	—	—	—	—	—
Net increase (decrease) in net asset value	.11	(.54)	.08	.48	(.36)	.26	1.20	(1.38)	(1.68)	(.41)
Net asset value at beginning of period	6.87	7.41	7.33	6.85	7.21	6.95	5.75	7.13	8.81	9.22
Net asset value at end of period	$6.98	$6.87	$7.41	$7.33	$6.85	$7.21	$6.95	$5.75	$7.13	$8.81
Ratio of operating expenses to average net assets	.53%	.52%	.54%	.57%	.60%	.73%	.99%	1.09%	.94%	1.09%
Ratio of net income to average net assets	9.85%	9.49%	9.93%	11.06%	11.70%	8.28%	10.20%	11.35%	10.86%	7.13%
Portfolio turnover rate	34.14%	52.92%	36.02%	9.27%	6.30%	59.57%	128.07%	71.91%	80.46%	33.71%
Number of shares outstanding at end of period (000's)	1,735,011	1,895,183	1,938,886	888,946	309,032	47,039	2,407	904	809	1,574

Source: A GNMA prospectus. Reprinted with permission.

example of why a few minutes spent looking at tedious columns of numbers may be rewarding.

Let's analyze these numbers. The high price for the fund was $9.22 in 1979; and the low price was $5.75, in 1982. This represents a decline in NAV of $3.47, or almost 38 percent of principal over that three-year period. To put that into perspective, if you had invested $10,000 in 1979, the value of the principal (your original shares) would have declined to $6,200 by 1982.

Note that for each of these three years, you would have been quoted (accurately) a dividend yield of approximately 10 percent. Your total return, however, would have been a disaster. To quickly calculate total return for the three-year period between 1979 and 1982, add the dividend yield (+10 percent, +10 percent, +10 percent) and the decline in principal value (-37 percent). That translates into a negative total return of approximately -7 percent. In other words, after three years of reinvesting 10 percent in dividend yields, that fund still posted a net loss.

If you are income-oriented, and if you invest mainly to receive the dividend income, please notice that as principal shrinks, so does the dividend yield. In 1979, the dividend yield would have been 10 percent of $10,000, that is $1,000. By 1982, with your shares now worth only $6,200, the dividend yield would have been 10 percent of $6,200, that is $620.

When you analyze similar tables, you should note all changes in NAV, even seemingly minor ones. For instance, between the beginning of 1987 and the end of 1988 (a two-year period), the fund's NAV dropped from $7.41 to $6.98, which represents a decline of almost 6 percent. Or take the point of view of a long-term investor. In 1988, NAV was $6.98, 24 percent below NAV of $9.22 in 1979. To be fair, note that in 1988, NAV was about 29 percent higher than in 1981.

What does all of this tell you? First, ask yourself: how did you feel when you saw these numbers? Would you have been comfortable holding this fund while its returns gyrated wildly? If not, then pay close attention to potential volatility before you buy a bond fund. High volatility means that returns are highly unpredictable and vary significantly from from year to year.

Second, don't buy a bond fund mainly on the basis of advertised dividend yield. Also consider potential stability of share price. Only buy a potentially volatile fund if you are prepared to experience significant price fluctuations and unstable returns.

The potential payoff is that, over time, in spite of the fluctuating NAV, you may earn higher total return than you would from a fund with a more stable NAV. However, there is no guarantee this will occur. Before you buy a potentially volatile fund, compare total return of that fund for a period of at least five years to that of a money market fund, or any less volatile fund. This will help you to evaluate whether potential gain appears significant enough to warrant the risk.

In case you are wondering, the numbers in Exhibit 10.2 are representative of those you would have found in a GNMA bond fund. Remember that GNMA funds have always been heavily advertised as providing both high safety (the securities are guaranteed by the U. S. government) and high returns. During the early 1980s, this did not keep GNMA funds from fluctuating wildly in response to prepayments and interest rate changes.

Exhibit 10.2 contains several other items of interest. They are the following:

- *Dividends from net income:* These are the actual dividends paid out every year. Dividend distributions are the combined coupons, distributed on a per share basis, usually monthly.

- *Ratio of net income to average net assets.* This is the dividend yield, averaged out for the year. It is probably close to the dividend yield the fund was advertising each year.

- *Distribution from realized capital gains.* This fund distributed a capital gain, once, in 1987. Mutual funds realize capital gains when they sell securities at a profit. Unless these gains are offset by losses, by law, mutual funds are required to pass these on to shareholders. For tax purposes, these distributions are taxed as capital gains, not as dividend income. All bond funds—including municipal bond funds—occasionally distribute capital gains and create a tax liability.

- *Ratio of operating expenses to average net assets.* Expenses of the fund for the past five years have been around the 1/2 of

1 percent mark. The fund gets good grades for a low expense ratio.

- *Portfolio turnover rate.* This indicates how actively the portfolio changes. Portfolio turnover of bond funds tends to be very high. Rates of 150 percent a year are not uncommon. Theoretically, portfolio turnover of 100 percent means that the entire portfolio changes once a year. In actuality, many portfolio managers maintain a core portfolio of perhaps 50 percent to 60 percent of their holdings and turn over the remainder.

  This category does not really help you to evaluate the fund. Different managers achieve good performance both with high and with low turnover.

What else in the prospectus should I read?

Always make sure that you understand *the objectives and policies of the fund.* You do not want to be like the shareholder who asked (after noticing catastrophic price declines in his fund): "why is this high yield fund full of junk bonds?"

The objectives of the fund are summarized in a brief paragraph, usually on the first page of the prospectus. This paragraph describes the types of securities the fund intends to buy (corporates, munis, GNMAs, Treasuries, etc.); the probable average maturity of those securities; and the major risks incurred by the fund.

If the language of the objective appears to be full of jargon, or unclear, ask the fund's information people for clarification. If for example, the objective states the "the fund will buy speculative securities that are well below investment grade," it is important that you understand that this fund will invest in junk bonds. If the objective states that the fund will purchase "high and upper medium quality securities," ask for specific rating information. Be sure that you understand the risk factors described in the objective. The risk factors should be taken seriously, even if recent fund performance has been excellent. Remember, however, that policies are usually defined in broad enough terms to allow fund managers enough latitude to deal with changing market conditions.

Elsewhere in the prospectus, under the rubric "Investment Policies," specific investment policies are described at greater length. Be sure to check whether the fund's charter permits the fund manager to engage in activities such as writing options or trading futures contracts. Sometimes, these activities are intended as hedges. Hedges are expensive, but not risky. But be on the lookout for indications that the fund may use speculative techniques in an attempt to boost yield. For instance, a number of bond funds have attempted to boost dividend yield by writing options or by buying future contracts. In practice, these forms of leverage sometimes backfired and resulted in actual losses to shareholders. Nonetheless, even funds holding government securities "only" (and which as a result advertised themselves as ultra safe) were guilty of these practices. (Some of these funds included a "plus" in their name; the "plus" referred to the intended use of leverage to boost yield.)

Annual expenses are included in the same section as Exhibit 10.2. Exhibit 10.3 shows what the expenses would look like for a typical no-load mutual fund. Note that for this fund, there are no commissions of any kind and no 12b-1 expenses. Annual expenses for this fund are extremely low.

Exhibit 10.3
Table of Fund Expenses for a No-Load Fund

The following table illustrates **all** expenses and fees that you would incur as a shareholder of the Fund. The expenses set forth below are for the 1989 fiscal year.

Shareholder Transaction Expenses	
Sales Load Imposed on Purchases	None
Sales Load Imposed on Reinvested Dividends	None
Redemption Fees	None
Exchange Fees	None

Annual Fund Operating Expenses	Prime Portfolio	Federal Portfolio	U.S. Treasury Portfolio
Management and Advisory Expenses	0.10%	0.11%	0.09%
Shareholder Accounting Costs	0.11	0.10	0.10
12b-1 Fees	None	None	None
Distribution Costs	0.04	0.04	0.04
Other Expenses	0.03	0.03	0.08
Total Operating Expenses	0.28%	0.28%	0.31%

Exhibit 10.4
Table of Fund Expenses for a Load Fund

Expense Table

The purpose of this table is to assist an investor in understanding the various costs and expenses that a shareholder will bear directly or indirectly in connection with an investment in the Fund. These figures are based on actual amounts recognized for the fiscal year ended September 30, 1988.

Shareholder Transaction Expenses

Maximum Sales Load Imposed on Purchases (as a percentage of offering price)............	4.00%
Maximum Sales Load Imposed on Reinvested Dividends (as a percentage of offering price)	4.00%
Deferred Sales Charge...	NONE
Redemption Fees..	NONE
Exchange Fee (per transaction)...	$5.00

Annual Fund Operating Expenses (as a percentage of average net assets)

Management Fees..	0.45%
Other Expenses...	0.08%
Total Fund Operating Expenses..	0.53%

Exhibit 10.4 is taken from the prospectus of a typical load fund.

This fund clearly shows a 4 percent load. It has no 12b-1 fee. Note, however, that if you elect to reinvest dividends, you will be charged 4 percent of each dividend reinvested. Note also the $5.00 fee for exchanging from one fund to another.

Finally, in addition to all of the above, when you read the prospectus, be sure to check the procedures.

- for investing in the fund
- for redeeming shares
- for receiving dividends

Also check:

- available services (checkwriting privileges, telephone redemption, telephone switching privileges and so on).
- whether the fund can be used for tax-deferred plans such as IRAs or KEOGHs.

These are all easily understood, but should be noted to avoid nasty surprises.

Is there any important data not contained in the prospectus?

Certain key data not in the prospectus should be checked with the fund's toll free number. The first is the current average maturity of the securities in the fund. This will determine its exposure to interest rate risk. The prospectus of a fund states parameters that are broad enough to allow the manager a good deal of latitude in determining where on the yield curve he wants to be as market conditions change. As a result, the actual maturity of a fund may vary significantly from one year to the next. For instance, it might vary from 9 to 20 years for a long-term fund. Under normal circumstances, volatility will be lower at the 9-year mark than at the 20-year mark.

The second key data not in the prospectus is the fund's total return over specific periods. Suppose, for example, that you are considering buying an intermediate municipal bond fund. It is useful to compare the total return data of several funds in order to evaluate how management has done under the same market conditions.

If you do compare total return for several funds, make sure that you are comparing performance over the same period of time. Also try to include a long enough time span so that it includes both strong and weak markets. You will want to know not only how much a fund gains in strong markets; but also, how it navigates weak markets. Total return data may be included in the statement of additional information or in the fund's annual reports. It can also be obtained from the marketing people.

Finally, it is not generally realized that a fund may have up to 35 percent of its portfolio in securities other than those listed in the fund name. It is important to find out what securities a fund actually holds.

Why not just buy the fund that had the highest return last year?

For a number of reasons. First, determine how comfortable you would be with the fund's volatility. If the best-performing fund last year was highly volatile, and volatility makes you uncomfortable, look for another fund.

Second, fund performance varies with changing market conditions. Generally, bond funds track the sector of the market in which they are invested. If a particular group of funds does well one year and conditions change, so will returns for these funds. It is important to look beyond last year's performance numbers and to try to figure out why the fund went up or down in value and whether the trend is likely to persist.

If, for example, a fund is long-term, and its NAV went up, it is probable that the rise was due to a significant decline in interest rates. The fund's NAV is likely to drop just as steeply if interest rates turn around and go up. If international funds do well one year, this may have been the result of a decline in the value of the dollar. If the value of the dollar rises the following year, then the NAV of those funds would decline (see the next chapter for a fuller explanation).

Ironically, the popularity of bond funds groups has become almost a contrary indicator. Junk bond funds became wildly popular, for example, just before they tanked.

How are taxes computed when selling mutual funds?

Suppose you invested $10,000 in the "many happy returns" bond fund three years ago. You sell the shares today for $20,000. What are the tax consequences?

Simple, you say, the difference between my purchase price and my sale price is $10,000. That represents a capital gain, and it will be taxed at the current long-term capital gains rate. Simple, but wrong. And yet, it appears, a very common error.

To calculate your tax liability, you have to determine what is called in financialese the "cost basis" of your shares. This includes not only the money you invested directly, but also reinvested dividends and capital gains distributions. (These distributions are listed on each year's tax returns, and taxes are paid annually on them).

Let us assume, for example, that for the three years that you have owned the "many happy returns" bond fund, you have received dividends totalling $1,000 annually, as well as capital gains distributions of $500 two years in a row. Dividends and capital gains together add up to $4,000. When you sell all your shares, the total amount of the distributions (that is, dividends plus capi-

tal gains) has to be added to the $10,000 that you initially in-
vested. The cost basis rises to $14,000 (instead of $10,000). This
lowers the tax liability. To determine capital gains taxes, subtract
the cost basis ($14,000) from the sale price ($20,000). You owe
taxes on capital gains of $6000—and not $10,000.

If you are selling only part of your shares—not all the shares
in the fund—this procedure has to be modified. The important
point to remember is that distributions, including dividends paid
out by municipal bond funds that are not taxable, should be
added to your cost basis. This raises the cost basis and lowers
taxes due.

When you switch money out of one mutual fund into another, even within the same family of funds, this is considered a
sale for tax purposes, and will create a tax liability, which may be
either a capital gain or a capital loss.

Finally, there are tax consequences to owning funds, even if
you just hold them and sell nothing. Each fund generally sends
out exact tax information on dividend and capital gains distributions at the end of each year. Dividends are federally taxed (unless the fund is a municipal bond fund). Capital gains
distributions are federally taxable, as capital gains. Currently, this
tax is the same as the one on dividends, but that may change if
the tax law changes again.

It is a good idea to inquire about the schedule for capital
gains distributions before you buy a fund. If you buy a fund just
prior to a capital gains distribution, you are taxed immediately,
even if you have owned the fund for one day, or if the fund immediately declines in value.

Paper losses or paper gains, create no tax liabilities, but you
may want to sell a fund in which you have a paper loss, either to
redeploy assets, or to offset a capital gain. Similarly, you may
want to protect a capital gain by selling shares.

It is essential to maintain good records if you own mutual
funds. A simple method is to keep all your records for one fund
in one folder and to keep those together as long as you own the
fund. Even if you do not do all the computations yourself, an
accountant will need this information to compute your tax liability accurately.

SUMMARY: QUESTIONS TO ASK BEFORE BUYING A BOND FUND

What securities does the fund hold? what are its objectives and investment policies?

What is the average maturity of the fund?

What is the credit rating of most of the securities in the fund?

What has been the total return for the last year? For the last three years? For the last five years?

How much has the NAV varied from year to year? Am I comfortable with that amount of volatility?

What has been the fund's dividend yield? What has been its 30-day SEC yield?

Is there a commission? An exit fee? A 12b-1 plan?

What are annual expenses?

How long has that fund existed? Has it existed long enough to have a meaningful track record?

How does its track record compare to that of similar funds?

What services are available to shareholders?

11

Varieties of Bond Funds

This chapter discusses the risk factors and past performance
of the following types of bond funds:

- *money market funds (taxable, tax-exempt).*

- *short-intermediate funds (taxable, tax-exempt)*

- *intermediate funds (taxable, tax-exempt)*

- *long term bond funds (taxable, tax exempt)*

- *Junk bond funds*

- *GNMA funds*

- *International bond funds*

- *Zero bond funds (Target funds)*

- *Index funds*

Selecting a fixed-income fund can appear thoroughly bewilder-
ing. There seems to be a bond fund for every type of security, in
every maturity length. How is one to choose?

This chapter is a start. It classifies funds based on risk factors, potential total return, and volatility. In differentiating among
funds, I used a number of criteria.

The most elementary distinction between bond funds is based on share price; that is, whether it remains constant or can be expected to fluctuate. Only money market funds have a constant share price. NAV of every other kind of bond fund can be expected to fluctuate: some, very little; and some, a lot.

In most instances, interest rate exposure—and therefore, maturity length—is the primary determinant both of a fund's volatility and of its total return. Funds with longer maturities have higher yields, but more volatility, than funds with shorter maturities. For this reason, funds are grouped first of all based on their maturity length.

In addition, the types of securities held by the fund (for instance, taxable vs. tax-exempts, junk vs. governments) also affect both total return and volatility. Therefore, funds are differentiated by sector.

For several types of bond funds, total return and riskiness are determined by a combination of factors unique to that type of fund. The funds that come readily to mind are GNMA, international, junk, and zero bond funds. I am calling this group "bonds with unique risk factors" and analyzing them separately.

Finally, there is the inevitable miscellaneous category. It includes funds that do not fit either of the previous two categories.

FUNDS WITH A CONSTANT SHARE PRICE: MONEY MARKET FUNDS

Over one-third of the assets in mutual funds are in money market funds. Money funds are now available from mutual fund groups, from banks, and from brokerage firms. They come in taxable and tax-exempt form. Amazingly, new wrinkles in the money fund market are constantly appearing.

As a group, money funds have been an extraordinarily successful product. They have been profitable both for shareholders and for the companies offering them. In spite of the enormous sums slogging around this market, it has proved remarkably free of scandals, scams, and losses. It is probably almost a forgotten fact that before money market funds existed, individual investors seeking risk free investments were limited to passbook savings accounts at miserly regulated rates. The major innovation of money market funds was that they made available to the individual investor the high money market yields previously available only to institutional investors.

The defining characteristic of money funds is that share price is a constant $1.00. Therefore, the value of principal in money funds does not fluctuate. The interest yield fluctuates with the market. If interest rates rise, so does yield. If interest rates decline, so does yield.

Money market funds invest in short-term paper. Average maturity of these funds is now required by the SEC to be 90 days or less. (Note, however, that money funds may purchase Treasuries that go out two years and individual paper up to one year, as long as the average maturity of the fund remains at 90 days or less). Taxable money market funds invest in securities such as bank notes, commercial paper (issued by corporations), bank CD's, and short-term government securities. Tax-exempt money funds invest in tax anticipation notes, bond anticipation notes, and commercial paper issued by tax-exempt issuers (for example, hospitals, states and so on). Generally, yields on money market funds are close—within 50 basis points of each other.

Nonetheless, money market funds compete fiercely for the investor's dollar. Through advertising, money funds attempt to stress differences between their fund and all others. Some funds stress yield; others safety.

Money funds emphasizing safety invest primarily in U. S. government securities and insured CDs. As a result, their yield at the lower end money market yields. Note that if the fund holds only Treasury securities, the dividends are not taxed at the state and city level, and this may boost return, particularly in high tax states.

Money funds stressing yield hold a mix consisting of government paper, CDs, and commercial paper. The mix varies from fund to fund. A tremendous amount of ingenuity is being deployed to create new variations. One fund family is now investing in dollar denominated assets issued by U. S. corporations abroad, chiefly in Europe. There is no currency risk, since these funds are purchasing dollar denominated assets. These money funds have been at the higher end of the yield spectrum because interest rates have been higher in Europe. But this is not necessarily permanent.

Over time, one of the main determinants of yield for money funds is the efficiency of the fund; that is, its expense ratio. This is another area where funds are competing in order to to attract new investors. Some new funds try to attract buyers by initially absorbing all management expenses. This can result in a yield advantage of from 30 to 50 basis points for as long as the management continues to absorb expenses. While this is never permanent, there is no harm in enjoying the extra yield as long as it lasts. Other funds, in an effort to attract permanent, large, long-term deposits are now charging for such services as checkwriting, say $2.00 per check. The rationale is that charging for services will hold down fund expenses and will result in higher net yields for those shareholders who do not require these services. One hallmark of these money funds is that they require minimum deposits of $20,000.

How safe are money market funds? A spate of articles published in late 1990 has created the impression that money funds may not be as riskless as most investors assume. The facts behind these articles are not in dispute. A number of money funds were caught holding short-term paper of companies that defaulted. This could have resulted in a drop in the value of the funds of 1 percent to 2 percent, depending on the size of the fund. The parent companies running the funds chose to absorb the loss; no investor lost a penny.

If similar occurrences were to continue or to increase, however, the possibility exists that the share price of some money funds might not remain at $1.00 and that money fund investors might experience some losses. I am not predicting such losses. But while such an occurrence appears unlikely, in the opinion of some experts, it is a real possibility. If this concerns you, there are a number of strategies to follow. You might want to invest only in very large money funds (that is, with total assets exceeding one billion dollars). Another strategy would be to invest in funds that hold mainly or only Treasury paper. But note that commercial paper is rated and that money funds are permitted by law to invest only in highly rated paper.

To the average investor, small differences in yield are not significant. On a $20,000 account, a 50-basis point difference in yield amounts to $100.00 per year. Moreover, money market funds continue to be among the safest available investments. Selecting a money market mutual fund should therefore be determined by the features that are most important to you. The following is a brief listing of the principal features of various types of money market mutual funds.

Brokerage Money Market Funds (Cash Management Accounts)

Large brokerage firms, as well as discount brokerage firms, offer accounts known as cash management accounts. These are intended for affluent individuals. They require an initial minimum deposit of $5,000 (Schwab) to $20,000 (Merrill Lynch) and offer an extraordinary range of services. They come with a choice of a credit or a debit card (when you use a debit card, charges are automatically deducted from your current balance); offer unlimited check writing privileges; a choice between taxable or tax-exempt money market funds; and can be used to buy (and hold) either stocks or bonds.

In addition, interest income from stocks, bonds (or any other source you designate) is automatically swept into the account; and any monies deposited start earning interest on the day of deposit. If you have a Treasury-direct account, interest income and redeemed principal can be directed automatically to the cash management account. Large brokerage firms also sell insured bank CDs through their cash management accounts, and they shop the country for the best current rates. The cash in cash management accounts is covered by SIPC, for amounts between $100,000 and $500,000. Yields on money market funds in cash management accounts are competitive. Annual maintenance fees vary between $80.00 and zero.

Mutual Fund Money Market Funds

Most of the major mutual fund groups include one (or sometimes several) money market funds. If you invest money in either the equity or the bond funds of the group, the money market account enables you to transfer monies from those funds into the money market account (or vice-versa), often with just one telephone call.

The money market accounts also have checkwriting privileges (generally limited). Mutual fund money market funds are not insured and are governed by the same rules that govern mutual funds.

Bank Mutual Funds

These were started with great fanfare by the banking industry in the early 1980s. Many banks advertised initially high teaser rates; but these lasted only a short time. Bank money market funds have significantly lower yields than either brokerage firm or mutual fund money market funds, as much as 200 basis points. Their main advantage is that they are the only money market funds that are actually federally insured (up to $100,000); and if that helps you sleep better at night, by all means, take your money out of the bank's passbook account and put it in its insured money market fund. You will still boost your yield (compared to a passbook account) and have a totally safe investment.

Tax-Exempt Money Market Funds

These have the same features as taxable money market funds except that income from the money market funds is federally tax-exempt. Tax-exempt money market funds are offered by mutual fund groups and by brokerage firms, but not by banks. Minimum required for investment is usually $1,000.

Deciding whether to invest in a tax-exempt or taxable money market account comes down to arithmetic. You have to calculate whether the net-after-tax return is higher with a taxable or a tax-exempt money market fund, and the calculation is the same as that for municipal bonds. Generally, for most investors, differences in yield between tax-exempt and taxable money funds are not significant, unless the extra income lifts your marginal tax bracket to a higher level. Slight differences in net-after-tax yield are continually being created by changes in tax rates and changing yields in the marketplace.

If safety is a paramount concern to you, consider investing in money funds holding mainly Treasuries. Even though such funds might be expected to yield somewhat less than funds holding commercial paper, the taxable-equivalent yield is boosted by the fact that interest income of these funds will be exempt from state and local taxes. Particularly in high tax states, this exemption may bring the net-after-tax yield of these funds close to that of tax-exempt money funds; or to funds holding lower quality paper.

Single State Tax-Exempt Money Market Fund

These are the newest entrants among tax-exempt funds. As their name indicates, these funds invest only in paper issued by a single state. They are, therefore, tax-exempt to residents of that state as well as federally tax-exempt. Such funds have been established by mutual fund groups for California, Massachusetts, New York, New Jersey, Minnesota, and Pennsylvania. New single-state funds are being created almost daily because demand for them is high.

The appeal of these funds is the double tax exemption. Nonetheless, they may not be a good buy. The reason has been the high demand and the scarcity of available paper in some states. This has resulted in very low yields, compared to general tax-exempt (or even taxable) funds. Additionally, some funds are occasionally unable to buy enough paper from their state and have had to purchase some out-of-state paper, resulting in a probably unexpected, and certainly unwelcome, tax liability to shareholders.

What Percentage of Your Assets Should You Keep in Money Funds?

Because of their relatively high yields, safety, and convenience, money market funds have become a permanent alternative to bank passbook and checking accounts, as well as a place to keep liquid cash or contingency reserves. Over long stretches of time, however, returns of money funds are lower than those of stocks or longer term bonds and bond funds. Two questions then arise: what percentage of your total assets should you keep in money funds? and should you maintain a permanent percentage of a large portfolio in money funds?

One intriguing aspect of money fund returns is that there are occasional periods when money market funds outperform all other investments. This generally occurs when long-term rates are rising steeply so that both long-term bonds (and also stocks) may be falling steeply.

Some financial planners believe that investors should keep a percentage of their permanent investment portfolio in money market funds, in order to "smooth out" annual returns. Over time, however, real returns from money funds are not likely to outpace inflation. (While I have not seen statistics on money funds per se vs. inflation, return on T-bills—a reasonable proxy for money fund returns—averaged 1/2 of 1 percent annually for the period between 1926 and 1989). (Ibbotson and Sinquefield, SBBI, *1990 Yearbook*). For that reason, the permanent percentage of assets in money funds should never exceed 25 percent to 30 percent of total assets. As a general rule, the longer term your investment horizon is, the less should be permanently in money funds.

Keeping Informed on Money Funds

Every Thursday, the financial pages of the *New York Times* and of the *Wall Street Journal* list tables of the most recent seven-day yield of major money market funds (both taxable and tax-exempt). So does *Barron's,* on the weekend. Exhibit 11.1 shows the format of these tables.

Exhibit 11.1
Format of Table of Money Market Fund Yields

	Taxable Assets Avg. 7-day ($ mil.) Mat. Yld.				Assets Avg. 7-day ($ mil.) Mat. Yld.				Assets Avg. 7-day ($ mil.) Mat. Yld.		
				ZweigGvt	49	6.21	6.40	UST Master	68	4.62	4.73
PW RMA	51	6.23	6.43		**Tax Exempt**			ValLinTxE	39	4.27	4.36
PW Reir	59	6.05	6.24	ASO TxEx	51	3.98	4.08	VangCA	67	4.54	4.64
PW RM US	56	5.99	6.17	AT Ohio Tx	33	4.42	4.52	VangNJ	87	4.76	4.87
QuestCSP	49	6.01	6.19	ActAstTx	35	4.37	4.46	VangOH	79	4.82	4.93
QustCsG	69	5.72	5.88	ALXB TF	48	4.35	4.44	VangPA	45	4.79	4.91
QuestValue	...	...		Allia Tax	61	4.13	4.22	VangMB	72	4.89	5.01
RNC Liq	65	6.11	6.30	AllTxCal	56	3.83	3.90	VistaTF	51	4.33	4.42
RegisDSi	71	5.92	6.10	AllTxNy	56	3.73	3.80	VistaNY	62	3.67	3.74
RenaisGvt	35	5.94	6.13	AllurTF	32	4.56	4.66	WPG TX	47	4.84	4.96
RenaisMM	31	6.29	6.50	VanKmpTF	68	4.76	4.87	WoodTE	43	4.44	4.53

Note that in addition to the yield, the table lists the size of the fund and its average maturity. The article that accompanies this table includes such data as whether yields are rising or declining; as well as taxable-equivalent yields for tax-exempt money funds.

If maximum safety is one of your priorities, Donoghue (P. O. Box 6640, Holliston, MA 01746) publishes a newsletter that rates money funds for safety.

FUNDS WHOSE SHARE PRICE GOES UP AND DOWN: FUNDS WITH INTEREST RATE RISK

For this group of funds, both total return (dividends plus any change in the share price) and volatility of share price (that is, how much share price goes up or down) are related directly to the average maturity length of the fund's portfolio.

This is due to two factors. Assuming a normal "upward sloping" yield curve, dividend yield is higher for longer maturities, and lower for shorter maturities. Therefore, funds with longer average maturities normally yield more than funds with shorter maturities.

But higher yield always comes at a cost. The cost here is that the share price of funds with longer average maturities goes up and down more steeply in response to interest rate changes than that of funds with shorter maturities. A bond fund responds to changes in interest rates very much like an individual security. Price changes (both up and down) would be similar to those described for individual bonds in Chapter 3. For example, if interest rates rise, from 8 percent to 9 percent, long-term bond funds may decline in value by 6 percent to 10 percent (depending on the structure of the fund and the surreal level of interest rates) in a matter of months. Smaller declines would be registered by funds holding intermediate maturities; and no declines at all would occur in the price per share of money market funds.

For this reason, over short-term holding periods (under one year), the total return of long-term funds is unpredictable. It may be higher than the dividend yield if interest rates decline (because there will be a large capital gain); about the same as the dividend yield if rates remain stable; but lower than the dividend yield if interest rates rise (there would be a capital loss).

Over long holding periods (higher than five years), long-term funds should have higher total return than shorter term funds. But that needs to be qualified. If interest rates are stable or decline, long-term bond funds will continue to post higher total returns than shorter term funds. But because of the high interest rate risk, during a period such as the 1970s when interest rates climbed inexorably for most of the decade, long-term funds would be miserable investments.

Before discussing these funds in greater detail, let's first look at Exhibit 11.2 which lists the cumulative total return for various types of bond funds for the 1 year, 5 year and 10 year periods ending Dec. 1990. The total return is the cumulative total return, based on reinvestment of all dividends and capital gains distributions, if any, plus changes in share price. For purposes of comparison, money funds are also included in this exhibit). If you are considering purchasing a bond fund, you might find it useful to compare its total return against the average for that group, for the same time period. Note also that my classification differs somewhat from that of Lipper.

As Exhibit 11.2 demonstrates, over the past decade, for the one-year, five-year and ten-year time periods, it has paid, and very handsomely to buy the longest term funds for each category and just hold. But note also the exceptional return of intermediate (five-to-ten-year funds) for the same period.

The exceptional returns of long-term (and intermediate) bond funds for the past 10 years were due both to the extremely high level of interest rates in the early 1980s, and to the fact that long-term interest rates declined, irregularly, from 1982 onwards, for most of the decade. (There were some spikes; the worst occurred in 1987.) Nonetheless, the general trend of declining interest rates added a very large chunk of capital gains to the already high dividend income earned by the funds. The highest returns were earned in the early 1980s. The most recent returns are lower.

What this table does not show, however, is the variability of returns for long-term funds over short-term holding periods. During 1987, for example, the price per share of long-term bond funds declined by between 10 percent and 20 percent ($1,000 to $2,000 per $10,000 investment) between March and October, as in-

Exhibit 11.2
Performance Summary, through Dec. 1990

All distributions—dividends and capital gains—are assumed to be reinvested.

	1 Year	5 Years	10 Years
Money Market Funds (Taxable)	7.77%	41.69%	141.31%
Money Market Funds (Tax Exempt)	5.51	27.46	69.25
Taxable			
Short (1-5 Years) U.S. Gov't. Funds	8.99	47.82	NA
Intermediate (5-10 Years) U.S. Gov't. Funds	8.51	48.82	159.75
Intermediate (5-10 Years) Investment Grade Debt	7.20	49.02	198.14
U.S. Gov't. Funds (Long Term)	7.39	49.61	190.87
Corporates—A Rated (Long Term)	6.79	48.76	210.21
Tax Exempt			
Short (1-5 Years)	6.39	35.76	99.25
Intermediate (5-10 Years)	6.48	41.70	153.11
General Municipal (Long-Term)	5.93	52.42	189.21
Insured Municipal (Long-Term)	6.49	50.43	179.28
High Yield Muni Funds	5.05	51.82	196.76

NA—Not available.

Source: Derived from *The Fixed Income Fund Performance*, Jan. 1991, pp. 128-129, published by Lipper Analytical Services, Inc. N. J.

terest rates on long-term Treasuries rose from 9 percent to 10 1/2 percent, and rates in all other sectors went along. Most bond funds tracked their sector of the bond market.

Finally, one of the more mysterious characteristics of bond funds is that the name of a fund may not accurately reveal either the holdings of a fund, or its chief risk factors. First, any fund may hold up to 35 percent of its total assets in something quite different from the securities in its name. Second, the name may be so general that it can designate a variety of possibilities.

Any number of confusing possibilities exist. A fund holding "government only" securities may hold primarily Treasuries, primarily GNMAs, primarily zero coupon bonds, or a combination of all of those. A high yield fund may hold long-term, high quality securities (high yield because long-term) or junk bonds (high yield because the credit quality is speculative). A fund calling itself long-term may actually maintain an average maturity of 10 to 12 years, which is closer to the intermediate range. The possibilities are numerous.

The following section will briefly discuss the major categories of bond funds whose return and volatility are related to maturity length. Before buying any fund, make sure you know what securities it holds; then read the description corresponding to the actual holdings.

Remember, however, that even if the credit quality of the securities in a bond fund is impeccable, any long-term fund will have significant market (interest rate) risk.

Short-Intermediate Funds: 1-3 Years

This group has a somewhat shorter maturity than Lipper's "short" category which consists of funds with maturities of one to five years. I have singled it out as a separate category because a number of large and well managed fund groups have funds that specifically limit maturity length to three years or less. The rationale behind this group is that this maturity sector will capture a higher yield than is available in money market funds; and that the very short maturities will reduce volatility, compared to long-term portfolios.

There are not many funds in this group. But it includes both taxable and tax-exempt funds. Taxable funds invest at both ends of the credit quality spectrum, in governments, for higher credit quality; or in corporates, for higher yield. Tax-exempt funds invest in a variety of credit qualities.

Since their inception, these funds have achieved their objectives with mixed success. Volatility has been dramatically lower than for longer term funds (the largest declines to date in the price per share have been on the order of 5 percent to 6 percent); but so has total return. Current yield numbers are usually about

50 to 100 basis points higher than those of the higher yielding money market funds.

However, this relationship varies depending on the current shape of the yield curve. In late 1991, short rates dropped far more steeply than long rates. As a result, the yield curve became much more steeply upward sloping and the pick-up in yield of short-intermediate funds compared to money market funds became much more significant: about 130 basis points for tax-exempt funds, and over 250 basis points for taxable funds. At that point, these short-intermediate funds were particularly attractive to an investor seeking to increase yield without significant interest rate exposure. During 1988, however, when the yield curve was inverted, the yield of short-intermediate funds went below that of money market funds.

Total return for these funds is variable. In 1987, for example, total return for the year for both taxable and tax-exempt short-intermediate funds was close to zero, because a significant rise in interest rates caused a decline in NAV approximately equal to the dividend distributions. But for 1991, total return of these funds will probably exceed that of money funds by a significant amount.

For the most recent three years and five years, total return has been either close to or somewhat better than for money market funds, as is shown in Exhibit 11.3.

Exhibit 11.3
Total Return of (Short-Intermediate) and of Money Market Funds, through Dec. 1990

	Tax-Exempt		Taxable	
	Short Intermediate	Money Market	Short-Term Bond	Money Market
3 Year	18.9%	17.1%	25.9%	25.7%
5 Year	33.4%	27.8%	44.4%	42.2%

Note: There is no general source of data for these funds. Data was obtained directly by contacting the management company. This data, for the T. Rowe Price funds, is typical of what you would find for this group.

Alternatives to these funds would depend on your objectives. For maximum liquidity, consider a money market fund. For higher total return, go out a little further on the yield curve to the next group. If you have more than $10,000 to invest and if you can hold the security for two to five years, consider either short-term tax-exempt paper or Treasuries. (See the sections on Treasury-direct, and on pre-refunded tax-exempt bonds.)

Intermediate Funds (4-10 years)

This group corresponds approximately to the group called intermediate by Lipper, with a maturity of five to ten years. The rationale behind this group is similar to that of the shorter (1-3 year funds); but the position further along the yield curve captures a higher yield, while holding down volatility (compared to the longest term portfolios).

During the 1980s, funds whose maturity has clustered between 7 and 10 years have proved to be unusually attractive investments. This has been partly due to a demand anomaly. During that period, the longer intermediate maturities (corresponding to the 7-10 year mark) have been orphans, with relatively fewer buyers than either longer or shorter maturities. At the beginning of the 1990s, this continues to be the case. As a result, as is shown in Exhibit 11.2, total return for this maturity sector has been almost equal to that of long-term funds in the taxable sector; and only somewhat lower for the tax-exempt sector. Volatility for this group, however, is significantly higher than it is for the short-intermediate group, closer in fact to that of longer term bond funds. In 1987, for example, when some long-term bond funds suffered declines of close to 20 percent, declines for intermediate funds were generally no more than 15 percent. On the other hand, short-intermediate funds, with maturities under three years, experienced declines of 5 percent or less.

This category includes both taxable and tax-exempt bond funds; credit quality varies somewhat from fund to fund; but it is not a critical variable. Tax-exempt bond funds have been the stars of this group (again, because the yield curve for municipals tends to be more steeply sloping than that of Treasuries).

Funds in this group are suitable to diversify a bond portfolio. There is a significant difference between the best and the worst performing funds in this sector, so look at a number of alternatives before you leap.

Long-Term and High Yield Funds

Funds that are called either long-term or high yield are among the oldest bond funds. In this section, high yield refers to funds that are called high yield because they hold long-term securities (junk bond funds are discussed elsewhere).

The key characteristic of this group is an average maturity of between 15 and 25 years. Swings in NAV can be violent over short term periods. In 1987, the worst year to date, long-term funds suffered declines of close to 20 percent of principal value within a six month period. Total return for that year was negative for the worst performing funds and it was close to zero for the best.

Some fund managers in this group vary maturity length a good deal from one year to the next. If managers anticipate a rise in interest rates, maturity is shortened to reduce volatility (maturity may be dropped to the intermediate range). If they anticipate a decline in rates, maturity length is increased to capture capital gains. Current maturity of a long-term fund can be checked with the fund's marketing people.

Because the share price of these funds goes up and down a lot, they should be not be bought for holding periods of under one year. There is no way to predict what share price will be if you need to redeem within a short period of time.

Consider buying such a fund to diversify a large portfolio. Also, if you think interest rates are about to go down, these funds are an attractive speculation. Remember finally that while many of these funds appeal to safety minded investors by stressing credit quality, high credit quality does not protect against interest rate risk.

Long-term taxable and tax-exempt funds will be discussed separately.

Taxable (Long-Term) Funds   Funds in this group have average maturities of between 15 and 25 years. Alternate names for funds in this group might be: "income," "corporate," "governments" and the like. These funds may hold corporate bonds, Treasuries, government agency paper, GNMAs, and so on, in any combination. Many of the names in this fund group do not identify the actual securities in the fund. More importantly, many fund names also do not contain any meaningful clue concerning the average maturity of the fund. This is important because the long average maturity of these funds is their chief risk factor.

Because of the publicity surrounding junk bonds in 1989 and 1990, and their extremely poor performance during those years, a number of taxable funds with average maturities around the 20-year mark, which might formerly have been called "hi-yield" or "high income" funds are taking the term "hi-yield" out of their name, and renaming themselves "high income."

Returns for this maturity sector have varied from fund to fund. The best among the long-term funds have had the highest total returns of all fixed-income funds (about twice those of money market funds for the decade of the 1980s). You might expect total return to be highest for funds holding corporates, rather than governments. But this has varied from year to year. Funds holding mainly Treasury or government agency paper have done particularly well going into recessionary periods; or whenever there is market instability and a so-called "flight to quality" takes place.

Funds holding Treasuries may yield more than corporates on a net-after-tax basis because of the exemption from state taxes. For tax-sheltered accounts, consider high quality corporate funds.

If you do not want to risk any loss of principal, and if you are investing in Treasuries, remember that buying Treasuries individually is actually safer than buying them through a bond fund. That is because if you buy individual Treasury issues, you are guaranteed to get your principal back in full when the Treasury matures. But you cannot know what the price of a bond fund will be when you want to sell your shares.

Tax-Exempt (Long-Term) Funds

General Municipal Bond Funds.   The general, tax-exempt bond funds are the veterans of the industry: a few had their inception in the 1970s. Average maturity for these funds is typically in the

16 to 25 year range and the portfolio is extremely diversified: geographically; by type of bond (both revenues and GOs); and by credit quality. Income from dividends is federally tax-exempt, but taxable in most states.

What was stated for long-term taxables applies equally to this group. Short-term price swings are highly unpredictable and can be significant. On the other hand, because of the high degree of diversification and continual monitoring of credit quality, shareholders are protected against significant credit risk. For the decade of the 1980s, total returns of this group have been very high. Indeed, for investors in the higher tax brackets, these funds would have outperformed any taxable bond fund.

Because municipal bond funds have proved so popular, a number of more specialized variations have emerged.

Municipal High Yield Funds.   The first to emerge were the tax-exempt high yield funds. In spite of the similarity in name, there is simply no credit analog in the municipal market to the "high yield" junk bonds issued by leveraged corporations. Tax-exempt high yield funds hold issues in the riskier sectors of the tax-exempt market (for instance, hospitals, electric power, private purpose bonds, and the like, as well as some of the riskier GOs). Credit quality for these funds clusters around investment grade, or just below; but that is a far cry from corporate junk bond funds.

Since their inception in 1985, high yield municipal funds have performed exceptionally well. As a group, they have outperformed all other municipal bond funds, including those holding higher quality paper. In addition, and for reasons that are not entirely clear to anyone, volatility of high yield muni funds has actually been somewhat lower than for general municipal bond funds (you would expect the exact opposite). If a severe recession were to occur, however, the lower credit quality of these funds (compared to general municipal bond funds) would become a more significant risk factor. Also, if an interest rate spike were to occur, one would have to anticipate a price decline about equal to that of any fund in the same maturity sector.

Municipal—Insured (Long-Term) Bond Funds.   These are very recent, with the oldest dating back only to 1988. They invest in insured municipal bonds. Although called long-term, some of these funds have maturities of 10 to 12 years. Volatility for those funds should therefore be lower than for longer term funds.

Insured bonds yield somewhat less than uninsured bonds. Therefore, one would expect insured bond funds to have lower total returns than either general or high yield funds. However, during 1989, total returns of insured bond funds were as high as those of high yield funds. No one is quite sure why. In a recession, insured funds may outperform other municipal bond funds.

The combination of lower volatility (compared to the longest term funds) and high returns is particularly attractive. But because these funds are so recent, it is a bit early to predict whether they will continue to do as well as they have during the past two years.

Municipal—Single State Long-Term Bond Funds. Another recent wrinkle in tax-exempt bond funds has been long-term single state bond funds (average maturity anywhere from 10 to 20 years). These are tax-exempt to residents of the state as well as federally tax-exempt. (Some of these funds are also called high yield—in order to distinguish them from tax-exempt single state *money market* funds.) Advertising of these funds is based heavily on the dual tax exemption.

There are two disadvantages to funds in this group. Because they have become very popular, the net-after-tax yield may be significantly lower than for general municipal bond funds. (The phrase "high yield" in this instance is either meaningless or misleading). The other disadvantage is a lack of diversification. If the region experiences an economic downturn, the credit quality of all the bonds in the fund deteriorates, and this may result in a decline in the fund's NAV. Moreover, the NAV of these funds goes up and down like that of any other long-term bond fund in response to interest rates. I do not recommend these funds unless there is a significant yield pick up (net-after-tax) compared to long-term general bond funds.

Single State Insured Long-Term Bond Funds. Yes, there are long-term, insured, single state bond funds, with double tax exemption. Again, these are very recent, but they represent an improvement compared to single state general bond funds since the insurance protects somewhat against price volatility due to deteriorating credit quality. Check the maturity length (which will be

an important clue to potential volatility) and the track record before purchasing. Monitor new funds before committing a lot of
money.

Let's briefly summarize some key points relating to long-
term municipal bond funds. Before buying any municipal bond
fund, compute the taxable-equivalent yield illustrated in Chapter
7 to determine whether tax-exempts will net more for you than
taxables.

Curiously, if one excludes single state bond funds, total return for all long-term municipal bond funds (whether general,
high yield, or insured) has not varied significantly from group to
group during the past few years. The riskiness of these funds so
far seems to have been governed more by maturity length than
by the credit quality of the fund. That, however, may be due to
conditions in the credit markets that were unique to the 1980s. It
would be prudent, for example, in spite of their excellent total
return over the past few years, to consider muni "high yield"
funds as somewhat riskier than funds holding higher quality
credits.

Like long-term taxable funds, these funds should be not be
purchased for holding periods under one year. They should be
purchased to diversify a very large portfolio; and possibly, for
those wishing to speculate, to make interest rate bets (if you think
interest rates are about to decline).

FUNDS WHOSE PRICE GOES UP AND DOWN:
BONDS WITH UNIQUE RISK FACTORS

This section will discuss funds whose total return is governed by
factors that are unique to each group.

Exhibit 11.4 shows the cumulative total return of funds in
this category through December of 1990. Cumulative total return
includes the reinvestment of all dividends and capital gains distributions (if any), and any changes in share price.

High Yield Funds (Corporate - Junk)

So-called "junk bond funds" invest in corporate bonds rated
highly speculative. That rating indicates a strong possibility of de-

Exhibit 11.4
Performance Summary, through Dec. 1990

All distributions—dividends and capital gains—are assumed to be reinvested.

	1 Year	5 Years	10 Years
GNMAs*	9.63%	51.68%	210.34%
High Current Yield (Junk)	−11.08	11.12	131.39
Short World Income	18.33	NA	NA
World Income General	12.42	114.22	NA

*10 Year Result for GNMAs (through Dec. 31, 1989)   153.51%

NA—Not available.

Source:Derived from *Fixed-income Fund Performance*, Jan. 1991, pp. 128-129, published by Lipper Analytical Services, Inc., N. J.

fault. This is the only type of bond fund where the primary source of risk is credit quality.

These funds are a perfect illustration of the fact that high yield does not necessarily translate into high total return. As of December 1990, total return was negative for the preceding two years, in spite of a current yield averaging an astronomically high 13 percent to 15 percent for 1990. This means at the end of two years, even after adding back the high dividend, an investment was worth less than two years earlier. For the previous five-year period, cumulative total return was lower than for virtually risk-less money market funds.

That was not always the case. After their inception, junk bonds (and junk bond funds) had very high total returns for four years. Indeed, directly as a result of these high returns, junk bond funds attracted large cash inflows: "experts" theorized that junk bonds would always generate excess returns. Then, in 1989 and 1990, in spite of diversified holdings, NAV of the funds plummeted as buyers disappeared and the market for junk bonds essentially shut down. Junk bond funds lost an initial 30 percent of NAV in about 6 months, and another 15 percent to 25 percent the following year.

When NAV began declining, investors in junk funds began bailing out. As outflows increased, bond fund managers were forced to sell into the decline, causing the decline to steepen. In order to cope with the continuing outflow of monies from their funds, managers of junk bond funds instituted a variety of measures. Some cut dividends. Others changed the name of their fund. Still others merged the junk bond funds with other funds in the same fund family, or changed the investment policies of the funds.

As a direct result, in 1991, there were few genuine "junk bond" funds left. The mutual fund groups that continued to provide the real article adopted the policy of routinely advising anyone asking for information on junk bond funds that these are considered speculative; and furthermore, that the high dividend yield was the result of a dramatic drop in price and was unlikely to be maintained.

Of course, because the market is perverse, 1991 was also the precise point that a rally in junk bond funds occurred. Between January and September, the NAV of these funds rose by about 10 percent. That translates into a total return for that time period in excess of 20 percent. However, cumulative total return for the last five-year holding period is still low because of the disastrous declines of 1989 and 1990.

Because of the imperative need to diversify, mutual funds represent the only practical way for the average individual to invest in junk bonds. Nonetheless, junk bond funds should continue to be considered highly speculative.

If this area attracts you, you should be aware that whereas even a poorly managed junk bond fund will at least be somewhat diversified, a number of the worst performing junk bond funds have had truly abysmal total returns, well below the average for the group. The worst performing junk bond funds suffered losses of close to 50 percent in 1990, after losing 25 percent in 1988. (This means that an investment worth $10,000 at the beginning of 1988 would have shrunk to approximately $2500 at the end of 1990, even after adding back the dividends).

These funds are suitable only as a speculation (that is, for money that you can afford to lose) and only for investors holding a very large, and otherwise well diversified portfolio.

Long-Term GNMA Funds

As a group, GNMA funds continue to attract enormous sums: the largest bond fund is a GNMA fund that has about $11 billion in assets. GNMA fund advertising focuses on two very appealing themes: their high dividend yield (GNMAs yield more than Treasuries); and the unconditional government backing, which eliminates credit risk. It is therefore a shock to some buyers of GNMA funds to discover that the high credit quality does not eliminate market risk.

On the plus side, GNMA funds require a much lower initial investment than individual GNMAs (usually, $1,000 compared to $25,000). Because of the unpredictability and complexity of GNMA cash flows, bond funds represent the best way to invest in this security. The size of the funds results in more predictable cash flows (compared to individual GNMAs). Also, investors in GNMA funds are able to reinvest interest and mortgage prepayments automatically, and at a high rate, thereby boosting total return. Finally, GNMA funds can buy GNMA instruments far more economically than individuals.

GNMA funds, however, share the negative aspects of the underlying instruments. Their NAV is as volatile as that of long-term bond funds, but the behavior of GNMA funds is as quirky as that of GNMA securities. In strong markets, when interest rates decline, GNMA funds generally underperform long-term funds. Also, if interest rates drop massively, prepayment risk is high. A speed-up in prepayments would result in a decline in NAV; and it would also lower dividend yield. If interest rates go up, the NAV of GNMA funds plummets. There have been several periods when GNMA funds experienced very substantial drops in NAV (between 1979 and 1982, for example, NAV of some GNMA funds declined up to 30 percent in a few months).

Total return for GNMA funds is difficult to predict. When interest rates are stable, these funds do well, because of the high dividend yield. In volatile markets, total return may be disappointing. Between 1985 and 1989, total return for GNMA funds was about the same as that of shorter intermediate funds, and well below that either of long-term funds or longer intermediates. At the end of 1989, total return was significantly lower for 10 and 12 year holding periods (based on average yields published by

Lipper) than that of long-term funds, but it improved the following year.

Since 1988, a new type of GNMA fund has come on the scene. It invests in adjustable rate mortgages. The rationale is that the yield will fluctuate with prevailing interest rates, and as a result, principal value will remain stable. This stability, however, is accompanied by a lower dividend yield, which may significantly lower total return (compared to "normal" GNMA funds). These funds are too recent to generalize about future price and return performance.

Because GNMA advertising focuses so heavily on yield, some of the more poorly managed funds used to play games in order to boost the advertised yield. Prior to 1987, advertised GNMA yields included return of principal as income (it is actually a return of your own money). SEC regulations have eliminated this abuse. Nonetheless, be aware that total return for GNMA funds (from the best to the worst) varies significantly from fund to fund. The best performing GNMA funds manage for total return. Before purchasing a GNMA fund, be sure to check the fund's history and total return, compared to other GNMA funds.

If you already own a GNMA fund, and if you are happy with it, by all means continue holding it, especially if you have already paid a commission. But if you are investing new money, also consider other alternatives. If stability of principal is a primary concern, consider five-year Treasuries. If you are looking for high total return, consider longer intermediate bond funds. Also, for IRA or Keogh accounts, consider mutual funds investing in zeros if rates are attractive.

If you are investing in GNMAs through a fund, be sure to read the chapter on GNMAs in order to understand the nature of these very complex instruments. It is important to understand that whenever long-term interest rates drop massively, this increases prepayment risk for holders of GNMA securities.

International Funds

This group corresponds to the category called "World Income General" by Lipper.

If I had to pick the most beleaguered bond fund manager, the manager of an international bond fund would be a strong candidate. This manager may purchase bonds issued in any country, in any maturity. Consider his dilemma. Bonds issued by foreign corporations or foreign governments are subject to the same risks as U. S. securities: credit risk and interest rate risk; and these vary enormously from country to country.

But international bond funds are subject to additional risks. The most important of these is currency risk since bonds are purchased in American dollars. Currencies fluctuate even more unpredictably and dramatically than interest rates. There is also what is known technically as sovereign risk; that is, the risk deriving from the political and the economic system of foreign countries, some with highly unstable governments, and even less stable economies. Finally, physical purchase of the securities can be very difficult. Settlement dates vary all over the lot, and delivery of the securities can take as long as a year in some of the less developed countries.

Because of these difficulties, individual investors will find that mutual funds represent the easiest method of investing in international bonds. (If you would like to try investing on your own, you should be aware that although Standard & Poor's and Moody's are establishing a toehold in Europe, most foreign bonds remain unrated.) In no other aspect of bond fund investing are returns so variable from fund to fund, and so unpredictable.

Most of these funds represent a bet against the dollar: they prosper when the dollar declines against foreign currencies. The first international bond funds were introduced in 1985. For the first three years, as the dollar declined steeply, these funds soared. The greatest part of total return was capital gains, resulting from the decline in the value of the dollar. In 1988 and 1989, as the dollar rose, the funds sank: total return was dismal. In 1990, the dollar dropped; once again, international funds were stars. But in 1991, the dollar rallied: once again, return for these funds was dismal.

There are several types of international bond funds. Global funds invest in U. S., as well as foreign bonds. International funds, on the other hand, invest only in foreign securities. Maturities of either global or international funds are in the short to intermediate range (between five and ten years). The main risk in these funds is currency risk (and not interest rate risk).

Short World Income Funds   In 1989 and 1990, a number of "short world income" funds were introduced. These are similar to the longer international bond funds, but their average maturity is shorter—between one and three years depending on the funds. Because average maturity is short, interest rate risk is low. The chief risk factor of these funds is the currency risk.

In 1990, total return for these funds was very high (18.3 percent, according to Lipper). There were two reasons for this. Interest rates outside the United States were higher than in the United States. And the dollar declined against most foreign currencies. Because 1990 returns were so high, these funds became very "hot." In 1991, however, the total return of these funds has been far lower.

If these funds appeal to you, remember that if the dollar rises against foreign currencies, or if short-term interest rates abroad decline, then total return of "short world income" funds will necessarily decline and may become negative.

The potential total return of any international fund is unpredictable. Risk is high and derives from the inherent unpredictability of currency fluctuations.

International bond funds are suitable as a speculation; to diversify a portfolio; and as a hedge against the dollar.

Zero Coupon Bond Funds

These funds invest in zero coupon bonds (strips). There are several important differences between zero bond funds and other bond funds. Unlike other bond funds, zero bond funds buy securities that all mature at the same date. As a result, the price of the fund can be expected to return to par on the maturity date of the fund. But because the fund is made up of zeros, the price behavior of these funds is analogous to that of an individual zero with the same maturity length. Some of these funds are called "target" funds, the target being the maturity date. Average maturities for these funds vary from short to long.

The key risk factor for these funds is interest rate risk. But these funds are singled out as a special category because their price behavior is unique. Since U. S. Treasuries are used for strips, the credit quality of these funds is impeccable. But because zero coupon bonds are about 2 1/2 times as volatile as other bonds of comparable maturity, "zero" coupon funds (even those with inter-mediate maturities) are the most volatile of all bond funds, even more volatile than the longest bond funds. When interest rates decline, funds holding longer zeros are invariably the best per-forming bond funds as measured by total return. If interest rates rise, however, total return plummets.

Zero coupon bond funds in effect represent a way of lever-aging bond fund returns. (Indeed, many managers of corporate or government bond funds buy a few zero coupon bonds to boost total return if they anticipate that rates will drop.)

The maturity of zero bond funds can be selected to coincide with known future expenses (for instance, a child's admission to college; retirement; a trip, and so forth). If the funds are held to that maturity date, there is no credit risk, no interest rate risk, and no reinvestment risk. The actual total return is known and guar-anteed. But if they have to be resold before their maturity date, their volatility turns these funds into very high risk investments.

The main advantage of investing in zeros through funds is that transaction costs may be lower than for individual securities. Individual zeros, when sold in small amounts, have high mark-ups.

Because volatility is so high, funds holding mainly zeros should be bought as short-term holdings only if you are frankly speculating on short-term interest moves. "Zero" funds are suit-able as long-term holdings in order to fund future expenses whose dates are known, such as retirement, or a child's college education. Note that the tax treatment of zero bond funds is like that of individual securities. (There is currently no Lipper data available for this group; but volatility is so high—and returns so variable—that cumulative total return for long holding periods would be meaningless.)

Index Funds

The rationale behind bond index funds is analogous to that un-derlying equity index funds; namely, that few managers have bettered extremely broad, well-diversified indices. Portfolio turnover and expense ratios are low (because to manage the fund, the manager needs only to mirror the chosen index). Price behavior and total return mirror that of the chosen benchmark index.

These funds are a recent innovation. To date, Vangard—which pioneered stock index funds—is the only management company to offer index funds. Currently available are: a bond index fund keyed to the Salomon Brothers high grade index (high quality corporates); and an international bond fund keyed to several international benchmark indices. The funds are too small, and too recent, to permit any kind of generalization.

Because benchmark indices track a very large number of securities (numbering sometimes into the thousands), it would be impossible for any individual investor to put together a portfolio that would mirror an index. To date, the bond index funds also have held far fewer issues than the benchmark indices. But through the use of mathematical models, they are able to approximate the chosen index. Unmanaged equity index funds have been highly successful. Any investor interested in diversifying a core bond portfolio would do well to investigate these funds.

Total Return, Flexible Funds

These again are quite recent. They are called such names as "total return fund" or "flexible fund." The objective of these funds is to manage for total return. They therefore try to boost the dividend yield by selecting the fund sectors, or the maturities, that are likely to appreciate the most over the short term. Leveraging techniques (buying or selling futures contracts, writing options) may also be permitted.

It is impossible at this point to generalize about total return for this group. This is because the key characteristic of these funds is to give the fund manager total freedom to select any sector, any security, and any maturity length. Some rely heavily on mathematical, quantitative models, which until recently had been available only to institutional investors. Since the track record of these techniques for institutional investors is uneven, it is hard to say whether they will be of benefit to individual investors. I would suggest investing in such a fund with the greatest caution, and with only a small amount of money, until they compile a more meaningful track record.

Evaluating Future Possibilities

Bond funds have been proliferating so rapidly that, no doubt, new varieties will continue to appear. The criteria used in the preceding sections should enable you to evaluate both potential risk and potential total return. The questions to ask yourself are the following:

- what is the average maturity of the fund's portfolio? If it is short (under two years), interest risk is low. If average maturity is intermediate (4 to 10 years) interest rate risk is higher. Long-term funds will have the highest risk.

- Is there a currency risk?

- Is there credit risk? Credit risk would be significant only if the credit quality of the fund is below investment grade.

- How high is dividend yield expected to be, and what is that based on? Remember that very high yield translates into high risk. Investigate the risk factors before you buy.

- Finally, how much freedom does the manager have in determining what to buy? If he has total freedom, then what kinds of track record has he established?

- As a result of all these factors, how volatile is NAV expected to be?

CONCLUSION AND SUMMARY

The preceding discussion indicates that over the past 10 years, certain types of funds (long-term funds, intermediate funds, high yield municipal funds, GNMA funds) have had exceptional total returns. For this period, also, total return has been almost directly related to maturity length. The longest term funds outperformed intermediate funds; and those in turn outperformed money market funds.

One would naturally want to know: will longer term funds continue to have higher total returns than shorter funds? The answer to that question is a qualified yes. Over long holding periods, longer term funds should continue to have higher total return than shorter term funds, if for no other reason than dividend yield is higher. Because of compounding, and because dividends will be reinvested at higher rates, longer term funds should have higher total returns than shorter term funds.

But this scenario is contingent on what happens to interest rates. If rates remain relatively stable, or if they continue to decline from current levels, the longest term funds will continue to have higher total returns than shorter maturity funds and money funds by a substantial margin. But if rates rise, or if they are turbulent, then total return of long-term bond fund would be highly unpredictable for short holding periods and may very well be negative long term.

Moreover, the exceptional returns enjoyed by certain categories of bond funds (for instance, the longer intermediate funds or high yield municipal bond funds) may very well be tied to a combination of factors unique to the 1980s, and these factors may not repeat. Therefore, it would be prudent to take very literally the standard disclaimer that one finds on all prospectuses; namely, that past performance should be not taken as a prediction of future results.

A related question is whether during the 1990s, total return from bond funds is likely to match the exceptional returns of the 1980s. The answer to that is no. Even if long rates were to continue to drop through the 1990s, total return would be lower than during the 1980s because interest rates, and as a result, reinvestment rates, are currently a lot lower than they were at the beginning of the 1980s.

Of course, rates could rise from current levels. But if that prospect makes you smile, remember this: a substantial rise in yields from current levels (say 200 to 300 basis points) would translate into a very substantial loss of principal for the longest term funds (as much as 25 to 30 percent).

Finally, let me add a caveat. One of the problems in evaluating bond fund performance and returns is that so many bond funds were established comparatively recently (within the last five years). Hence, many of the conclusions in these chapters must be considered preliminary and tentative. When more funds have been around for longer periods, more meaningful conclusions should be possible.

Some Do's and Don'ts for Buying Bond Funds

Let's summarize some general principles that should guide the purchase of bond funds.

- Don't buy any fund whose share price fluctuates if you are going to need the money in less than a year: you cannot know at what price you will be able to redeem.

- If you are investing primarily for "income" and safety of principal is important to you, don't buy the longest term funds or those with the highest stated yields. Those will be the riskiest funds. Instead, stick to funds that have intermediate (or shorter) maturities (whether taxable or tax-exempt) and that invest in high quality bonds.

- Where possible, for new money, buy no-load funds, with low expense ratios and no 12b-1plans. Fund groups that meet those criteria are listed in the preceding chapter.

- Before buying a fund, make sure you know exactly what securities are in it; check the current maturity length.

- Don't invest more than 20 percent of your bond portfolio in any bond fund that is long-term; international or junk. Only invest in these funds if you have a large, well-diversified bond or bond fund portfolio (minimum: $100,000). It's not necessary to own one of each.

- The more complex the security, the more expertise it requires, then the more appropriate it becomes to buy a fund rather than individual securities. Funds are the most efficient way for individual investors to own international bonds, GNMAs, junk bonds and corporates.

- Taxable bond funds are particularly useful for tax-deferred (or tax-sheltered) monies that you want to place in fixed-income securities.

■ Bond funds enable you to invest small sums efficiently, and to reinvest dividend interest effectively, thereby increasing compounding. (For tax-deferred monies, consider high quality corporate, GNMA, or zero funds).

Keeping Informed about Bond Funds

A number of prominent financial magazines periodically include bond funds in their mutual fund surveys. These guides are confusing because they normally do not include either maturity length or total return. Indeed, while some of these surveys assign letter ratings to indicate risk, those letter ratings tell you very little about the potential volatility of a fund. If you investigate the average maturity of a bond fund, that will tell you more about the riskiness of the fund than a letter rating. So will a brief look at the "per share data" table in the prospectus. Magazine surveys should be used primarily to locate funds that are no-load, have low expense ratios, and no 12b-1 plans, since that information is generally carried in the survey.

One excellent source of information concerning bond funds is a newsletter called *Morningstar,* located at 53 West Jackson Boulevard, Chicago, IL, 60604. The phone number is (800) 876-5005. *Morningstar* contains detailed and in-depth analysis of individual mutual funds. It rates fund management, details holdings of the funds, average maturities of the securities in the fund, and so on. *Morningstar* should be available in most large public libraries.

The most complete surveys of bond fund returns and performance are published by Lipper Analytical Services, on a monthly basis. Unfortunately, you will find them only in very large libraries or in the libraries of large business schools.

Another excellent source are the surveys published by Wiesenberger Financial Services. Wiesenberger publishes two monthly newsletters and an annual survey of mutual fund results. The Wiesenberger surveys are more readily available in large public libraries than the Lipper surveys. They can also be found in the libraries of large business schools.

One excellent but easily overlooked source of information on no-load funds is the literature put out by the no-load mutual fund groups listed in the preceding chapter. Its purpose is to guide you to funds within each fund family that are most appropriate to your needs. These mutual fund groups want happy shareholders. Their general literature and periodic reports are informative and clearly written. These groups also usually send periodic newsletters to shareholders which include historical performance data for their funds; and information on the interest rate outlook of their economists.

Several of these groups have truly distinguished themselves in the level of additional information that they provide to shareholders. T. Rowe Price, for example, has developed planning kits (for retirement planning, and for portfolio planning) that are models of clarity. As another example, in 1988, Mr. Bogle, the chairman of the Vanguard group, sent out a letter to holders of its junk bond fund warning of potential trouble ahead.

12

Closed-End Bond Funds and Unit Investment Trusts (UITs)

This chapter discusses

- *the main characteristics of closed-end bond funds*

- *when to buy closed-end funds*

- *Unit Investment Trusts (UITs)*

CLOSED-END FUNDS

Closed-end funds are an arcane and specialized corner of the market. Nonetheless, their popularity has increased enormously during the 1980s. Under the right circumstances, they represent attractive investment vehicles. But they are not for everyone because they require that the investor become familiar enough with this type of fund to know when the investment is attractive, and when it is not. The following questions and answers describe some of the major characteristics of closed-end fixed-income funds.

How do closed-end funds differ from mutual funds?

Like mutual funds, closed-end funds are comprised of a diversified portfolio of a specific kind of financial asset (stocks, municipal bonds, government bonds, etc.) managed by a professional manager. There is an enormous variety of closed-end bond funds. They are available for munis, for international bonds, for convertible bonds, for corporate bonds, and so on, and with varying average maturities. Individuals may buy or sell into the portfolio by buying or selling shares of a fund.

There are, however, important differences between closed-end funds and mutual funds. You will recall that mutual funds are technically known as open end investment trusts. That means that they continually issue new shares. When investors buy shares in a mutual fund, the manager buys more securities and the fund grows. The net asset value (NAV) of the mutual fund is determined entirely by the value of its assets.

A closed-end fund, on the other hand, issues a fixed number of shares. Even though the portfolio may change, the number of shares of the fund remains fixed. That is why it is called a closed-end fund. After issue, a closed-end fund trades on one of the stock exchanges. Its price is determined like that of any stock: namely, by the demand for that particular stock. A closed-end fund share may sell for more than its net asset value (NAV). When that happens, the closed-end fund is said to be trading at a premium. A closed-end fund share may also sell for less than its net asset value. It is then said to be trading at a discount.

Like bond mutual funds, a closed-end bond fund has a continually managed portfolio, typically consisting of 30 to 60 issues. Also, like bond mutual funds, a closed-end fund never "matures." Therefore, its price will not, like that of an individual bond, return to par automatically. Finally, again as for bond mutual funds, the price of a closed-end fund will fluctuate with interest rates; and those fluctuations are governed by the average maturity of the closed-end bond fund. That means that closed-end bond funds with longer maturities will have greater price volatility than closed-end bond funds with shorter maturities.

But the price fluctuations of closed-end bond funds are more complex than those of bond mutual funds because the price of the closed-end bond fund will also fluctuate depending on demand. For instance, if interest rates decline, demand for closed-end bond funds with high yields may increase, therefore driving up their price. In fact, the price of a closed-end fund may be going up while its NAV is going down; and vice versa.

Why should closed-end funds not be bought at the time of issue?

When a closed-end fund is issued, its initial offering price includes a hidden cost, typically between 7 percent and 8 percent. This is the so-called underwriting spread, which goes to the underwriter. This spread means that about $700 to $800 is taken out of an initial investment of $10,000. That is only the first injury to your pocketbook. Typically, once a closed-end fund starts trading, its price goes to a discount. That is to say, its price declines; and the value of your principal declines. Why closed-end funds move to a discount after they start trading is somewhat unclear. But the existence of this phenomenon has been extensively documented.

The obvious conclusion is that one should never buy any closed-end fund at the time of issue. Unfortunately, this is precisely the time that brokers are most likely to tout these funds because this is the time that they earn the highest commission.

If you are buying a closed-end bond fund for income, why not buy at the time of issue?

During the 1980s, the most popular closed-end funds have been those investing in fixed-income securities, perhaps due to the general popularity of bond funds. New issues have been snapped up.

Caution, however, is in order. When you buy a closed-end bond fund at the time of issue, the portfolio has not been constituted. The manager has no money with which to buy bonds until the shares of the fund are sold. You cannot know accurately what securities will be in the portfolio (therefore credit quality is unknown); or what its yield will be. It may take the fund three to six months to become fully invested, and in the interim, your money is likely to be parked in Treasury bills.

The bottom line is that, when you purchase a closed-end bond fund at the time of issue, you are purchasing an unknown portfolio and yield. Remember also that you will be paying a hidden cost of 7 percent to 8 percent; and that the price of the fund is likely to move to a discount. Therefore, if you are investing primarily for income, purchasing a closed-end bond fund at the time of issue would appear to make no economic sense, particularly since there are any number of more attractive alternatives.

When should I buy a closed-end fund?

Many investors purchase closed-end funds primarily as trading vehicles: that is, for speculative purposes. The opportunity for profit derives from the changing size of the discount, as well as from fluctuations in the share price. When the discount narrows, or when the price of the fund moves closer to its NAV, the investor realizes a profit. The ideal trade would involve buying at a wide discount to NAV, and selling when the fund moves to a premium. To realize a profit, however, the fund need only to move to a narrower discount.

This piece of advice, however, is deceptively simple. Complex strategies have been developed for trading closed-end funds. For example, one leading expert, Thomas Herzfeld, suggests that before you buy any closed-end fund, you track its price for a lengthy period of time. He suggests buying only when the discount is 3 percent wider than the normal discount for that fund. If you want to invest in closed-end bond funds, then you either must be willing to research the patterns that determine discounts for specific funds; or you should seek out someone who is a specialist and can demonstrate a track record in that area, to you.

When are closed-end bond funds attractive vehicles for income?

If you can buy a closed-end bond fund in the secondary market at a discount to NAV, you are, in effect, purchasing the underlying bonds for less than you would have to pay for similar bonds on the open market. That raises the net dividend yield that you will earn. Suppose, for example, that you purchase a fund at a 10 percent discount to NAV. Suppose further that the fund has a current yield of 6 percent based on NAV. The net yield of the fund, compared to the discounted price you paid, will be 6.7 percent. You will, moreover, be purchasing a continually managed, diversified portfolio, at an attractive commission cost since the transaction costs of buying closed-end funds trading in the secondary market are low.

If you are purchasing such a fund primarily for income, another guideline is to compare the expense ratio of the fund (expenses as a percentage of assets), and its income ratio (net income per share divided by net assets). If the discount exceeds the expense ratio, then you are essentially not paying the management fee.

Some other factors to consider would include:

- The exchange on which the fund trades (the largest funds trade on the NYSE, which would mean greater liquidity).

- The credit quality of the bonds in the portfolio.

- The fund's average maturity (funds with average maturities of under 10 years would be less volatile).

- How often the dividend is paid (some funds pay dividends quarterly; others monthly).

Closed-end funds occasionally become "open ended." When that happens, the fund's NAV becomes its price. If the fund was purchased at a discount to NAV, that would provide a windfall profit. If, however, it was purchased at a premium (or at issue), that would result in a loss of principal. There is no certain way to predict which funds will become open-ended, but it happens occasionally.

Also, even if you purchase a closed-end bond fund primarily for income, if it is purchased at the right price, total return may be boosted by capital gains resulting from a narrowing of the discount. This is likely to happen if interest rates fall. But remember that this is a two-edged sword. If interest rates rise, the investor may suffer a double whammy as the price falls for two reasons: because of rising rates; and because investors are selling.

How do I determine the yield?

To determine the yield, total up net investment income per share and divide by the share price.

Some published yields of closed-end bond funds include capital gains distributions and return of capital (that is your own money being returned to you, and not earned income). The true yield is the interest income. It is, of course, a current yield. There is no yield-to-maturity since the fund does not mature. Total return will depend on price fluctuations for the fund, in addition to dividend yield.

How Can I Get Information on Closed-End Funds?

Closed-end bond funds are not extensively covered by the financial press. The *Barron's* weekend edition has the most complete listing, but even that information is sketchy. *The Wall Street Journal* publishes partial tables Monday and Wednesday: the two together constitute one complete listing. The *New York Times* also publishes partial listings. Exhibit 12.1 shows the format of a typical listing.

Reading from left to right, the table lists

- the name of the fund;

- the Net Asset Value (NAV) of one fund share;

- the price of the fund on the exchange (remember that a closed-end fund is a stock);

- the difference between the price of the fund and its NAV.

A minus sign indicates that the fund is selling at a discount to its net asset value; a plus, that it is selling at a premium. The yield of the fund portfolio is not quoted, nor is its average maturity length. The price you would pay would be the listed stock price, which is likely to fluctuate daily, plus the broker's commission. The commission structure is the same as that of any stock.

To obtain information on any fund, contact the funds directly. If the fund is trading in the secondary market, the prospectus will be unavailable. Ask for the latest annual and quarterly reports. Also, be aware that closed-end funds do not publish total return numbers. In any case, if you do find total return information for these funds, beware of comparing total return numbers for closed-end funds unless you know whether they are calculated based on price, or on NAV.

Exhibit 12.1
Format for Closed-End Bond Fund Listings

Tuesday, March 19, 1991
Unaudited net asset values of closed-end investment bond fund shares.

Bond Funds				Convertible Bond Funds		
	NAV	Stk. Price	% Diff		NAV	Stk. Price	% Diff
ACMGv	10.10	10⅞	+7.67	LnNCv	15.41	13⅜	−13.21
ACMGSp	8.76	8⅞	+1.31	PutnHi	6.82	6½	−4.69
AIMStra	8.63	7⅞	−8.75				
AmAdjR96	9.63	10⅛	+5.14	**International Bond Funds**			
AmGvt	7.17	7⅜	+2.86	FirstAusP	10.24	9⅝	−6.01
AmOplF	9.72	9⅞	+1.59	GlobalYd	8.73	8¼	−5.50
BlkStrTer	9.43	10¼	+8.70	WorldIn	8.87	8⅝	−2.76
Cigna	5.44	5⅜	−1.19				
ColInfT	10.90	10¼	−5.96	**Municipal Bond Funds**			
Currinc	12.06	11¾	−2.57	AllsMunIncO	9.28	9⅝	+3.72
1838Deb	20.06	21	+4.69	AllMuInT	10.14	10⅛	−0.15
FBosStr	9.21	8¾	−4.99	AllMuPre	9.35	9¼	−1.07
HanJl	15.19	15⅛	−0.43	ColInv	10.82	11¾	+8.60
HiIncAd	4.52	4⅝	+2.32	DrSIM	9.75	10½	+7.69
HiYlFd	6.73	6	−3.69	KmpStra	11.36	11⅝	+2.33
				MuniIns	9.97	10	+0.30

SUMMARY: QUESTIONS TO ASK BEFORE BUYING A CLOSED-END FUND

Am I buying at issue? If so, what is the underwriting spread?

What is the NAV of the shares?

Is the fund selling at a premium or at a discount?

What is the average discount for this type of fund?

What kinds of bonds are in the portfolio?

What is their average maturity and credit quality?

On what exchange does this fund trade?

Additional References

The most complete source of information on closed-end funds is the annual *Encyclopedia of Closed-End Funds,* published by Thomas J. Herzfeld Advisors, Inc. (The Herzfeld Building, P. O. Box 161465, Miami, Florida 33116). It is expensive ($125.00), but exhaustive. Most of the information contained in it is unavailable elsewhere.

UNIT INVESTMENT TRUSTS (UITs)

Unit investment trusts (UITs) represent a third type of bond fund. They are sold through brokers, either in brokerage firms or in banks; and on a commission basis, usually around 5 percent. When you buy a UIT, you are purchasing a diversified portfolio of securities. But that portfolio is quite different from either a mutual fund or a closed-end fund. The key characteristic of a UIT is that, once constituted, its portfolio remains unmanaged. With few exceptions, no bonds are added or sold out of the portfolio. Because the portfolio remains unmanaged, its price should rise towards par as the UIT approaches maturity.

The portfolio of a UIT is typically much less diversified than that of a mutual fund, consisting of perhaps as few as ten issues. While the portfolio is assigned a maturity date, that date is simply the date when the longest term bond in the portfolio matures. Each of the bonds in the portfolio may actually mature at a different date, over a span of time that may last as long as ten years. Each individual issue in the UIT is also subject to call risk. As each bond matures, or is called the principal is returned to the shareholders. Varying   percentages of the entire portfolio must then be reinvested.

There are UITs for as many purposes as mutual funds and individual securities: corporates, governments and municipals; in a variety of maturities, from intermediate to long. Merrill Lynch, Van Kampen and Merritt, Bear Stearns, and Nuveen are major sponsors. Some municipal portfolios are insured (the entire portfolio is insured, not each individual issue). There are also single-state municipal portfolios. Sponsors of UITs generally maintain a secondary market. But selling a UIT before it matures is somewhat more cumbersome than selling a mutual fund. Particularly during market downturns, UITs can be illiquid (that is, difficult, and expensive, to sell).

Note also that while a UIT quotes two yields, a current yield and a yield-to-maturity, the yield-to-maturity must be calculated with a formula that takes into account the different maturities of the bonds in the UIT. Therefore, the yield-to-maturity is not comparable to the yield-to-maturity quoted for individual bonds.

Brokers point to a number of features as advantages. Income is paid monthly, and since the portfolio does not change, the monthly amount is fixed. Moreover, since UITs are not actively managed, there is no annual management fee. This should theoretically result in a higher yield than for mutual funds with comparable credit ratings and maturities.

These arguments do not appear compelling. The yield advantage may be illusory or based on low credit quality. And the coupon is fixed only until the first bond matures out of the portfolio. Thereafter, as various bonds mature, the monthly coupon changes. Moreover, the shareholder will have to reinvest returned principal and coupons at an unknown rate.

In addition, compared to the purchaser of a mutual fund, the purchaser of a UIT has no protection of any kind against either interest rate risk or the deterioration of individual credits in the portfolio. You are purchasing a portfolio of issues, which will not change, and not a manager.

Finally, because each UIT is unique, each portfolio must be scrutinized with great care. Since UITs are advertised on the basis of yield, some UITs play games in order to quote higher current yields. For example, they buy high coupon bonds which might be subject to call. Or they buy bonds with questionable credit ratings. Municipal UITs were widely criticized after the Washington Public Power (WPPSS) default for stuffing their portfolios with the bond of the project which ultimately defaulted. This resulted in substantial losses that were passed on directly to shareholders.

The only advantage UITs offer compared to mutual funds is that, since the portfolio has a maturity date, its price rises towards par as the fund nears maturity. This might make UITs attractive to an investor who does not have sufficient funds to buy a diversified portfolio of individual securities; but who wants to know that principal will be returned in full, when the fund matures.

In sum, UITs offer somewhat more diversification than individual bonds; but few advantages compared to mutual funds. Because of the high initial commission, they should considered for purchase only as long-term holdings, and only after careful scrutiny of their portfolio and yield.

SUMMARY: QUESTIONS TO ASK BEFORE BUYING A UIT

What securities does the UIT hold?

What is the maturity of the portfolio?

What is the credit quality of the portfolio?

What are the call provisions of the issues in the UIT?

What is the size of the commission?

To whom could I resell the UIT if I need to sell before the UIT matures?

Do you stand ready to buy back the UIT? At what price?

PART IV

Portfolio Management

Investing is sometimes considered a complicated and mysterious process that is comprehensible only to initiates. Moreover, earning, spending, and investing are so bound up with deep emotions and needs that rational analysis often falls by the wayside. As a result, some of us invest like schizophrenics: we put some of our money in investments thought to be totally risk-free; and then we turn around and buy securities or investments that we don't understand, on faith, based on advice we fail to investigate.

Actually, anyone able to balance a checkbook can formulate and carry out an investment strategy. Anyone can accumulate assets, indeed, substantial assets. For most people, financial security is the result, not of making it big on one or more stocks, but rather, of patience, a reasonable game plan, a willingness to save some money—and time, which gives compounding a chance to work. The magic of compounding has been discussed elsewhere. What has not been discussed is how, simply by systematically investing some money each month, you can build up a very substantial nest egg. Exhibit A demonstrates how much can be accumulated by putting aside $100 a month, and allowing it to compound at a rate of return of 8 percent, for a period of thirty years. (I am illustrating an 8 percent rate of return because it is achievable.)

Convinced? The next question is: how do I manage this money? No topic in finance has caused more ink to flow. Millions of words and thousands of pages have been devoted to it. I won't

Exhibit A
The Magic of Compounding: What Happens to an Investment of
$100 per Month Earning an 8% Return, Compounded Monthly*

Year	Cumulative Investment	Cumulative Interest + Interest on Interest	Total Value
1	$ 1,200	$ 61	$ 1,261
4	4800	904	5,704
8	9,600	3,933	13,533
12	14,400	9,882	24,282
16	19,200	19,838	39,038
20	24,000	35,294	59,294
25	30,000	65,544	95,544
30	36,000	113,408	149,408

*(All dividends reinvested at 8%)

pretend that this section will contain the magic sesame that will make you really rich. There are, however, some basic principles that most financial professionals would subscribe to, and that anyone can put to use.

Chapters 13 and 14 will discuss how to formulate a game plan for investing and managing a portfolio. Let's start with one important caveat, however. It is not wise to put all of your financial assets entirely in fixed-income instruments. A discussion of a bond portfolio really makes very little sense if it is divorced from the larger concerns that drive overall portfolio management. Chapter 13 will therefore discuss overall portfolio management and the role of a bond portfolio within an overall investment strategy. Chapter 14 will then focus entirely on strategies for buying and managing a bond portfolio.

13

Overall Portfolio Management

This chapter discusses

- *a game plan for investing*

- *the defensive vs. the enterprising investor*

- *the historical returns of stocks, bonds, and cash equivalents*

- *a model portfolio of stocks and bonds for the defensive investor.*

A GAME PLAN FOR INVESTING

The first and most basic question about money management concerns you, and not money. It is this: how much time and effort are you prepared to spend on this endeavor? Some of us are really fascinated by finance. We like numbers. We like to get into the nitty-gritty of every security. And some of us lack either the time, or the interest to expend a great deal of time and energy on investment choices and decisions.

If you are reading this book, chances are that you are interested in managing your money better. But quick, ask yourself:

how have you invested money in the past? On what basis? How much time and effort have you devoted to finding out about potential investments? What is the level and depth of your information concerning investments? Have you simply asked a broker (or a friend) for suggestions and followed them? Or have you attempted to find sources of information that would lead to genuine expertise?

The Defensive vs. the Enterprising Investor

This distinction is important. In his classic book, *The Intelligent Investor*, Benjamin Graham distinguished between two types of investors: the defensive and the enterprising investor. The defensive investor is content to forego the highest possible rate of return in exchange for safety and freedom from concern. The enterprising investor, on the other hand, must have the time and the interest to thoroughly study investment choices.

This does not mean that the defensive investor buys securities that he does not understand. Quite the opposite! The important distinction between the two is the degree of involvement. The enterprising investor, as described by Graham, is someone who has the time, the training and the inclination to develop genuine expertise and skill, equal to or better than that of any professional who manages investments for a living. This is the key point. The enterprising investor has knowledge and skills at least equal to those of a professional money manager. Indeed, according to Graham, the enterprising investor considers his investments equivalent to a business enterprise.

This distinction remains as germane today as when Graham formulated it. Because few of us have the time and the disposition required of enterprising investors, it follows that most of us should consider ourselves defensive investors. This means that we should limit ourselves to securities that we understand, and which do not demand more time and expertise than we have.

Only you can decide what kind of an investor you are, where you are on solid ground, and what your limits are. On the other hand, a defensive investor, following some basic principles, can achieve very solid investment results. Indeed, Graham points out, that while it is not difficult to achieve quite good performance, it is extraordinarily difficult to do much better than that. Even extremely skilled professionals seldom succeed in consistently achieving results that are significantly above market averages.

The second important factor to consider is what is usually called "risk tolerance;" basically, how you react to losses. How much money are you willing to actually lose? What causes you to be uncomfortable or to actually lose sleep? What happens to you, to your ability to function, and to your gut, if you make a lot of money, or if you lose a lot of money? Are you investing for excitement and adventure, or for income? No one but you can answer those questions, and they have to be based on a knowledge of how you react to real life investing in assets that move up and down in price.

These questions should determine the proportions of your portfolio that you would want to place in riskier assets, and the kinds of risks you are willing to assume. Selecting instruments and strategies inappropriate to your risk tolerance will not only result in psychological distress. It can also cause you to lose a lot of money. The main culprit is panic, that is, panic buying or panic selling. In other words, buying high and selling low, which is the perfect recipe for investment disaster.

What Are Your Financial Goals?

Before you invest any money, you have to determine how you will ultimately use this money. You may be saving for an immediate goal such as a major purchase or a downpayment on a home. Or you may be saving to buy a car or an expensive vacation. You may also have more distant goals in mind such as planning for retirement and beyond, or for a child's college education. Alternatively, you may not have a specific goal in mind. You may simply be trying to accumulate assets for the distant future, in order to achieve a measure of financial independence and financial security. In that case, you would be managing mainly for long-term growth.

For investment purposes, the basic distinction between these goals is time. If you are saving for a specific purpose, and cannot afford to lose any of this money, then your choices are limited (this will be discussed in the next chapter). But if you are saving for the long term, and mainly for overall growth, then time becomes your most important ally because time means compounding. As explained previously, the power of compounding is truly astonishing, even for comparatively low yielding investments. When high yielding investments are allowed to compound, then it becomes truly awesome.

RISK AND TOTAL RETURN

Often, individual investors associate risk with safety of principal. An investment is considered riskless if there is no risk to principal. Conversely, an investment is considered risky if the value of principal goes up and down from year to year; or if returns vary from year to year.

That perspective, however, lacks one important dimension, namely, time. Risk has to be evaluated both short term and long term. The price of stocks, for example, goes up and down violently from year to year; short-term risk is extremely high. You may earn 30 percent one year; and lose 20 percent the next. But on a long-term basis, over long periods of time, stocks provide higher returns than so-called "riskless" investments.

One of the few guides to potential investment performance is a rearview mirror; that is, knowing the returns of different categories of assets over time. Such a perspective does not in any way predict short-term results, but it does establish reasonable expectations for long-term results.

Historical Returns of Stocks and Bonds

Let's briefly consider the total return of four classes of financial assets:

- stocks (often considered the riskiest asset);
- long-term government bonds (mistakenly considered a very conservative and safe investment);
- intermediate bonds;
- a "riskless" asset, T-bills.

One widely quoted source, the *1990 Yearbook* published by Ibbotson Associates[1], shows that between 1926 and 1989, stocks (as measured by the Standard and Poor's 500 Index) provided average annual returns of about 10 percent. Among fixed-income instruments, intermediate bonds provided the best returns, averaging 4.9 percent annually. Long-term government bonds (that is, 30-year Treasuries) came next, averaging about 4.6 percent. T-bills returned only 1/2 of 1 percent. If the returns from fixed-income instruments appear low, bear in mind that interest rates were very low through the early 1950s.

Another study[2] covering the period between 1950 and 1989 shows similar results. Once again, stocks (measured by the Standard and Poor's 500 Index) had the best overall returns, averaging 11.7 percent annually. And once again, intermediate (two-to-five-year) Treasuries led the fixed-income returns, averaging 6.4 percent. But for this period, T-bills, surprisingly, averaged slightly more than long Treasuries: 5.4 percent for T-bills vs. 5.1 percent for long-term Treasuries. (Remember that these are total returns: do not confuse with yield).

Viewed from this perspective, over long periods of time, the riskiest asset provided the highest return. Whatever their maturity range, bonds, the apparently more conservative asset, provided significantly lower returns than stocks. The higher returns of intermediate bonds were no doubt due to two factors noted previously; They yield more than shorter instruments; but they protect principal far better than the more volatile long-term bonds.

To really grasp what these numbers mean, and how compounding affects investments returns, let's translate these rates of return into dollars. Sinquefield calculated how much one dollar would have grown if invested in 1926 and dividends were reinvested through 1989. That dollar would have grown to $7.03 if invested in T-Bills; to $17.30 if invested in 30-year Treasuries; to $21.50 if invested in intermediate (two-to-five-year) Treasuries; but to $534 if invested in stocks.

---

1. Ibbotson and Sinquefield, *Stocks, Bonds, Bills and Inflation, 1990 Yearbook*. Chicago: Ibbotson Associates, 1991.
2. Neuberger and Berman Management Inc., 1990 Study by Research department.

Exhibit 13.1
**Table of Average Annual Total Returns of Stocks, Long-Term
Government Bonds, and T-Bills for every decade since the 1920s**

	1920s*	1930s	1940s	1950s	1960s	1970s	1980s
S & P 500	19.2%	0.0%	9.2%	19.4%	7.8%	5.9%	17.5%
Long Term Gov't	5.0	4.9	3.2	−0.1	1.4	5.5	12.6
T Bills	3.7	0.6	0.4	1.9	3.9	6.3	8.9
Inflation	−1.1	−2.0	5.4	2.2	2.5	7.4	5.1

*Based on the period 1926–1929

Source: *Stocks, Bonds, Bills and Inflation, 1990 Yearbook™,* Ibbotson Associates, Chicago (annually updates work by Roger G. Ibbotson and Rex A. Sinquefield). All rights reserved, p.16.

Finally, for some additional perspective, Exhibit 13.1 shows average annual returns for every decade since 1926 (again, total returns) for the same financial assets, and compares these to the rate of inflation during those decades:

Overall, over long periods of time, total return from stocks has been much higher than that of bonds. However, Exhibit 13.1 demonstrates that stock returns are highly unpredictable. For example, during the decade of the 1970s, which had the highest rate of inflation of any decade during the 20th Century, returns for stocks were far below average—about 5.9 percent. (That bear market cycle in bonds actually lasted from 1969 to 1982). Returns for long-term bonds during that same period were close to those of stocks—about 5.5 percent. But remember that during the 1970s, yields on long-term bonds soared, with long Treasuries yielding 16 percent in 1982. That 5.5 percent long-term bond return actually masks an enormous drop in the value of principal. In fact, during that entire period, both stocks and long-term bonds failed to keep up with inflation!

The most recent decade—the 1980s—stands out because it is totally exceptional. Stock returns for that decade almost matched those of the 1920s and the 1950s, the two best previous decades. Bond returns, however, were unprecedented. The exceptional total returns of bonds can be attributed first, to the very high level of interest rates at the beginning of the 1980s; and second, to the significant decline from those levels that occurred over the decade, adding significant capital gains to the dividend yields. Paradoxically, these spectacular bond returns followed three decades that can only be characterized as a bond crash that lasted three decades. Indeed, the investment returns of the 1980s are so exceptional that it is unrealistic, in the light of historical data, to expect that either the stock or the bond market will continue to have equally spectacular results.

What does this mass of data tell you? First of all, it says that it is always wise to put some assets in stocks. But also, it says that no two consecutive decades have been exactly alike. Don't plan on repeats! Finally, it says that investing only in the "safest instruments" (that is, money market funds, short-term CD's, as well as T-bills), carries a very high cost, namely, significantly lower returns than any other category of asset. This cost is particularly high since inflation further erodes real returns and causes a genuine loss of purchasing power.

Any investor will want to consider not only long-term returns (which the data demonstrates), but also, short-term volatility (not illustrated above). Short-term volatility is the extent to which returns vary from year to year. It may come as a surprise that during the 1980s, volatility of stock returns has been about average, that is, not unusually high for stocks. But it may come as an even bigger surprise that during the 1980s, the volatility of long-term bonds has been almost as high as that of stocks; and that consequently, total return of long-term bonds has been as difficult to predict as that of stocks over short term holding periods.

A Long-Term Portfolio for the Defensive Investor

The preceding perspectives can be put to use in formulating an investment plan for long-term growth; that is, any plan envisioned to last over several decades. A prudent investor would allocate his portfolio among stocks and bonds. The stock portion would constitute the volatile, but potentially higher return, part of the portfolio. Logically, bonds should then provide both safety of principal and predictable income.

This suggests two questions: First, is it possible to put together a portfolio comprised of both stocks and bonds that is uncomplicated enough to meet the needs of a defensive investor? And second, which bonds will provide the best combination of safety of capital and predictable returns?

The answer to the first question is: most definitely. Here is the model portfolio. It should be divided as follows:

- 60 percent two-to-five-year Treasuries (I shall call this the core bond portfolio);

- 40 percent a stock mutual fund—preferably, an index fund.

This looks very boring and ultra-simple. But actually, it meets every criterium for sound portfolio management. Let's consider each portion in turn.

Let's first look at the stock portion of the portfolio. I have suggested an index fund; that is, a fund that exactly duplicates a benchmark index. The most frequently used index is the Standard and Poor's 500 stock index. By its very nature, an index fund will never beat the market but it will mirror market performance almost exactly. Returns from an index fund will normally be slightly lower than the index. The difference is due to the fact that the index fund has some management expenses. An index does not.

An index fund offers a number of advantages when compared to other types of stock funds. First of all, while you might assume that if a fund does only as well as the market, its performance will be average, think again. Historically, 70 percent of mutual funds fail to do as well as the Standard & Poor's 500. Or, to put it differently, over time, an index fund beats 70 percent of all stock mutual fund managers. Second, an index fund usually has lower expense ratios than actively managed funds. You keep more of what the fund earns. Third, index funds make fewer capital gains distributions than most stock funds. As a result, over time, a larger portion of your stock investments compounds without annual taxation. Finally, an index fund eliminates the worry that if you select the wrong mutual fund, the market may do well while your fund does not. There is no need to pick the hot manager of the year, or the decade. (The oldest, largest, and most efficiently managed index fund—i. e., with the lowest expense ratio, is the Vanguard 500 Index fund.)

Now let's look at the bond portion of the portfolio. There is no need to repeat in detail what was stated in the chapter on Treasuries. But a brief review of the advantages of this core portfolio may be helpful:

■ This maturity sector yields more than short instruments. It captures about 85 percent to 95 percent of the return available on long-term bonds, but with far less volatility (and therefore far less risk to principal) than long-term Treasuries. Indeed, as the studies quoted elsewhere have shown, over two different time periods, the first lasting about 60 years, and the second lasting about 30 years, two- to five-year Treasuries have had higher total returns than either long-term bonds or T-bills.

■ Such a portfolio has zero credit risk. No diversification among different kinds of securities is required since the principal of any Treasury is 100 percent safe, whether you own $10,000 or one million.

■ For most individuals, the total return of Treasuries will probably be close to that of seemingly higher yielding fixed-income instruments for two reasons. First, individuals can buy Treasury securities more cheaply (that is, with lower commission costs) than any other debt instrument. In fact, if you buy through Treasury-direct, and hold to maturity, commission costs are zero. Second, a portfolio of Treasury securities is not taxable at the state and local level.

That's it. One can't imagine a portfolio that is simpler to buy and to manage. On the bond side, you eliminate credit risk entirely and a good deal of interest rate risk. On the stock side, you can stop worrying about which stocks or stock fund to buy; and when to buy. Annual expenses for managing such a portfolio are under 1/4 of 1 percent for the stocks; zero for the bonds if you buy through Treasury-direct.

Will this approach to investing earn the highest returns possible? No, that is unlikely. But remember that this portfolio is intended for an investor who does not wish to pursue complicated strategies. Moreover, over time this portfolio should do quite well. It will beat chasing hot tips or pursuing strategies that you may not understand. At the other extreme, it will also beat keeping your money entirely in CDs.

Studies have shown that over time, the most important factor in determining total return is not which specific assets you buy (that is, not whether you buy IBM stock as opposed to General Motors), but which categories of assets you own (that is, whether you own stocks as well as bonds). Timing of stock purchases is less important than many believe, as long as stocks are bought and held for the long term. A study conducted by T. Rowe Price Associates, for example, simulated the returns that an investor would have earned on stocks if that investor consistently bought at the top of every market, but then held his stocks for the long haul. Surprisingly, even this luckless investor would have done well, compared to one holding nothing but short-term instruments.[3]

In doing research for this book, I spoke to a number of professionals whose firms manage money for high net worth individuals, that is, individuals whose portfolio totals one million dollars and up. I was delighted to find that while these managers differ in their approach to stock investing, they all view the fixed-income portion of the portfolio very much as I describe it above. They concentrate their purchases (or limit them entirely) to intermediate securities, mainly Treasuries, and for the reasons described.

Variations on the Basic Portfolio

This portfolio is not intended as a rigid recipe. Rather, it embodies a number of principles:

- allocation among both stocks and bonds;
- uncomplicated securities and strategies;
- low transaction costs;
- diversification;
- a growth component and a stable, income producing component.

---

3. *The Price Report, No. 25, Fall 1989.*

All of these combined should produce long-term growth. Moreover, such an allocation can be adapted to almost any size portfolio. Diversification is not needed for Treasuries; and the index fund is inherently diversified.

The basic portfolio can easily be altered to meet a variety of needs. Suppose that you are in your thirties. Furthur suppose that you are beginning to put some money aside for retirement which seems to be forever away. You consider yourself a risk taker and you want to emphasize growth, rather than preservation of capital. Fine, then switch the proportions around. Invest 40 percent of your portfolio in 2-5 year Treasuries and 60 percent in the stock index fund.

Watching money compound is about as exciting as watching grass grow. If you like more excitement in your finances, investigate other possibilities (for instance, individual stocks, mutual funds, options, whatever strikes your fancy). Put up to 10 percent of your total assets (and 100 percent of your energies) into that exciting portion of your portfolio. Divide the remaining 90 percent as suggested above. This unexciting portfolio will guarantee an attractive return on the bulk of your investments until your results with the exciting 10 percent show you what kind of an investor you might be.

If you have a large portfolio (say, $200,000 or more) and are particularly troubled by the thought of reinvesting at lower rates, you might put a percentage of your bonds in longer dated Treasuries (up to 20 percent). Or, if you are in a high tax bracket, and can benefit from tax-exempt income, substitute high quality municipals for up to half of the core portfolio. In either case, it is best to include intermediate maturities. For municipals, the best returns have been earned by going out somewhat further along the yield curve than for Treasuries, to the five- to ten-year maturity sector.

Portfolio management for retirees is often singled out for unique treatment. Retirees, even those with substantial assets (say $400,000 or more) are sometimes advised to place their entire portfolio of financial assets in long-term bonds and usually, in long-term municipals. The rationale for this approach is that the retirees need "maximum" income but they also need to protect capital. This need to protect capital (or so the thinking goes) rules out "risky" investments such as stocks. That thinking, however, misses a number of important points:

- that a portfolio entirely in bonds is unlikely to grow;
- that total return of long-term bonds is volatile and unpredictable;
- that inflation is likely to erode the real purchasing power of a portfolio entirely in bonds.

The basic consideration in structuring an investment portfolio for retirees—as for anyone else—is total return. The model portfolio described above, with 60 percent in a core bond portfolio of intermediate securities and 40 percent in a stock index fund, is likely to provide greater stability of principal and higher total return than one entirely in fixed-income instruments, particularly if they are long-term. The stock component should provide growth. And choosing intermediate—rather than long-term—bonds, should protect principal.

What about income? After all, retirees depend on a monthly check. That check, however, need not come entirely from dividends. It can come from a combination of dividends and principal. Yes, that may spend down principal. But remember that assets will continue to compound and to grow while withdrawals are being made.

It is not difficult to set up this type of plan. Most mutual funds enable shareholders to set up automatic withdrawal plans which make it very easy for anyone to withdraw monthly income. Investors who manage their own portfolio can create their own withdrawal plan, by automatically withdrawing a specified sum each month.

For most individuals, the main difficulty in setting up a portfolio such as the one I suggest is psychological. It flies totally in the face of much conventional "wisdom" and much of what has been bred into your bones. You will have a thousand objections. You may not believe, in spite of historical evidence, that an unmanaged stock portfolio (that is, an index fund) will do better than most fund managers. Or you may not believe that a portfolio containing stocks will preserve your purchasing power better, in the long run, than keeping your money in "riskless" instruments such as bank CDs. Or you may hate paying taxes and for that reason, want to own nothing but municipals. If nothing will move you, then buy municipals (but then reread the chapter on munis and stick to maturities under ten years).[4]

Finally, I can't resist passing along two dumb (but tried and true rules). The first rule for making money is not to lose any money. The second rule is not to forget the first.

You have probably heard both of those rules. But what do they really tell you? Well, suppose you lose 50 percent of an investment. How much do you have to earn to make up for that loss? No, the answer is not 50 percent. It is 100 percent. If you are not convinced, calculate that in dollars. Suppose you have a $10,000 investment, and it declines by 50 percent. It is then worth only $5,000. A 50 percent gain gets you back only to $7500. Your money has to double for your investment to be worth $10,000 again.

SUMMARY

This chapter discussed some of the overall principles that should guide a game plan for investing over the long term. The first is an investment style appropriate to your temperament and the time available for investing. The second is diversification among both stocks and bonds. A model portfolio was proposed for the defensive investor consisting of a core portfolio of intermediate bonds (mainly Treasuries) for stability of principal and predictable income, and of stocks (or stock funds) for growth.

---

4. This issue was discussed by Michael Lipper in an article entitled: "A Costly Misperception," *Barron's*, August 13, 1990, p. M10. The major point of the article was that a portfolio made up entirely of fixed-income instruments was likely to show less growth and have lower total return than one invested in both stocks and bonds. For an in-depth discussion of portfolio management, as well as index funds, and modern investment theory, you might want also to read a very lucid and clearly written book by Burton G. Malkiel, entitled *A Random Walk Down Wall Street*, New York: Norton, 1990.

14

Management of Bond Portfolios

This chapter discusses

- *a game plan for investing in bonds*

- *how to spot undervalued fixed-income instruments*

- *yield spreads*

- *market timing in the bond market*

- *swaps*

- *how to structure your bond portfolio*

- *managing a bond portfolio for total return*

A GAME PLAN FOR INVESTING IN BONDS

Any investment in bonds starts with a number of questions: What is the ultimate use of the money? What is my time frame? Can I afford to lose any part of my investment? Should the money be in a taxable or in a tax-exempt investment?

Evaluation of alternative choices requires that you determine which security will give you the best combination of probable total return and risk. In a sense, this entire book has dealt with

259

matters that relate to these issues. The introductory chapters, for example, dealt at length with the management of both interest rate risk and credit risk. Chapters on individual securities discussed specific uses for each.

Evaluating investment choices should consist of putting to use the information in the preceding chapters. This chapter will illustrate the process of choosing from among alternative investments. In addition, it will introduce a number of concepts that are used by professionals in the management of bond portfolios, and that can be adapted by individual investors in the management of their own bond portfolios.

When Will I Need The Money?

If you are saving for a specific purpose and the money will be needed in less than a year, and if your resources are limited, then your options are equally limited. You have to confine your choices to instruments that guarantee that principal will not fluctuate in value. That limits you to money market funds, CDs, or to short-term paper such as T-bills.

You might wonder why it is not advisable to buy longer term bonds with higher yields and enjoy these yields until you need the money. There are two reasons. First, you cannot be certain that you will recover the entire principal when you need it because you do not know where interest rates will be when you want to sell. Also, as explained elsewhere, commission costs are particularly high when you sell small lots. Honest brokers will tell you that small investors get killed by commissions when they sell.

However, if the intended use goes out somewhat further in time, say between two and ten years, then you have a different alternative, which professionals call "maturity matching." Put more simply, that means that you would buy a security which will mature at the time principal is needed. Typical intended uses include saving for retirement; for a downpayment on a home; and for a child's college education. Buying securities that will mature at the time the money is needed enables you to go out further along the yield curve, and therefore to buy securities that are higher yielding than the shortest cash equivalents. At the same time, maturity matching eliminates the risk that principal will have declined in value because of interest rate changes when principal is needed.

Maturity matching does not dictate which instruments you should choose. If, for example, the money is needed in five years, you might buy a five-year Treasury note; a five-year pre-refunded muni; a five-year bank CD; or a five-year Treasury zero.

To decide which security to buy, consider the credit quality of the securities you are considering. Also compare either the net-after-tax yield, or the taxable equivalent yield of these instruments. That would vary depending on market conditions and on current tax laws.

What about long-term uses, that is, anything over ten years? If the money will not be needed for at least 10 years, then I would suggest that you stick to the growth portfolio described in the preceding chapter, and include both stocks and bonds.

How Do I Choose Among Investment Alternatives

You want to buy some bonds. How do you decide which securities to buy?

Let's illustrate with a concrete example. On a radio talk show, I heard an elderly caller wondering what the opinion of the guru might be. He was considering purchasing a unit investment trust (UIT) of municipal securities, as a vehicle for investing $20,000. He wasn't quite sure what the maturity of the UIT was, but he guessed that it was around 15 years. The UIT was insured by MBIA, and quoted a yield of 7 percent. He wanted to hold the UIT for approximately five years, and then he intended to sell it.

Now, it was evident to me that this caller violated some basic rules of investing. Most importantly, his questions made it clear that he did not understand the product he was considering. He did not realize that a 15-year maturity exposed his money to considerable interest rate risk. He clearly thought that the insurance feature eliminated risk to principal. Finally, he did not understand the transaction costs he was incurring. The guru, incidentally, was not much wiser.

How should our caller have proceeded? First of all, if the money was needed in five years, his best bet was to stick either to a riskless instrument, or, for a somewhat higher yield, to a security with a five-year maturity.

On the day of the call-in show, a quick glance at the *New York Times* revealed the following alternatives:

- Tax-exempt money market funds were yielding about 5 1/2 percent. The taxable equivalent yield in the 28 percent bracket was approximately 7.65 percent.

- Two-year Treasuries had a yield of about 8.5 percent, federally taxable. Five-year Treasuries yielded slightly more, approximately 8.7 percent.

If the caller had telephoned a broker, he would have been told that tax-exempt paper, maturing in five years, rated in the A+ or higher range, was yielding between 6 percent and 6 1/2 percent. This translates into a taxable equivalent yield of 8.3 percent to 9 percent in the 28 percent bracket.

The caller was clearly leaning towards the UIT because of its apparently higher yield. But how much was he really earning?

For comparison purposes, do a quick approximate calculation. Assume that the UIT will continue to yield 7 percent per year. Multiply by five, and you get 35 percent. But consider that in five years, when the caller sells the UIT, he will incur a commission cost of about 5 percent. Subtract the commission cost from the total dividend yield. The actual return declines to 30 percent. Divide by five, and you get 6 percent per year, tax-exempt.

You can now compare the yield of the UIT to the other alternatives. After subtracting commission costs, the actual yield of the UIT is only slightly higher than the tax-exempt money fund. It is equal to or somewhat lower than five-year tax-exempt paper. It is only marginally higher than a five-year Treasury. To put that into further perspective, consider that a difference of 1/2 of 1 percent in annual yield on a $20,000 investment amounts to $100 a year.

But of course, the approximate return of 6 percent a year is based on the assumption that interest rates won't change, and that when the caller sells the UIT in five years, he will get back the entire principal. I can't tell where interest rates will be in five years, but one thing is certain: they are unlikely to be where they are now. Because of the interest rate uncertainty, it is impossible to predict the actual total return of the UIT. If interest rates rise, the price per share of the UIT will decline and the total return of the UIT will be be higher than 6 percent a year. If interest rates decline, the price per share of the UIT will rise, and the total return will be higher than 6 percent.

The interest rate uncertainty disappears for any of the other listed alternatives. Since safety of principal was clearly the paramount consideration of the caller, any of the other listed alternatives would have been a better choice.

If safety of principal was the the highest priority of the caller, then the five-year Treasury provided a return that was only marginally lower than the UIT, with total safety of principal. If tax exemption was a high priority, then the five-year muni provided a higher net tax-exempt return, again with greater safety of principal. If the caller was looking for the highest degree of safety, as well as tax exemption, then a five-year prerefunded muni, or any five-year AAA rated muni would have been better choices.

The caller was clearly chasing yield. More importantly, he did not realize that the fifteen year maturity exposed his principal to considerable interest rate risk, for very little incremental gain.

Whenever you are considering alternatives among bonds, the main consideration should always be: what kind of risks am I taking on? and how much am I earning to take on that risk? Is $100 a year on a $20,000 investment sufficient compensation for taking on considerable interest rate risk? (If the concept of interest rate risk is unclear, then please reread Chapter 3.)

For the sake of simplicity, I chose a relatively straightforward investment decision, involving a sum of money which in the bond market is considered a small investment. Again for the sake of simplicity, I ignored such considerations as reinvestment risk and compounding. Actually, for that size investment, and for a five year period, neither of these factors makes a significant difference. Reinvestment risk and compounding should be considered mainly if you are investing larger sums, and if you are investing for longer time periods.

It bears repeating that if you are a defensive investor, you cannot get hurt if you limit your investment choices to Treasuries in the two-to-five year maturity range; or to high quality municipals, with maturities of between two and ten years. Under no condition should you ever buy any security whose risks you do not fully understand.

If you have the time and the interest to compare alternative investments in greater depth, then it pays to cast as wide a net as you can. One method would be to fill in a grid like the one in Exhibit 14.1.

This type of exhibit is intended as a quick guide to relative values between maturities and sectors. You would be comparing currently available yields-to-maturity. Because of the spreading use of computers, some brokerage firms are now supplying this type of information to their customers. Remember, however, that any dealer will supply information based on his own markups. When comparing investments, remember the following check-list:

- Shop around and compare prices.

- Consult the newspaper for currently available yields on Treasuries, corporates and GNMAs and the Blue List for munis.

- Consider tax consequences. Invest in the highest yielding taxable instruments for tax-deferred or tax-sheltered monies. For non-sheltered investments, calculate the net-after-tax yield.

Exhibit 14.1
Comparing Yields for Fixed-Income Investments for Different Maturities

	GOVTs	GNMAs	Munis	CDs	Mutual funds
1 Year					
1-3 Years					
3-5 Years					
5-10 Years					
Long Term					

Elsewhere in the book, specific uses were suggested for fixed-income instruments as they were analyzed. Exhibit 14.2 pulls together and summarizes investment choices and alternatives for specific purposes.

Exhibit 14.2
What Should I Invest In?

Cash Equivalents
    Money Market Funds (Taxable)
    Money Market Funds (Tax Exempt)
    T-Bills
    Bank CDs

Short Term Uses—1 To 5 Years
    T-Notes
    T-Zeros
    Pre Refunded Munis
    Munis up to 5 years
    Bank CDs

Long-Term Uses—More Than 5 Years (for Taxable Money)
    T-Notes
    T-Bonds
    Munis

Tax Deferred—More Than 5 Years
    Zeros (or zero bond funds)
    Corporate Bonds—High Quality
    GNMA (Bond Funds)
    Corporate Bonds (or Corporate Bond Funds)

High Cash Flow (Current Income)
    Premium Bonds
    GNMAs (or GNMA bond funds)
    Closed-End Bond Funds (Bought at a Discount)

To Make Interest Rate Bets
    Long Term Treasuries
    Zero Bond Funds (Target Funds)
    Long Term Zeros
    Accrual or Z Tranches of CMOs

For Call Protection
    Discounts

To Lock in Yield
    Zeros
    Discounts

To Fund Child's College Education
    EE Bonds
    Muni Zeros
    Muni College Bonds

MORE COMPLICATED STRATEGIES

In addition to comparing currently available yields, a buyer of bonds, like a buyer of stocks, may try to find securities that are currently undervalued. Several criteria may be used to spot undervalued bonds.

Yield Spreads

Yields in different sectors of the bond market do not all move together. The reasons for this are diverse. Often, supply increases dramatically in one sector. If Treasury borrowings are particularly heavy, for example, Treasury paper floods the market. Invariably, at that point, yields go up. Periodically, certain sectors of the bond market fall into disfavor. Other sectors become popular. If demand increases in a particular sector, yields fall in that sector. If demand drops, or sell-offs occur, yields can rise dramatically.

The key indicator for comparing values in different sectors of the bond market is the yield spread; that is, the difference in yield between various sectors of the bond market with comparable maturities. Professionals make extensive use of yield spreads, based on extraordinarily detailed data. Individual investors, however, can get a sense of those spreads through some readily available information.

Basic yield spread information is contained daily in the financial pages of major newspapers in tables that list key rates. Yield spreads can also be found in graphs that compare yield curves in different sections of the bond market. Exhibit 14.3 shows some of the key interest rates that would have been listed April 2, 1991.

First, let's define some of the rates. Readings from top to bottom, the rates are:

- 3-month T-bills, a proxy for a risk-free rate of return.

- 7-year Treasury Notes, a proxy for longer intermediate highest quality yield.

- 30-year Treasury Bond. The yield-to-maturity of the bellwether long bond.

- ■ Telephone bonds. Average yield of high quality, long-term corporate debt.

- ■ Municipal bonds. Average yield of a benchmark index of long-term municipal bonds compiled by the *Bond Buyer*.

The spread that would probably be of greatest interest to individual investors is the spread between munis and Treasuries. To calculate that spread, subtract the 7.33 percent muni yield from 8.26 percent, the yield-to-maturity of the Treasury long bond. The yield spread is 93 basis points.

The size of the spread indicates whether munis are a good buy, compared to Treasuries. Spreads between munis and Treasuries occasionally narrow to as few as 30 to 50 basis points or less. (This occurs for instance, when there is an unusually large supply or a panic in some sector of the muni market.) When that happens, long-term munis are generally an excellent buy, because spreads usually revert to "normal" over time. When they do, the price of munis rises.

On the other hand, if the spread widens (to above 135 basis points), munis are less attractive and are probably overpriced. This is a poor time to buy. The spread in Exhibit 14.3—93 basis points—is neutral.

The basic spread information can also be used to calculate the ratio of muni yields to Treasuries. To calculate that ratio, divide 7.33 percent (the muni yield) by 8.26 percent (the Treasury yield). At that ratio, munis yield 88 percent of Treasuries, which means that munis are reasonably attractive to buyers even in the 28 percent bracket. Occasionally, when there is a large supply of

---

Exhibit 14.3
Key Interest Rates (in percent)

3-Month Treas. Bills	5.80
7-Year Treas. Notes	7.93
30-Year Treas. Bonds	8.26
Telephone Bonds	9.31
Municipal Bonds	7.33

munis, the ratio may be a lot higher (say, 90 percent of Treasuries or above), indicating that munis are a particularly attractive buy.

A striking example occurred in 1986. During that year, a proposed change in the tax laws resulted in a momentary panic in the muni market. As a result, for a few months, yields on munis were actually 115 percent of Treasuries; that is, 15 percent *higher* than those of Treasuries. Historically, munis have normally yielded between 80 and 90 percent of Treasuries. The ratio varies as a result of changes in the tax laws; and also as a result of current supply and demand for municipal bonds.

During the 1986 panic in the muni bond market, it should have been evident that at some point, muni yields would again drop below those of Treasuries; and that they would in all likelihood decline once more to a ratio of 85 percent of Treasuries. A decline in long-term yields of that magnitude (about 30 percent) implies a dramatic possibility for capital gains. And, in fact, at that point many managers of institutional assets bought munis (rather than corporates) both for the very high yield (above that of Treasuries) and for the potential capital gains. While it is unlikely that munis will again yield more than Treasuries, it is not uncommon for munis to yield 90 percent to 95 percent of Treasuries, and when this happens, they are usually an excellent buy.

Another good example of changing yield spreads traces yields in the junk bond market. Before junk bonds became a household word, yield spreads between Treasuries and junk were about 400 basis points. As their popularity increased, yield spreads narrowed to about 200 basis points. The narrowing spread was a signal to alert buyers that the yield on junk bonds was no longer high enough to compensate for the high default risk of these bonds. Thereafter, the junk bond market crashed. At the beginning of 1991, the spread had widened to an unprecedented 700 to 1200 basis points (depending on which index you consult). At that point, the very wide spread indicated that junk bonds were then a far better buy than they were at the height of their popularity, when the spread had narrowed to 200 basis points.

Professional money managers rely on yield spreads to determine which sectors of the bond market might be undervalued at any particular time. Since their transaction costs are very low, they often seek to exploit imbalances between sectors that are uneconomic for individual investors. But the kinds of imbalances described above are wide enough to be exploited profitably by individual investors. In any case, they are certainly useful in evaluating the attractiveness of one sector, when compared to another and they can be used by a buy-and-hold investor to determine which sectors of the bond market are attractive at a given time.

Using the Yield Curve

As explained in Chapter 5, the yield curve is the most basic tool for determining buy-points for any particular security. Over the past five or six years, the most attractive buy points for Treasuries have been in the two-to-five-year maturity range; and for munis, in the five- to ten-year sector. This intermediate sector has captured about 90 percent of the yield available on long-term instruments, but with far lower volatility.

Even during that time period, however, significant anomalies occurred. If you get into the habit of comparing yields, anomalies become readily apparent, whenever they occur. Between 1988 and 1989, for example, the Treasury yield curve became steeply inverted. Yields on two-to-five-year Treasuries climbed to above 9 percent for a brief period of time. If you had had any money to invest during that time, and you had checked the yield curve both for Treasuries and for munis, you would have seen that on a net-after-tax basis, two-to-five-year Treasuries were yielding close to 7 percent, whereas longer munis, on a net—after-tax basis, were yielding a lot less. As a result, the safest securities (two-to-five-year Treasuries) actually yielded more than munis, even those with low credit ratings. That was an excellent time to load up on two-to-five year Treasuries.

Historical Data

If you have some basic information concerning historic rates of return, just reading the daily financial press will tell you on a relative basis, which sectors appear to provide good value. For example, 30-year Treasuries have seldom yielded above 9 percent for very long periods (with the notable exception of 1979 to 1982, when they reached 15 percent). A yield above 9 percent (again for Treasuries) is seldom available for maturities of two years or above. Whenever such yields have occurred, they have turned out to be excellent buying opportunities. Yields of above 9 percent or 10 percent on long-term Treasury zeros are particularly attractive since those are compounded rates, and they are guaranteed if you hold to maturity. To put that in perspective, remember that the historic rate of return on stocks is about 10 percent.

Let's look at another example. In a recent book a noted expert, Burton Malkiel stated that based on historic valuation criteria of stocks, the stock market appeared somewhat expensive. However, based on historic real rates of return of bonds, he considered bonds particularly attractive. Because yields of high quality corporate utility bonds were high relative to Treasuries, he recommended that investors purchase those bonds (then yielding somewhat over 9 percent).[1]

Active Strategies

Professional money managers differentiate between active and passive strategies. Passive strategies "maturity matching," for instance, are essentially buy-and-hold. Their purpose is to insure that when principal is needed, it will be there. The buyer selects securities with a specific maturity; and those securities are held until principal is redeemed. This strategy minimizes transaction costs and also eliminates the need to formulate an interest rate scenario.

Active strategies are more speculative. They are designed to take advantage of opportunities for capital gain resulting from interest rate shifts or from temporary shifts in bond sector valuations. They require far more sophistication than passive strategies since they must be based either on interest rate forecasts or on the ability to evaluate different sectors of the bond market.

Not surprisingly, since interest rate forecasts are notoriously unreliable, "incorrect" active strategies may wind up losing—rather than making—money. Many money managers opt for passive strategies in the belief that on the whole, they are more

---

1. Burton Malkiel: *A Random Walk Down Wall Street*. New York: Norton, 1990, pp. 331-335.

successful. For most individual investors, particularly for anyone describing himself as a defensive investor, passive strategies usually prove more satisfactory.

As I have emphasized, the bond market is dominated by institutions. It bears repeating that many of the newer instruments that have come on the market in the last few years are designed to be used by so-called sophisticated investors. These are the professionals who earn their living buying and selling bonds, and who have the clout that comes from trading the enormous sums traded by institutions. The individual investor is at a disadvantage in this market in a number of ways. He incurs much higher transaction costs both in buying and selling; and he has limited access both to information and to certain types of securities. Finally, the individual investor does not have access to the enormous array of mathematical models and data that institutions have developed. All of this means that many of the strategies available to sophisticated institutional investors simply cannot be duplicated by individual investors.

Where does one draw the line between "investing" and "speculating"? Anyone who invests has an intuitive grasp of what the terms mean to him. To some extent, any investment contains a degree of speculation. Where you would draw the line depends partly on your risk tolerance, partly on your skill and experience as an investor, and partly on the size of your portfolio. Where bonds are concerned, purchases should be considered at least partly speculative if you are buying in order to capture capital gains and not primarily for the dividend income. It implies further that the investor intends to trade securities, and does not necessarily intend to hold them to maturity. It goes without saying that speculation only makes sense for large, well-diversified portfolios, and if commission costs are low.

An investor interested in investing in bonds partly as speculative instruments would want to identify those sectors of the bond market likely to result in the highest total return for a specific time period. This requires evaluating the different sectors of the bond market (that is, Treasuries, corporates, munis and so on) in all maturities in order to select those sectors and those maturities which will appreciate the most over the near term.

There are many kinds of criteria that might apply. Money managers would start by using yield spread data. Another tool would be sensitivity analysis. Sensitivity analysis describes the impact of a decline or a rise in interest rates on the total return of various securities. Such an approach is illustrated in Exhibit 14.4.

Sensitivity analysis requires an interest rate scenario. The information in Exhibit 14.4 is targeted to an investor who trades actively and who is attempting to take advantage of market inefficiencies.

The type of securities that you select will depend on your goals as an investor (or trader). If for example, you expect that interest rates will decline, you might consider buying long-term bonds. Certain bonds give you more "leverage" than others. Long-term munis provide the least leverage since they are usually callable after ten years from the issue date, and that limits potential price appreciation. Treasuries are not callable and that would give you higher leverage. The most leverage (about two and one half times as much) would be provided by zero coupon Treasuries or the accrual tranches of CMOs.

The risks you incur depend partly on what you intend to do if interest rate changes fail to follow your scenario. Suppose you think interest rates will decline. You decide to purchase long-term bonds, partly for income and partly as a speculation. If rates drop, you can sell your bonds, cash in your capital gain, and reinvest your principal. If rates do not drop as you anticipate, however, you have incurred no loss of principal but you may now lose liquidity and potential income if rates go up.

The greatest degree of leverage is obtained—not by buying in the cash market—but by buying either options or futures contracts. The most widely traded contract is the Treasury bond contract, but there are also several less widely traded municipal contracts. This kind of analysis is beyond the scope of this book. For a detailed discussion, either of sensitivity analysis, or of leverage, you would need to read a book targeted to institutional investors. The standard reference text is *The Handbook of Fixed-Income Securities*, Frank Fabozzi and Irving Pollack, editors, published by Dow Jones Irwin, Homewood, Illinois, 1987.

If analysis of spreads, or sensitivity analysis, interest you, you can also get useful information by requesting the literature written for institutional money managers from one the larger national brokerage firms that has a large institutional clientele. It may take some persistence; but if you are insistent, you can get it.

Exhibit 14.4
Sensitivity Analysis

HORIZON ANALYSIS - PERIODIC TOTAL RETURN
One-Year Holding Period - Workout Date 7/23/91

Issue		Yield Down		0	Yield Up	
		-100	**-50**	**0**	**+50**	**+100**
U.S. Treasury 8 1/2% due 8/15/95 * $102.06 - 7.99%	Yield	6.99	7.49	7.99	8.49	8.99
	Price	105.25	103.47	101.73	100.03	98.35
	Total Return	11.32	9.64	8.00	6.45	4.87
U.S. Treasury 8 7/8% due 5/15/00 * $104.34 - 8.22%	Yield	7.22	7.72	8.22	8.72	9.22
	Price	110.63	107.27	104.03	100.92	97.93
	Total Return	14.42	11.25	8.20	5.31	2.49
Refcorp STRIPS 1/15/01 * $40.68 - 8.79%	Yield	7.79	8.29	8.79	9.29	9.79
	Price	48.48	46.32	44.26	42.30	40.43
	Total Return	19.17	13.86	8.80	3.98	-0.62
Ford Holdings (AA/AA) 9 1/4% due 3/01/00 * $101.5 - 9.0%	Yield	8.01	8.51	9.01	9.51	10.01
	Price	107.59	104.43	101.40	98.48	95.67
	Total Return	14.85	11.85	8.97	6.26	3.59
GNMA 9 1/2% Current-Coupon * 101.625 - 9.33% Total Return	Yield (Bond Equiv.)	8.43	8.88	9.33	9.78	10.23
	Spread (1)	90bp	85bp	80bp	75bp	70bp
	Price	105.97	103.87	101.55	99.12	96.63
		13.07	11.27	9.23	7.06	4.82
U.S. Treasury 8 3/4% - 5/15/20 * $104.28 - 8.36%	Yield	7.36	7.86	8.36	8.86	9.36
	Price	116.51	110.08	104.20	98.84	93.93
	Total Return	19.92	13.85	8.32	3.30	-1.34

*Price as of 7/23/90 (Note: All prices represent Merrill Lynch Consumer Markets offerings.)
(1) Due to the prepayment option embedded within mortgage-backed securities, yield spreads to Treasuries are expected to vary at different interest-rate levels.

The table illustrates a total-return analysis of alternative investments available in the short to intermediate sector of the taxable fixed income markets. It is designed to indicate the expected returns on those instruments if market yields rise, fall or remain unchanged over a 12-month in- vestment period. We include those sectors that we are recommending now and, as a benchmark, the 30-year Treasury bond. Since we expect yields to decline moder- ately over the next 12 months, the "-50" column is the most relevant. If yields do decline, the Refcorp zeros and the corporate notes should produce the best total returns among the intermediate maturities. If yields are un- changed, the mortgage-backed (GNMA) and corporate is- sues perform best, but the Refcorp zeros outperform the Treasury notes and bonds.

Source: *Fixed Income Digest,* July 27, 1990, p. 2. Published by Merrill Lynch, Pierce, Fenner & Smith, Inc. Reprinted with permission.

MISCELLANEOUS

Swaps

When you swap bonds, you trade one bond for a different bond, rather than for cash proceeds. During the 1970s, swaps used to be an annual ritual for many holders of long-term bonds. These swaps were usually done for the purpose of generating a tax loss. They represented a means of recouping partially the erosion of principal that resulted from annually rising interest rates.

During the 1980s, most holders of long-term bonds have capital gains, rather than capital losses, and for that reason the annual rite of tax swapping of bonds is disappearing. Note also that the significantly lower income tax brackets that resulted from the Tax Reform Act of 1986 (33 percent for the top bracket as compared to 70 percent in the 1970s) have reduced the value of tax losses, even when they do exist.

However, there are other motivations for swapping than generating tax losses. Bonds may be swapped:

- to upgrade credit quality (a good time for that is when yield spreads between credit ratings narrow);

- to increase dividend income (either by extending maturities or by lowering credit quality);

- to take advantage of anticipated changes in interest rate levels (going shorter or longer along the yield curve).

Any of these swaps might be viewed at different times as improvements of the basic bond portfolio and as a means of increasing total return.

Whatever the purpose of the swap, however, there are good swaps and bad swaps. The chief difficulty in evaluating swaps is that transaction costs are not obvious. Prices are usually quoted net so that the actual commission cost is hidden. On a large trade, for long-term bonds, you should assume that commission costs will equal perhaps 2 percent to 3 percent of the value of principal, that is, $2,000 to $3000 per $100,000.

But there may be costs to a swap in addition to the commission. To evaluate a swap, you need to compare the total par value of the bonds that are being swapped; the annual coupon interest income; the credit quality of the issues involved; and the maturity of the bonds. Suppose, for example, that you own a $25,000 par value municipal bond, rated A+, with a 20-year maturity, and a 7 percent coupon. You receive annual dividend income of $1,750. Further suppose that you are offered a swap for this bond. Costs of the swap would include any of the following:

- you are offered a bond with a lower credit rating (say B+);

- coupon income declines by $100 a year;

- the par value of the potential swap is lower than the par value of the bond you own (say $22,000 compared to $25,000); and

- you are offered a swap which lengthens maturity to 22 years.

Any of these represents a cost.

To evaluate whether or not to do the swap, you need to compare all of the cash flows of the two bonds; their maturity; and their credit quality. For an in-depth discussion of swaps, see Sidney Homer and Martin Leibowitz, *Inside the Yield book*, pp. 78-96.

Market Timing in the Bond Market

If you could forecast interest rates perfectly, you would want to keep your money in long-term bonds (or in long-term bond funds) when interest rates are declining, in order to capture capital gains; and you would want to switch to money market funds when interest rates are rising, in order to preserve principal and take advantage of rising yields. Unfortunately, it is often difficult to know whether interest rates are rising or declining; and it is even more difficult to predict what they are going to do next week, month, or year.

In spite of this, investment advisors and brokerage firms routinely offer asset allocation advice that suggests what percentage of one's assets should be in cash or cash equivalents, in stocks, and in bonds. For cash, you can read: money market funds. Within the last few years, a number of specialized newsletters have begun to offer "timing" advice entirely for the fixed-income sector that suggests when to put your money in long-term bond funds, and when to put it in money funds. Brokerage firm asset allocation strategies have had very mixed results. So have timing newsletters. According to Mark Hulbert, who tracks investment results of newsletters, only a couple of newsletters have outperformed a buy-and-hold strategy for bonds. In addition, the newsletters dispensing timing advice are quite recent. They have not had enough time to build up a meaningful track record.

Whether timing can ultimately beat buy-and-hold strategies is open to question. But if timing interests you, when you read the hype on switching, remember that timing has hidden costs. One occurs if the timing is off. The investor is "whipsawed" which means that he sells low and buys back high. In addition, switching involves buying and selling. You incur commission costs when you buy and when you sell. Sales generate still another transaction cost, namely, taxes. Market timers usually do not include any of these costs in their results. These costs, however, lower returns, even if the switching turns out to be "correct." Given all of these uncertainties, if timing strategies interest you, it would be prudent to start with only a small percentage of your funds.

According to Hulbert, in *The Hulbert Guide to Financial Newsletters* Chicago, Probus, 1990, as of July 1990, the two newsletters with the best timing record in the bond market were *Fund Exchange*, edited by Paul Merriman, located in Seattle, Washington; and *Systems and Forecasts*, edited by Gerald Appel, in Great Neck, New York. (*Nota bene*: This should not be construed as a recommendation of market timing. At this point, most services have been around too little time to build up a meaningful track record).

Structuring Your Bond Portfolio

Throughout the book, I have recommended that you stick to intermediate maturities for the greater part of your portfolio. That strategy is called a "focused" strategy. Managers of large individual portfolios sometimes recommend a different approach known as a "barbell" strategy. Half the portfolio is invested in very short-term maturities (under two years); and the other half in long-term instruments (20 to 30 years). During certain periods, this strategy has worked extremely well. Under some interest rate scenarios, however, this strategy can backfire. Suppose, for example, that short-term rates drop and long-term rates rise. This happens whenever the yield curve becomes steeply inverted. At such times, a barbell portfolio suffers a double whammy. The principal value of the long-term securities declines. At the same time, yields in the shortest term sector also decline.

Another popular strategy for structuring a large bond portfolio is to ladder maturities; that is, to buy a combination of two-year, three-year, five-year, seven-year, and ten-year maturities. The average maturity of such a portfolio is about half that of the longest maturities. If the longest maturities are around seven or ten years, the average maturity of the entire portfolio would be between three and five years. That is short enough to protect principal. As the bonds mature, replace them with equivalent maturities. This enables you to benefit from interest rate swings whether or not you correctly anticipate the future direction of interest rates.

One variation for a large ladder portfolio is to include a small percentage of long-term maturities (up to 15 percent). That variation would result in a portfolio similar to an index developed by the Ryan labs, called the "Ryan Index." For the two years preceding 1990, this unmanaged index outperformed most government bond funds, and produced total returns about as high as long-term bonds, but with far less volatility. This index consists of equal weightings of the most recent issues of Treasury notes and bonds: the two-, three-, four-, five-, seven-, ten-year bonds, and the 30-year bonds.[2] The minimum required to set up a reasonable replica of this portfolio is $35,000. But the actual Ryan index always includes the very latest bond issued for every maturity, and that would be impractical for individuals.

On the other hand, if you are not that systematic, and if you prefer to invest as money becomes available, and buy whatever seems to be most attractive within the two- to five-year maturity range, as long as you stick to Treasuries or other very high quality instruments, the risks remain low.

---

2. See "Current Yield," by Randall Forsyth, in *Barron's*, Nov. 5, 1990, p. 50.

Managing a Bond Portfolio for Total Return

As was explained in the sections on bond yields and total return, managing for total return involves taking into account all aspects of a bond's total return; namely, transaction costs, capital gains (or losses); and reinvestment rates. This implies a strategy that minimizes transaction costs, maximizes reinvestment rates, and preserves capital.

The following is a summary of some guidelines that will maximize total return:

- To minimize transaction costs, comparison shop. Buy Treasuries at auction. Buy munis at issue when you can. Buy maturities and securities with low spreads: that means intermediate maturities; and high quality credits.

- Buy and hold rather than trade; commision costs are particularly high when you sell.

- If you are investing new money in bond funds, stick to no-loads, with low expense ratios, and no 12b-1 plans.

- If you are investing in securities other than Treasuries, always check the yield against Treasuries of comparable maturities; and only purchase if the spread to Treasuries is high enough to warrant the additional risk.

- Some securities are bought most economically and efficiently through bond mutual funds: GNMAs, junk bonds, international bonds.

- The longer you extend maturities, the higher the credit quality you should require.

- If you are investing large sums, don't buy too many small lots. It is preferable to buy lots that are at least $25,000. Buying too many small lots raises transaction costs, both when you buy and when you resell.

- If you are putting money away for the long term, reinvestment rates are particularly important. This is because interest-on-interest constitutes a greater proportion of the total earned. Boosting reinvestment rates results in higher compounded interest income. To reinvest at higher rates, consider sweeping reinvested interest income into intermediate (or long term)—rather than money market—bond funds.

■ For most investors, two-to-five-year Treasuries, and five-to-ten year munis, will provide the best combination of risk and return.

Discount vs. Premium Bonds

In a number of sections, the disadvantages and advantages of discounts vs. premiums were mentioned. Again, since this comes up so often, a summary may be helpful:

For instruments with long-term maturities, bonds selling at a premium usually have higher yields than either par or discount bonds. The higher coupon also provides both a high cash flow; and a cushion if interest rates rise. The chief disadvantage of premium bonds is that if interest rates decline, they are more likely to be called. Before buying any bond selling at a high premium, be particularly careful in checking call provisions, since an early and unexpected call could result in a significant loss of principal. In addition, if interest rates decline substantially, premium bonds generally do not appreciate as much as par or discount bonds.

If you are buying long-term bonds, discounts are more interest rate sensitive. If interest rates decline, they will appreciate more in value than either par or premium bonds. Bonds selling at a deep discount also provide a form of call protection they are less likely to be called if the coupon is very low. Also, you are more certain to earn the quoted yield-to-maturity on those bonds than on premiums since a greater portion of the total return is locked in as a capital gain. This, however, is an advantage only if rates are historically relatively high: say above 9 percent for long-term Treasuries.

In general, investors looking for maximum growth would favor discounts; whereas those looking for high cash flow and price stability would favor premiums.

CONCLUSION

This book was initially started about two years ago. As this book is going to press, in October of 1991, the most recent three month T-bill rate has declined to about 5.5 percent, the lowest rate since the early 1970s. On the other hand, the Treasury long bond, a reasonable proxy for 30-year interest rates, is yielding about 8 percent, not much less than it did one or two years ago. In other words, the yield curve has become steeply upward sloping; and the spread between the shortest rates and the longest rates has widened to approximately 250 basis points, far higher than at any time in the recent past. No doubt, anyone holding long-term maturities is currently smiling whereas investors holding short-term maturities are more likely to be troubled, particularly if a good deal of their income derives from fixed-income instruments. Some articles in the financial press are predicting a buying panic as investors looking for higher yield are forced to lengthen maturities.

In the light of these developments, the frequent warnings concerning the riskiness of long-term bonds may appear irrelevant or even cruel. Nonetheless, recent interest rate trends raise a number of important issues. Let's briefly look at them.

The most pressing issue is the one faced by individuals who need to reinvest fixed-income securities. If you rely on dividend income, how should you reinvest your money?

Overall investment strategies in this book have been based on studies which have shown that over long periods of time, Treasuries in the two-to-five year maturity range (and somewhat longer maturities in the muni sector), have had higher total returns than either the longest or the shortest maturities. If you will remember, the main concern behind this strategy is protection of principal; in other words, managing for total return. The strategy of investing in two-to-five year maturities has worked in the past because it captures a higher yield than the shortest maturities, but it protects principal if interest rates rise. Nothing in current developments suggests that this will not continue to be the case.

In turn, that suggests that for most investors, the best option is to continue to stay away from both the longest and the shortest maturities. If you had followed that advice, you would still be enjoying higher dividends than are currently available. But if you have to reinvest new money, you will continue to earn reasonably high yields by continuing to follow the same strategy. As of this month, if you look at the *Treasury Table of Bills, Bond and Notes,* you will see that two-year Treasuries are yielding about 6.2 percent. Because of the current steepness of the yield curve, five-year Treasuries are yielding approximately 7.2 percent, 100 more basis points. The five-year yield still captures about 90 percent of the yield on the long bond, with dramatically less exposure to interest rate risk.

Yields on municipal bonds have not declined as much as those of Treasuries: high quality municipals in the two-year maturity range yield about 5.5 percent, which represents a taxable-equivalent yield of close to 8 percent for an investor in the 30 percent tax bracket. Ten-year high quality munis yield about 6.5 percent, which represents a tax equivalent yield of over 9 percent to the same investor. (This also indicates that the yield spread between munis and Treasuries has narrowed, and that munis are currently attractive when compared to Treasuries.)

If you prefer to invest through mutual funds, the maturity sector that would be most appropriate is the "short-intermediate sector," which limits the average maturity of the fund to three years or less. Yields in this sector again are well above money market yields: approximately 7.2 percent on taxable funds and approximately 5.4 percent on tax-exempt funds.

Nothing in current interest rate developments is cause to repeal any of the previously issued warnings about the perils of investing in long-term bonds. It is a mathematical certainty that if interest rates rise, the value of long-term bonds will fall. (If you have any doubt about this, please reread Chapter 3).

Having said that, it remains true that higher yielding instruments must currently appear particularly tempting. Is this the time to be buying junk bond funds currently advertising yields of around 11.5 percent; or CMOs, currently advertising yields of 9 percent; or 30-year Treasury zeros, for maximum capital gains if interest rates continue to decline?

Once again, forgive me for repeating: the highest yields, in the world of bonds, always go hand in hand with the highest risk. If you have a large, well-diversified portfolio, and if you want to place a percentage of your assets in these instruments, fine. But if your bond portfolio is small—under $50,000 in the world of bonds—(some experts would say under $100,000)—then you are taking a chance. Before you take such a step, please reread the sections on junk bonds, or on CMOs, or on zeros, or on whatever it is that is "hot" when you read this book.

One more caveat. If rates were to drop massively, long-term bonds in all sectors would appreciate in value. But a continuing steep decline in mortgage rates would spell trouble for holders of GNMA bond funds. That is because if rates decline steeply from current levels, prepayments would speed up significantly. Again, if that is not clear, please reread the sections on GNMAs.

Finally, let's consider one more possibility. Some experts are currently predicting that rates on short-term instruments will decline still further, and that the yield of the long bond will decline to 6 percent within the next two years. Does that mean that now is the last chance to buy bonds with higher yields?

I dearly wish I could predict interest rates and tell you what will happen next. But I can't. On the other hand, let's look at probabilities. Under what conditions could interest rates decline to levels significantly below current rates, and remain there over decades? Only if there was a prolonged and severe depression or if inflation remains at 2 percent, or less, over decades. In either scenario, even interest rates significantly below current levels would continue to provide a real rate of return, and you would not be hurt if you stick with the strategy of buying high-quality securities in the short to intermediate maturity sector.

But frankly, I doubt this will occur. Think back to the interest rate history of the last thirty years. Do you really think the next thirty years will be any less turbulent?

And when interest rates rise again, as they will, if you stick to the strategies outlined in this book, you will be able to take advantage of the higher yields and you won't lose any sleep because your principal will be protected. Isn't that a comforting thought?

So once again, many happy returns.   (*October 1991*)

I would like to briefly update the preceding conclusion as a paperback edition is going to press in November 1994. The main issue to be addressed is this: Was the strategy outlined above valid then? And is it still valid now? To answer these questions, a brief look at interest rate changes in the past three years is in order.

The past three years have witnessed dramatic ups and downs in interest rates. After the initial publication of the book, interest rates did continue to decline: the Treasury's long bond reached a low of 5.78 percent in September of 1993. Even more striking, at that point, the yields on three-month, six-month, and one-year T-bills were all under 3 percent.

These market conditions were the stuff of dreams for holders of long-term bonds, who were reaping handsome capital gains. For holders of short-term securities, however, declining interest rates created a major headache: how to roll over maturing fixed income securities so that income would be maintained. Investors were strongly tempted to chase yield, either by extending maturities or by investing in some of the riskier fixed income instruments.

All of this changed in October 1993, when the steady decline in interest rates that had marked the 1980s and early 1990s came to a sudden halt. Interest rates started an abrupt climb. Within a year, the interest rate on the long bond had climbed back up to 8 percent. As this is being written, the yield on the three-month bill is 5 percent and the one-year is approaching 7 percent. Some analysts view this as the start of a cycle of rising interest rates that may continue for several years, with the long bond reaching 9 or 10 percent within a few years. Others predict that rising yields will slow the economy, and that interest rates will then start to fall again. Which of these scenarios will come to pass? Unfortunately, at this time, no one knows.

Rising rates have had a dramatic and entirely predictable effect on total return for holders of all fixed income instruments. So far in 1994, total return for almost all fixed income securities has been negative. Dividend income has failed to compensate for the loss in the principal value of the bonds. Losses have varied directly with the maturity of the securities. This is most clearly visible in bond funds. Funds holding the shortest instruments, with an average weighted maturity of three years or less, have posted the best returns (indeed, a few of these funds are posting a positive total return). Funds holding securities with the longest maturities are posting significant declines in Net Asset Value, as much as 10 to 15 percent. Even after adding back dividend income, total return for these funds has been negative for 1994. Funds holding the highest quality securities (treasuries, insured municipals) have declined as steeply as funds holding lower quality paper. A small number of bond funds holding exotic instruments, or following complicated strategies, have declined even more steeply.

In short, current conditions are exactly those I was concerned about when I described the risks of investing in fixed income instruments.

Today's investor faces a situation that is exactly the reverse of what it was in 1991, when I wrote the first conclusion. Holders of short-term instruments are seeing their dividend income rise. Holders of long-term bonds or of bond funds are seeing the value of their principal erode. The temptation today is to sell anything that has a maturity of more than three months, and to retreat into cash, in order to protect principal.

What is striking, however, is that in spite of the dramatic turbulence in the credit markets for the past three years, the strategy outlined in 1991 would have protected bondholders then, and will continue to do so now.

The advice given in the conclusion written in 1991, namely, to stay away from both the longest and the shortest instruments for most of your bond portfolio, and to stick to relatively straightforward, high quality instruments, is clearly the best choice. If you are rolling over or investing new money, you will find that yields on maturities of two to five years for treasuries, and two to ten years for municipals, once again have reached attractive levels. Those maturities, moreover, will continue to protect the value of your principal.

What should you do, however, if you are holding long-term bonds or long-term bond funds? Difficult as it may be, don't panic. If you have a diversified portfolio, and if you are investing for the long term, or for maximum income, hold on. Interest rates will continue to move up and down. Total return is a combination of dividend return plus or minus changes in the value of your principal. In the short term, dramatic changes in the level of interest rates, such as those that occurred in 1994, dramatically affect total return. Over long periods of time, however, compounding dividend returns, particularly when dividends are reinvested at higher rates, will smooth over the bumps.

Finally, the steep losses suffered by holders of long-term or exotic securities should continue to serve as a warning not to invest in these types of instruments unless you hold a large and well-diversified portfolio (preferably more than $100,000) and unless you are prepared to experience significant fluctuations in the value of your principal, both up and down.

So, once again, many happy returns!   *(November 1994)*

Index

Annette Thau, former municipal bond analyst with Chase Manhattan Bank, received her Bachelor of Arts degree from Douglas College and a Ph.D. from Columbia University. She is the recipient of numerous fellowships including a Woodrow Wilson Fellowship, University Fellowships from Columbia University and a National Endowment for the Humanities Fellowship for Younger Humanists.